PENGUIN BOOKS

MULTILINGUALISM

John Edwards was born in Southampton in 1947. He is a graduate of McGill University and is currently Professor of Psychology at St Francis Xavier University in Nova Scotia. He has published a number of books on sociolinguistics, including *Language, Society and Identity* (1985) and *Language and Disadvantage* (1989). Professor Edwards is the editor of the *Journal of Multilingual and Multicultural Development*.

JOHN EDWARDS

MULTILINGUALISM

PENGUIN BOOKS

PENGUIN BOOKS

Published by the Penguin Group
Penguin Books Ltd, 27 Wrights Lane, London W8 5TZ, England
Penguin Books USA Inc., 375 Hudson Street, New York, New York 10014, USA
Penguin Books Australia Ltd, Ringwood, Victoria, Australia
Penguin Books Canada Ltd, 10 Alcorn Avenue, Toronto, Ontario, Canada M4V 3B2
Penguin Books (NZ) Ltd, 182–190 Wairau Road, Auckland 10, New Zealand

Penguin Books Ltd, Registered Offices: Harmondsworth, Middlesex, England

First published by Routledge 1994
Published in Penguin Books 1995
1 3 5 7 9 10 8 6 4 2

Printed in England by Clays Ltd, St Ives plc

To Suzanne

CONTENTS

PREFACE

A study of languages, of multilingualism and its ramifications, can be seen as part of sociolinguistics, or the sociology of language, or the social psychology of language.[1] Following a considerable period in which the social aspects of language were quite neglected, Joyce Hertzler wrote a paper in 1953, 'Toward a sociology of language', which advocated that more attention be paid to the interaction of language and situation.[2] In 1965 Hertzler published a book on the topic, in 1966 a sociolinguistics conference was held in California, and since then developments have accelerated rapidly.

There has been some debate over whether *sociolinguistics* or the *sociology of language* is the best title for the approach or, indeed, if the two terms represent different emphases altogether. While the latter term implies emphasis upon social behaviour elucidated through the study of language, sociolinguistics tends to stress the linguistic variation presented in different contexts. Perhaps the terms are best viewed as reflecting two sides of the one coin. However, the distinction just noted is not necessarily endorsed by all who use the terms, and some have alternated in their usage, while carrying on with the same sort of work. Also, sociolinguistics may have within it the seeds of its own demise, since it represents what many feel to be a necessary broadening of the larger field of linguistics. Once it is accepted that there can be no meaningful linguistics without attention to context, then sociolinguistics may be absorbed. This 'self-liquidation'[3] obviously does not apply to a field termed 'the sociology of language', which may be seen as a new, enduring and autonomous subtopic of sociology, a relatively loose conception 'falling easily into the growing company of sociologies of this and that'.[4]

So, the two terms may be different in emphasis and in degree of autonomy. In practice, they are used loosely and sometimes interchange-ably. In any event, given a mingling of context and language, it is possible that *both* terms might be more or less accurately used within the same investigation. One might, for example, use social-situational information to comment upon linguistic forms produced, or linguistic usage might be studied in order to understand the context better. After all, context can influence linguistic choice, and linguistic choice can be an index to perceptions of context (and may even *change* a psychological context).[5] This, incidentally, brings us more to a social *psychology* of language – with its traditional emphasis upon perception, attitude, belief and individual action – than to a sociological perspective (with *its* stress on group dynamics); again, however, we are not dealing here with watertight and mutually exclusive categories.

Whatever term is used, we *are* dealing here with the social life of language – we are not, then, primarily concerned with the technicalities of language itself (i.e., *linguistics*, with its various subdivisions – one of which, of course, could be seen as sociolinguistics or anthropological linguistics), nor with *psycholinguistics* – language acquisition, the relationships between language and thought, language and intelligence, and so on (though we must touch on some of these). Rather, the emphasis is upon interactions among language, society and culture; it is, consequently, a hybrid field of study, and one that sometimes sits uneasily on disciplinary fences.

Noam Chomsky, the most important contemporary linguist, believes strongly that linguistics is part of psychology; his work, therefore, is meant to illuminate the very nature of human language – largely through investigation of language 'universals' – and of human mental competence and its functioning. It is apposite, then, to consider what he has thought about sociolinguistics; 'self-liquidating' or not. In 1977, in a discussion of the relations between linguistics and the 'human sciences', he acknowledged that some descriptive work – such as demonstrating that Black English is a valid dialect – is perhaps useful for combatting educational prejudices but it is quite 'evident and banal' on a theoretical linguistic level; he was disturbed, however, by its 'theoretical pretensions'.[6] More pointedly, he claimed that 'the existence of a discipline called "sociolinguistics" remains for me an obscure matter', and that sociology in general lacks basic and explanatory principles. All such work, he feels, is not research, which is only successful when it grapples with underlying principles and structures. A counter-argument has been expressed which accuses Chomsky of restrictive practice. For example: 'a number of linguists [and others, too] have found Chomsky's *asocial* view of linguistic theorizing difficult to accept as anything but a rather sterile type of activity, with its explicit rejection of any concern with the social uses of language'.[7]

In pushing for his definition of research, Chomsky has in fact elevated 'sterility' into 'idealization': that is, he insists that, in order to get at those central principles (of language in his case, but his view applies, as well, to all scientific work) which promise explanatory insight, one must pare a subject down to essentials:

Opposition to idealization is simply objection to rationality; it

amounts to nothing more than an insistence that we shall not have meaningful intellectual work ... you *must* abstract some object of study, you must eliminate those factors which are not pertinent....
When you work within some idealization, perhaps you overlook something which is terribly important. That is a contingency of rational inquiry that has always been understood. One must not be too worried about it. One has to face this problem and try to deal with it, to accommodate oneself to it. It is inevitable.[8]

Chomsky's argument is, essentially, that the most important job for students of language is the uncovering of basic principles; later, perhaps, this asocial linguistics might form the basis of more broadly-based enquiries which would extend outward from the 'idealized' speaker to the world in which he or she speaks.

In summary, there appear to be three related strands in Chomsky's position here. The first is a concern for underlying structure, which requires an abstraction of language from its socially chaotic expression; to use Chomsky's own terms, studying linguistic *competence* is more scientific, more central and more interesting than describing actual *performance*. Second, Chomsky is critical of the whole empirical enterprise that under-pins so much of 'human science', claims that it trivializes research, and advocates a renewed attention to rationalist philosophy. Third, he demon-strates the familiar disdain 'pure' scientists have of 'applied' ones. Taken together, these points serve to separate a rational, intellectual search for truth with a capital 'T' from fact-grubbing and explanation in a changing social environment; while there has, historically and currently, been such a separation, such a pecking order among and within disciplines, the arguments as they apply to *language* have a particular immediacy, simply because everyone uses language. While both the pure and the applied aspects of physics and chemistry are closed books to most people, everyone is familiar (and expert) with the applied nature of language. Furthermore, many feel that it is *in* its applications that language is most interesting, that grammarians are a modern incarnation of medieval scholasticism, and that a linguistics which purposely ignores real-life variation is rather precious.

My own view here is that both Chomsky and his critics are right, because they are centrally concerned with quite different fields which are only apparently linked by a common linguistic element. Chomsky is not a narrow Schoolman, but nor is the study of language in society something which must wait until more idealized conceptions are solidified. Chomsky and his epigones are of course interested in the way language 'works', but rather more interested in what it may tell us about human mental functions, about (in Chomsky's words) linguistics as part of psychology (arguably the most important part). Sociolinguists are concerned above all with language variation as it occurs in actual usage, and sociologists/social psychologists of language are concerned with reactions to, and ramifications of, language as the pillar of social communication. It is not impossible to see links among all these approaches, but it is certainly not necessary since they are, for the moment at least, largely independent. The pure versus applied matter and, more pointedly, Chomsky's conception of research (which is probably too restrictive) remain open. Surely, however, we can agree that useful work can be done in many vineyards?

A BRIEF NOTE ON
REFERENCES

Having produced previous work in accordance with the Harvard system, I have found the writing of this book a refreshing change. I am very much in agreement with a recent piece in the *Times Higher Education Supplement* (24 April 1992) in which Rodney Barker points out the lunatic extremes to which the system has been taken. Intended to simplify things – by removing the little numbers, by no longer obliging the reader to jump to the bottom of the page or the end of the chapter (or book), by removing the necessity to swim upstream through masses of *op cit.*'s or *ibid.*'s – the Harvard arrangement placed references, repeatedly if necessary, directly in the text.

This has become the problem. References are now used not only to indicate vital referencing details, but also as 'academic credit cards', flashed incessantly and needlessly in front of a bemused reader, whose task now approximates pushing 'through treacle wearing Doc Marten's'. The treacle is hard to avoid, however; Barker says that Harvard references 'will not tolerate being skipped over. They demand attention, like [please insert evangelical religious group of choice] at the front door.' Hedging themselves in with superfluous references presumably gives even those with little to say a sense of authority and scientific validity. Alas, the pompous trappings often reveal shivering emperors. The Harvard system also seems to go hand-in-hand with endless qualification of the 'it might perhaps be suggested that, given the particular experimental context, some small correlation may conceivably exist, *mutatis mutandis*, between . . .' variety. A fictitious but not unfair example might be something like:

> Smith (1958) has demonstrated reasonably well – though one might quarrel slightly with his use of orthogonal rotation in the factor analysis (Zinot, 1945) – that coal miners are perceived as less feminine than young fashion models (see also Jones, 1962; White 1967a, 1967b; Young, 1968; and, for a slightly divergent view, Murphy, 1965, in press c), although there is some historical suggestion that the basic relationship was not unknown from earliest times (Plato, 1974; Rousseau, 1949; Wittgenstein, 1991).

The last three references, incidentally, demonstrate the curious practice of referring only to the most recent edition of venerable works – surely a referential disservice.

In this book, the reader who requires references is indeed obliged to do some searching – but not too much, I hope. I also hope that some of the extra material to be found with the basic references will repay the effort. I hope, finally, that the reader who never once turns to the back will still find the book of some interest.

ACKNOWLEDGEMENTS

My first thanks go to David Crystal, whose support for this and other undertakings is deeply appreciated. I also acknowledge the invaluable assistance of Suzanne de Larichelière; the book's appearance would have been seriously delayed without her labours. Third, I must thank Jane Aker for her help in the production. The book had its beginnings during a sabbatical leave in Dublin, and I am grateful to the Trinity College Library and Psychology Department for their aid and hospitality.

1

AN INTRODUCTORY OVERVIEW

Multilingualism is a powerful fact of life around the world, a circumstance arising, at the simplest level, from the need to communicate across speech communities. There have often existed important *lingua francas* which serve as aids to cross-group understanding, and which usually represent the language of a potent and prestigious society; thus, Greek, Latin, French, Arabic and, currently, English have all held sway, as have pidgins and 'artificial' or constructed languages (like Esperanto) in more restricted contexts. But the strong and obvious attractions of the lingua francas have generally co-existed with, rather than eliminated, more local forms and they have not spelled the death of multilingualism so much as they have been a product of it and, indeed, a contributor to it. Serious questions have been raised, however, about the greater language-killing potential of the present 'world language', English, and this is something to be discussed further; it is worth noting at the outset, though, that where a strong external variety actually pushes out a weakening indigenous one, the former has necessarily ceased to be merely a lingua franca, a language of intergroup convenience, and has come to possess – due to a variety of factors – outright replacement value.

To be bilingual or multilingual is not the aberration supposed by many (particularly, perhaps, by people in Europe and North America who speak a 'big' language); it is, rather, a normal and unremarkable necessity for the majority in the world today. A monolingual perspective is often, unfortunately, a consequence of possession of a powerful 'language of wider communication', as English, French, German, Spanish and other such languages are sometimes styled. This linguistic myopia is sometimes accompanied by a narrow cultural awareness and is reinforced by state policies which, in the main, elevate only one language to official status.

While there exist something like 5,000 languages in about 200 countries, a fact which itself argues for the prevalence of multilingualism, only a quarter of all states recognize more than one language. Also, even in those countries in which two or more varieties have legal status, one language is usually predominant, or has regional limitations, or carries with it

1

disproportionate amounts of social, economic and political power. Switzerland, for example, with its recognition of German, French, Italian and Romansch, shows clear linguistic dominance for one variety at the canton level and the four languages are not, in any event, anything like equal in cross-community utility. Singapore also has four official languages – English, Mandarin, Tamil and Malay – but the latter two are much less important than the former pair. Ireland recognizes both Irish and English as national varieties, but the first has, increasingly, only symbolic significance in the general life of the country.

Even in countries where more than one language has legal status, one cannot assume that multilingual encounters are common. On the other hand, they may not be rare in states officially recognizing only one or two varieties. Many African countries, for example, are societies so linguistically complex that multilingual interaction is commonplace; in officially English Nigeria some 80 million people speak about 400 languages. As we shall see, the occurrence of multilingualism at a personal level has a great deal to do with patterns of social interaction. You might live in the United States, where English has *de facto* status, and yet your life in a heterogeneous city like New York may require frequent switching between English and Spanish. Or, you might live in India – which recognizes fifteen languages – and never leave your monolingual enclave.

There is certainly a correlation between simple mobility and multilingualism. Scholarly and diplomatic interaction and exchange, for example, have always necessitated multilingual facility among an élite. But daily physical mobility is also important, accounting for a more widespread, non-élite multilingualism. Consider four illustrative examples from linguistically rich India.[1] A Bombay spice merchant has, as his maternal variety, a Kathiawari dialect of Gujerati, but at work he most often uses Kacchi. In the marketplace he speaks Marathi and, at the railway station, Hindustani. On internal air flights English is used, and he may watch English-language films at the cinema. He reads a Gujerati newspaper written in a dialect more standard than his own. A Bengali businessman who speaks both 'high' and 'low' Bengali has a 'primary' wife whose dialect is marked as a female variant and a 'secondary' wife who speaks Urdu. His office manager speaks Dhaki and his servants variously use Oriya, Bhojpuri, Awadhi, Maithili, Ahiri and Chatgaya. In a third case, we observe an Oriya married to a Tamil, who speaks English at home, whose children use Bengali, and who employs a Hindustani nurse and a Nepali watchman. Finally, consider a Sanskrit drama in which only the upper-caste characters speak Sanskrit, others in the cast using half a dozen other languages.

Two points suggest themselves here: first, and most obviously, these examples demonstrate the necessity for a multilingual competence; second, the fact that different domains and/or different social levels are associated with different varieties implies that the components of this competence need not be equally developed. That is, the knowledge of Marathi needed to buy rice in the market may not be sufficient to go beyond simple transactions; the level of Nepali required to deal with one's night watchman might not permit a deep discussion of current events. In fact, given the complexities here, and the social exigencies attaching to the various types of interaction, it would probably be rather non-productive to 'overdevelop' fluencies. Language use – here as elsewhere – generally extends only as required and, in cases in which more than one language is involved, different forms intertwine for different purposes. This is a phenomenon well known to students of *code-switching*, where individuals change languages frequently, often within one sentence. Here is an excerpt of a conversation between two Mexican Americans on the subject of cigarette smoking:

> Tu no fumas, verdad? Yo tampoco. Deje de fumar and I'm back to it again. . . . Se me acababan los cigarros en la noche. I'd get desperate, y ahi voy al basurero a buscar, a sacar, you know?[2]

It is a feature of much code-switching behaviour, by the way, that the language changes made are non-random, that a switch signifies something. In the full conversation from which the preceding lines are taken, speakers tend to use Spanish when self-conscious or embarrassed about their smoking, English when making more general or impersonal observations.

We come very quickly, then, to matters of linguistic balance, dominance and fluency. Is there such a person as a perfectly balanced bilingual (or multilingual), a person in whom all languages known are equally developed? The writer and critic George Steiner has claimed to be perfectly and maternally trilingual in French, English and German; perhaps closer inspection, however, would reveal that the balance among the three languages is not full – if it is, then Steiner is a rather exceptional individual.[3] The problems of assessing balance and fluency will be considered later and at least one of the issues relates to Steiner's observation that 'primary' multilingualism may be for some individuals (like himself) an 'integral state of affairs', that possession of several languages may not always be simply an extension from one original variety; this has some interesting psychological implications. Others have recently suggested a rethinking, too, of the 'ethos' of multilingualism,[4] and of the popular conception that monolingualism is somehow the norm. The linguistic complexities in the Indian examples just given certainly indicate a rich area of study, especially salutary, perhaps, for those linguists and others who 'inhabit the husks' of only one language themselves.[5]

Given the fact that multilingualism is a world phenomenon, but given also that official or prestige status is often restricted, it is apparent that attitudes towards multilingualism and language diversity in general are important. At an élite level, of course, multilingualism has always been encouraged, has been itself a marker of high status. In the Middle Ages those European scholars, diplomats and aristocrats who spoke Latin as a lingua franca enjoyed a level of education and privilege light years removed from the lives of the masses. The use of French in the royal courts of Europe is another example of an élite capacity. Voltaire (1694–1778), while visiting Berlin, noted that: 'Je me trouve ici en France. On ne parle que notre langue. L'allemand est pour les soldats et pour les chevaux; il n'est nécessaire que pour la route.'[6] Charles V, the Holy Roman Emperor (1519–56), is supposed to have neatly distributed his linguistic fluencies, speaking Spanish to God, Italian to women, French to men and German to horses. Education for the élite has always included a training in languages which evolved from a potent combination of necessity, snobbery and social boundary marking. Indeed, remnants of this are seen yet, and 'finishing' education still includes an important language component. Even Dotheboys Hall offered instruction in 'all languages living and dead'. Sadly, and particularly within the English-speaking world, the power of English has meant a progressive dilution of effort and achievement here, a retreat to be seen even at the highest postgraduate levels, where traditional language requirements are increasingly waived. Among other things, this has had the interesting effect of even more positively marking those with foreign-language competence.

It is hard to deny that proficiency in more than the mother tongue is an asset; the ease with which the trilingual Steiner, balanced or not, moves in a thicket of languages is enviable in his book on translation, *After Babel.* Members of the social élite, themselves multilingual, have often pointed to the advantages of their fluency. Emperor Charles V (again) observed that 'quot linguas calles, tot homines vales', meaning that one is worth as many people as languages known. Roger Bacon (1214–94), the thirteenth-century English Franciscan known as 'Doctor Mirabilis', wrote in his *Opus tertium* that *notitia linguarum est prima porta sapientiae* ('knowledge of languages is the doorway to wisdom').

There have been dissenting views. John Milton (1608–74) wrote:

> and though a linguist should pride himself to have all the tongues that Babel cleft the world into, yet if he have not studied the solid things in them as well as the words and lexicons, he were nothing so much to be esteemed a learned man as any yeoman or tradesman competently wise in his mother-dialect only.[7]

This appeared in Milton's essay, *Of Education* (1644) and was briefly referred to by Samuel Johnson in his great dictionary more than a century later (under the word *linguist*). Also in the seventeenth century, Samuel Butler (1612–80) – not the later author of *Erewhon*, but the writer of the rabelaisian and epic poem, *Hudibras* – composed a *Satyr upon the Imperfection and Abuse of Human Learning* in which the following lines appear:

> For the more languages a man can speak,
> His talent has but sprung the greater leak;
> And, for the industry he has spent upon't,
> Must full as much some other way discount.
> The Hebrew, Chaldee, and the Syriac
> Do, like their letters, set men's reason back,
> And turn their wits that strive to understand it
> (Like those that write the characters) left-handed.
> Yet he that is but able to express
> No sense at all in several languages,
> Will pass for learneder than he that's known
> To speak the strongest reason in his own.[8]

These few lines are interesting because they question the value of multilingualism *per se*, of having linguistic fluencies unmatched by wit. Butler's notebooks also reveal this view: 'He that has many languages to expresse his thoughts, but no thoughts worth expressing, is like one that can write all hands, but never the better sense, or can cast up any sum of money, but has none.'[9] One feels that Butler read with some appreciation the biblical story of Babel.[10] Butler's writing also reveals a belief that there exists some finite linguistic capacity, and that time spent on language learning must necessarily reduce that available for other pursuits – a theme I shall return to when discussing individual bilingualism. A final note here: given his remarks about the 'Hebrew, Chaldee, and the Syriac', one wonders what Butler made of *boustrophedon*, where alternate lines are written in opposite directions (i.e., right to left, then left to right, and so on; the practice was employed by the Greeks and others, and the term itself denotes turning like oxen ploughing a field).

A related point of interest here has to do with the historical equation of translation with treason (*traduttore–traditore*). This results from that identification with one's own language which has always been a marker of nationalism, and the perception (which is true, at least to some degree) that each language interprets and presents the world in a somewhat different way; the unique wellsprings of group consciousness, traditions, beliefs and values are thus seen as intimately entwined with language. One's language is one's inheritance and one's secret code. In fact, many writers – Wittgenstein in his *Tractatus* among them – have referred to the importance of language as a concealing, disguising medium co-existing with, and perhaps surpassing, its more obvious communicative role.

So translation is the revealing of deep matters to others, and may not be taken lightly. The translator, the one whose multilingual facility permits the straddling of boundaries, is then a type of quisling, but a quisling who must be allowed to do his spying, for obvious and practical reasons.[11] The alternative would be – and it is an alternative which might seem very appropriate and natural to a super-rational galactic visitor – a progressive and favoured reduction of languages; and this, even in (and perhaps because of) a contemporary world with several 'super-languages', is philosophically and nationalistically rejected by many.

There are as well, of course, many prejudices and preferences associated with languages. Charles V's choices have already been mentioned, and reflect what were considered appropriate selections according to context. This is also seen in code-switching behaviour. But preferences are often associated with language varieties *per se*, regardless of setting. We find Richard Carew (1555–1620), a sixteenth-century English poet and antiquary, writing about the 'excellency' of English, and going on to state that:

> The Italian is pleasant, but without sinews, as a still reflecting water; the French delicate, but ever nice as a woman, scarce daring to open her lips for fear of marring her countenance; the Spanish majestical but fulsome, running too much on the *o*, and terrible like the Devil in a play; the Dutch manlike, but withal very harsh, as one ready at every word to pick a quarrel.[12]

In the eighteenth century, G.W. Lemon observed that:

> Others then may admire the flimsiness of the French, the neatness of the Italian, the gravity of the Spanish, nay even the native hoarseness and roughness of the Saxon, High Dutch, Belgic and Teutonic tongues; but the purity and dignity, and all the high graceful majesty, which appears at present in our *modern English tongue*, will certainly recommend it to our most diligent researches.[13]

It is not surprising that most linguistic preferences – based upon historical pedigree, aesthetic judgement, 'logic' or whatever – reveal a liking for one's own variety. In his famous *Minute on Education* (1835), Thomas Macaulay (1800–59) wrote of English (as against Indian languages) that:

> The claims of our own language it is hardly necessary to recapitulate. It stands pre-eminent even among the languages of the West.... It may safely be said that the literature now extant in that language is of greater value than all the literature which three hundred years ago was extant in all the languages of the world together.[14]

At about the same time, Edwin Guest, in his *History of English Rhythms* (1838), noted that:

> That language, too [English] is rapidly becoming the great medium of civilisation, the language of law and literature to the Hindoo, of commerce to the African, of religion to the scattered islands of the Pacific. The range of its influence, even at the present day, is greater

than ever was that of the Greek, the Latin, or the Arabic; and the circle widens daily.[15]

George Marsh said, in 1860, that:

> English is emphatically the language of commerce, of civilisation, of social and religious freedom, of progressive intelligence, and of an active catholic philanthropy; and beyond any tongue ever used by man, it is of right the cosmopolite speech.[16]

And E. Higginson, in his English grammar of 1864, noted:

> For all the various and combined purposes of a language . . . for all the mixed uses of speech between man and man, and from man in aspiration to the one above him, we sincerely believe that there is not, nor ever was, a language comparable to the English. The strength, sweetness and flexibility of the tongue [recommend it].[17]

Furthermore, it is not only the 'large' languages of the world which have attempted to throw their weight around in this jingoistic way. The movement for the revival of Irish, for example, evoked similar sentiments. Towards the end of the last century, Irish was extolled for its 'perfection' and 'independence', which were so pronounced that it must clearly have been one of the first languages spoken on earth; indeed, an eighteenth-century scholar–soldier, Charles Vallancey, held that the origins of Irish lay with Carthage, that the language was a 'Punic–Celtic' compound, and that Ireland itself was the 'Thule of the Ancients'. Irish was seen as ideally suited for musical expression, and it was claimed that Irish vocal organs were naturally adapted for Gaelic speaking – thus Irish was already in the heads of non-Irish-speaking Irishmen, so to speak, and teaching it therefore necessitated a drawing-out rather than a putting-in. Finally, in a potent combination, Irish was seen as the 'casket which encloses the highest and purest religion that any country could boast of since the time of the twelve apostles'.[18] Similar associations and beliefs have probably been made concerning all languages and, indeed, many ordinary people are quite willing to pass judgements on languages.

The most important attitudes, prejudices and preferences about language and language choice are those enshrined in law or sanctioned practice, for these are the codified wishes of the socially dominant. The whole area of language planning, for example – which will be discussed later – can be seen in this light. Many of the difficulties encountered by minority-language communities in particular emerge because local desires do not mesh with state policy. The consequences of language contact here are fascinating, not only at the linguistic level itself, but also as a window onto the larger social scene, as a perspective from which to assess social movement. Struggles between 'big' and 'small' varieties will thus be central to the discussion, which is much more involved than might first be thought, and where problems abound at the most basic level (for example, just how are we to characterize a minority group, and why should so many 'small' communities rejoice in what Bertrand Russell once called 'the superior virtue of the oppressed'?).[19] Also, more evenly matched contests are being waged; the most widely known, perhaps, is that between English and French. The play here is occurring simultaneously in several contexts, two of the most instructive being in Canada – where linguistic matters have been particularly marked recently – and in Africa, where battles for linguistic hegemony take place on old colonial ground.

Whether we look at large or small combatants here, we shall have to deal with the ramifications of language contact, competition and conflict, with language maintenance, shift, decline and death and, in some instances, with language revival efforts. Many of these terms suggest an organic perspective on language and, historically, this has been a popular metaphorical treatment. An early expression of this notion is given by Thomas Jones in his seventeenth-century Welsh–English dictionary entitled *The British Language in its Lustre*:

> To Languages as well as Dominions (with all other things under the Sun) there is an appointed time; they have had their infancy, foundations and beginning, their growth and increase in purity and perfection; as also in spreading and propagation: their state of consistency; and their old age, declinings and decayes.[20]

Franz Bopp, the famous nineteenth-century linguist (1791–1867), also felt that languages were akin to living things: 'Languages are to be considered organic natural bodies, which are formed according to fixed laws, develop as possessing an inner principle of life, and gradually die out because they do not understand themselves any longer.'[21] The last few words of this quotation are curious, to say the least, but it is easy to see why the organic metaphor has proved appealing. Although languages themselves do not live or die, and obey no organic imperatives, their speakers do. In the sixteenth century, Joachim du Bellay (1523–60) was able to observe that:

> Languages are not born of themselves after the fashion of herbs, roots, or trees: some infirm and weak in their nature; the others healthy, robust, and more fitted to carry the burden of human conception; but all their virtue is born in the world of the desire and will of mortals.[22]

Languages *do*, then, have a span of existence which is granted by human society and culture rather than by natural laws. Linguists may no longer believe that languages 'behave like beans or chrysanthemums',[23] and they do not generally think that different languages are intrinsically stronger or weaker in some survival-of-the-fittest arena, but they do recognize that the fortunes of languages are inexorably bound up with those of their users. Perhaps we might consider languages as inorganic parasites on human hosts.

The organic view of language has, naturally enough, been most insistent at times of linguistic crisis. The Irish nationalist, Padraic Pearse, wrote about the nineteenth-century English educational system in Ireland as a 'murder machine' devoted to the elimination of indigenous culture and, especially, the Irish language, and more contemporary writers have also claimed that languages do not 'die naturally' but are, rather, killed by those seeking to destroy a nation. On the other hand, some observers (Irish among them) have suggested that languages may commit suicide, that it may be impossible to eradicate a language which its speakers truly wish to retain.[24] The popular Irish writer Flann O'Brien (Myles na gCopaleen) thus felt that: 'The present extremity of the Irish language is due mainly to the fact that the Gaels deliberately flung that instrument of beauty and precision from them.'[25] It is clear that terms like 'murder' and 'suicide' are highly charged and likely to obscure rather than clarify, to oversimplify matters into an us-versus-them format, where oppressors and oppressed kindly wear black or white hats, and where morality resides exclusively in one camp. We will have occasion to see later that it is, in any event, a profound error to think of language decline as other than a symptom of widespread social confrontation between unequal forces. The implication is that revival or restoration efforts, attempts to bring a language back to life, as it were, are quite unlikely to succeed if the focus is solely or mainly linguistic.

These comments notwithstanding, one would have to be very naive to imagine that treatments of language, even within the academic literature, will always prove to be disinterested assessments. For this reason, some recent efforts have been made to classify and organize features of importance for discussions of language contact, and it is felt that, because of the unequal forces involved, this exercise might be particularly worthwhile where minority languages are concerned. A comprehensive, multidisciplinary analysis of language situations would be, first of all, intrinsically useful context by context. It might also permit the isolation of generalities which would, in turn, allow helpful comparisons to be made. One might, as well, find it possible to make more accurate predictions about language maintenance and shift and, particularly from the perspective of minority-language speakers themselves, to indicate what is desirable, what is possible and what is likely in their multilingual settings.

Work here will be described more fully in due course, but a number of factors which seem especially salient in areas of language contact include the geographic, sociological, psychological, historical, religious and economic. In geographic terms, it seems useful to ascertain if a (minority) language in question is unique to one state, if it occurs in more than one, or if it is a minority variety in some settings but a majority language elsewhere. Also important are the types of connections existing between politically separated minority groups: do they adjoin one another (as, for example, the Basques in France and Spain) or is there a geographical gulf (as exists between the Catalans in Spain and Sardinia)? We might also want to know if communities exist in some cohesive manner (the Occitan group, for example) or if speakers are scattered, generally lacking a 'heartland' (the Saami community of Finland, Norway, Sweden and Russia; or the diffuse Romany-speaking population of Europe).[26]

Sociologically, we should consider the prevalence of in-group or out-group marriage as a factor in language viability, as is what has been termed 'institutional completeness' – roughly, the degree to which a language community finds it possible to live a normal and complete social life in and through its own tongue. Psychological factors will of course be central here, too. I have already touched upon the subject of *attitudes* to language, and there are clearly many dimensions. We need to be aware, for example, not only of a group's own views of its linguistic situation, but also of the attitudes held by those outside the group, particularly those whose social, economic and political positions are, or could be, powerful. It is quite common nowadays, for example, to find that mainstream tolerance for linguistic and cultural diversity within a society does not extend to active promotion of that diversity; an inability to perceive the difference between a passive goodwill and something more dynamic will clearly have serious consequences.

An historical dimension is essential in understanding multilingual matters. Although the history of language is an undeniable component of social history generally, one finds that historians – with some exceptions – have not paid attention to it. Equally, however, most students of language have not done their historical homework. Indeed, examination and interpretation of the historical record has sometimes been devalued for not producing data of the sort most familiar to social-psychological researchers; this surely indicates an impoverished conception of data.

Religious matters often interpenetrate with linguistics. As already pointed out, Irish revivalists made much of the connection they felt between the Irish language and Catholicism. The usefulness of this sort of linkage is that the strength of religion can be used to prop up and valorize a threatened language and, if the combination can be made firm enough, the united front can powerfully oppose a rival; thus, in the Irish case, English was attacked not solely as the linguistic foe, but more specifically as the vehicle of a materialist and secular society. A related but broader question worthy of more attention is whether secularization *per se* contributes to language shift. Finally here, economic factors must be considered.[27] It may not be the case that language-contact dynamics are simply reducible to economic underpinnings, but mundane economic and pragmatic facts have a great deal to do with multilingual interaction, and with minority-language vitality in particular. This is not, of course, a very popular line among the more romantically-inclined apologists for language maintenance and revival, but ordinary group members have historically proved very sensitive to the materially advancing or retarding aspects of language use.

One *setting* that obviously requires special attention is the school.[28] It is, first of all, a powerful and visible instrument of the state and one expects that officially sanctioned practices will be reflected in its curriculum and policies. Second, it can be understood as an arena in which interactions among groups (parents, teachers, children, speech communities) reflect wider social currents. Policies of cultural–linguistic assimilation or pluralism, for example, can be examined in detail here. Third, many more specific sociolinguistic issues are susceptible to interpretation in educational terms, issues including the acceptance of dialect and language variation, and the relationship between language and identity.

Just as the school exists as an arm of the state, so it is often singled out by language communities as the linchpin of their continuing cultural and linguistic identity. Wherever societal heterogeneity exists, schools may be asked to play a part – perhaps the central part – in maintaining and encouraging identities thought to be at risk. Schools and teachers have increasingly, in fact, played the role of agents of social change and have correspondingly experienced difficulties since this does not always mesh well with their more traditional task of transmitting core or basic skills. There has thus been created a tension between 'civism' and 'pluralism' in many jurisdictions in North America, Australia, Europe and elsewhere – that is, in settings of linguistic and cultural complexity.[29] Kedourie's view is worth noting, whether the 'nationalism' is that of an officially positioned majority, or that of some subgroup within a larger society, a group which contributes to that society's multilingualism and which pins its hopes for recognition, or status, or autonomy largely on the school:

> On nationalist theory ... the purpose of education is not to transmit knowledge, traditional wisdom, and the ways devised by a society for attending to the common concerns; its purpose rather is wholly political, to bend the will of the young to the will of the nation.[30]

There are many implications here that will have to be taken up later, but possibly the most important, and the most disturbing, is that under the banner of ethnolinguistic solidarity and language promotion children may become pawns in political machinations. Thirty years ago, a sensitive observer of the educational thrust of the Irish revival warned that 'children's minds must not be made the battleground of a political wrangle',[31] and another decried the use of schoolchildren as 'digits in the Irish revival statistics'.[32] These and other matters will take more specific shape when we consider such innovations as French immersion education in Canada, bilingual programmes in the United States and, of course, the attempted revival of Irish at school.

Of course, schools have very often made virtually *no* adaptations when faced with classroom heterogeneity. The most common practice, historically, has been for schools to cleave strongly to received policy – in content, structure, language and so on – leaving pupils to conform and change. Linguistically this has meant considerable hardship, and a sink-or-swim approach has surely led to miseducation and prematurely curtailed education for many. The school was, however, merely adopting a prescriptivist stance that was widely endorsed outside its gates. The essence of this position, in language matters at any rate, is a sense that one variety is 'correct', or uniquely appropriate for all members of society, or the sole carrier of prestige and power or, indeed, the particular repository of aesthetic, social and logical value. It will be clear, then, that multilingual settings provide a powerful incentive for prescriptive tendencies, especially where groups feel threatened by, or uneasy with, their linguistic neighbours. It also stands to reason that prescriptivism is closely allied with language defence, with efforts to maintain the 'purity' and integrity of a language, with attempts to prevent other languages from breaching the barricades.

One of the most obvious ways to protect a language is to establish a formal institution charged with this task.[33] The first important body here was the Accademia della Crusca, founded in Florence in 1582; it acted to safeguard the Tuscan dialect which Dante and Petrarch had championed in their work, and which had emerged as a sort of central mediator between northern and southern Italian dialects. Other academies followed in other countries. Spain had its Real Academia Española, established in 1713 by the Bourbon king Philip V, and its motto, *limpia, fija y da esplendor*, makes clear the desire to clarify, purify and glorify the language. This institution spread its influence with the Spanish empire and, in due course, Spanish-language academies were set up in more than a dozen states in the new world; these are now linked in an association pledged to the unity of Spanish. Academies in Europe also proliferated from the eighteenth century, and Arabic bodies exist in several countries.

The most famous academy, and the one upon which many others have modelled themselves is the Académie Française, founded by Cardinal Richelieu in 1635. Its aim was to promote its conception of clarity, simplicity and good taste in French, to encourage all that was 'noble, polished and reasonable'. The forty 'immortals' who made up the academy were given 'absolute power ... over literature and language'. The academicians were drawn largely from the church, the army and the nobility and were not trained philologists or lexicographers by any means. It is not surprising, then, that the dictionary produced in 1694 proved inadequate; in addition to the dilettantism of its makers, it omitted many words which, while current, were not thought sufficiently polite to be included. In modern times, the French academy has become best known for its efforts to purge foreign borrowings from the language – particularly English ones – and to create French terms where necessary. It has thus added a modernizing function to its original mandate.

Conspicuous by its absence is an English-language academy.[34] How did English remain 'uncaptured' and how has its 'haphazard and luxuriant growth' gone unchecked while French, Spanish and other languages have been given 'horticultural advice' for centuries? There have certainly been those who wanted an English-language body, including Daniel Defoe and Jonathan Swift. It should have come about, perhaps, in the seventeenth century; the Royal Society was founded in 1662, and it struck a committee for 'improving' the language – Dryden and Evelyn were among the members – but nothing was accomplished. What *did* happen, in both England and the United States, was the production of dictionaries by one-man academies. Samuel Johnson published his great work in 1755 and, in America, Noah Webster issued his dictionary in 1827. Both of these men were rather ambivalent about the prescriptive power and desirability of their efforts. Johnson certainly supported the potentially purifying function, hoping that his work might stabilize English and arrest its 'degeneration'. At the same time, he rejected what he called linguistic 'embalming' and implied that formal works could not, in any case, prevent linguistic innovation. Webster agreed, but also wanted to remove 'improprieties and vulgarisms [and] those odious distinctions of provincial dialects'. They each tried, then, to 'ascertain' English as they saw it while remaining aware of the dangers and improbabilities associated with prescription.

Contemporary linguists, particularly in the English-speaking world, have generally rejected prescriptive attempts of the academy or dictionary variety, and a widespread conviction is that common usage is the ultimate arbiter of 'correctness'. However, anyone who reads the newspapers realizes that a concern for 'good' English animates many people who have very clear ideas of what this variety is; moaning and worrying about the state of the language are often allied to a perception that school standards are falling, and that 'inappropriate' class or regional varieties represent a linguistic fifth column threatening the desired *status quo*. There are, as well, any number of popular books on the subject, with titles like *The Plight of English* and *Strictly Speaking: Will America be the Death of English?*[35] Given this continuing public concern, on the one hand, and the dislike many linguists have of entering into battle, it is apparent that more illumination is needed of that no-man's-land between academic linguistics and common usage.

In this brief introduction, I have tried to point to some of the salient aspects of multilingualism which will be taken up in the chapters following. The simple prevalence of multilingualism needs documenting, as does reaction to it from all quarters. Multilingual and bilingual usage, and matters of fluency, balance and switching will be addressed in a consideration of individual and group interaction. Classification of multilingual settings and the special problems of minority-language groups are of interest, not only intrinsically, but also because they provide a framework within which we can view broader social and linguistic relations. The school's role in multilingual societies is, as suggested above, important and sometimes pivotal. Finally here, prescriptive tendencies also have their part to play in multilingual reality. Overall, this book will outline something of the complexity associated with a world of many languages; and I hope that these introductory remarks have shown something of the breadth of the matter.

The book's aim could be seen as tracing the course of multilingualism, through individuals and societies, with a view both to understanding it and appreciating its influence upon human life. This requires a multidisciplinary approach, just as the classification scheme mentioned above did, but it also necessitates an interdisciplinary perspective. Not only, in other words, do we have to consider psychological, historical, educational and other approaches; we also must try to see how the interrelationships among them work. This is quite a formidable task and the result here is clearly an imperfect one. The idea of having, however, a fairly concise summary of the topic – suitably referenced for more specialized study – is sufficiently attractive to warrant an attempt. Not the least of my hopes here is that readers will find a treatment which is enjoyable as well as informative.

2

LANGUAGES IN THE WORLD

LANGUAGE ORIGINS

In the Tower of Babel story, in Genesis, the divine punishment for human temerity is the creation of a confusion of languages; this is remedied, in a curious way, with the glossolalia of Pentecost (noted in Acts) – that intriguing 'speaking in tongues' which still finds expression in some religious gatherings, but which is hardly a common language in any ordinary sense. Many linguists and others, of course, have felt that linguistic diversity is not a punishment but rather a vital component of human life, and if we go further back than Babel we may find some support for this. The famous injunction, once the flood had receded, to 'be fruitful and multiply' has been interpreted as including linguistic diversification; that is, Noah's descendants were commanded to develop new languages. By the time we reach the Tower of Babel we discover, of course, that they had not done so ('And the whole earth was of one language, and of one species': Genesis XI:1) and, thus, God's dissatisfaction with their presumptions was allied to the idea that they required a firmer nudge towards language diversity. But if diversity first occurred at this point, what was the original language?[1]

Herodotus reports that the Egyptian pharaoh Psamtik (663–610 BC) arranged for two babies to be nurtured without hearing any language. At the age of two, the infants apparently said *becos*, a Phrygian word meaning 'bread'. Frederic II of Hohenstaufen (1194–1250) attempted a similar experiment, but without success, for it was found that 'the children could not live without clappings of the hands, and gestures, and gladness of countenance, and blandishments'. Later still, James IV of Scotland (1473–1513) put two infants with a dumb woman, and Lindesay the historian noted that 'some say they spoke good Hebrew, but as to myself I know not but by hearsay'. All of these attempts were based on the assumption that, if left uninfluenced, children would somehow come out with the original language, an assumption not now widely shared! But the Mogul emperor Akbar (1542–1605) had also challenged it; he believed that children isolated from human speech would not speak themselves and in *his* experiment, children sequestered for four years in a *Gang Mahal* (dumb-house) supported this belief: 'No cry came from that house of silence, nor was any speech heard there. In spite of their four years, they had no part of the talisman of speech, and nothing came out except the noise of the dumb.'[2] In his *Essays*, Michel de Montaigne (1533–92) supported the earlier view:

> I believe that a child brought up in complete solitude ... would have some kind of speech to express his ideas, for it is not likely that nature would deprive us of this resource when she has given it to many other animals ... but it is yet to be found out what language the child would speak; and what has been conjectured about it has no great probability.[3]

Naturally occurring 'experiments' support Akbar's belief, however. 'Wolf-children', 'bear-children' and other such feral youngsters have been widely reported (if rather sparsely documented) for hundreds of years. None could speak or understand speech and, indeed, most efforts to teach them language were failures. Victor, the 'wild boy of Aveyron'[4] discovered in 1799 aged about eleven, is perhaps the best-described case but he too, although developing some comprehension, was unable to speak. All of this suggests what is now obvious to most people: although human beings may be 'prewired' and ready, in an evolutionary sense, to learn language, the manifestation and the specific form of this capacity are determined by social influence.

Apart from ill-considered (and unethical) speculations based upon experiments with infants, the question of language origins remains a puzzle. Was there one original language (the principle of *monogenesis*) or did several emerge simultaneously in different places (*polygenesis*)? And, in either case, how did language arise? We are obviously on shaky ground here, so much so that, in 1866, the Société de Linguistique de Paris forbade all further discussions on language origins, since all were deemed to be fruitless and speculative, and wasteful of linguistic scholarship better applied elsewhere.[5] Recently, though, the question has been given renewed attention and (again in Paris) a 1981 conference sponsored by UNESCO heard thirty-five papers on 'glossogenetics'.

The great Danish linguist Otto Jespersen (1860–1943) grouped some common theories into five types; the fact that they have all been given silly nicknames is an indication of their perceived seriousness:[6]

1   *The 'bow-wow' theory*: Words arose through onomatopoeic association: a dog's bark and the wind's noise became the names for dog and wind. Obviously this theory is limited, in that most objects in the world do not make characteristic noises. Furthermore, it fails to account for different languages' representations of the same natural sound: why do

roosters say 'cock-a-doodle-doo' in English and 'cocorico' in French?

2   *The 'pooh-pooh' theory*: Words derive from spontaneous exclamations of an emotional basis (*ouch!*). Again, however, this is a limited theory, to say the least.

3   *The 'ding-dong' theory*: People reacted to external phenomena by making specific noises (as a bell goes 'ding-dong' on impact) which somehow reflected them. There *is* some evidence for sound symbolism; in English, for example, many words beginning with *sl* mean something unpleasant, words with high front vowels convey smallness (*teeny, wee*), and so on. Again, however, this hardly accounts for a large percentage of vocabulary, even if we expand things by supposing that *mama* reflects the movement of lips approaching the maternal breast, or that *bye-bye* and *ta-ta* are the lips and tongue 'waving good-bye'.

4   *The 'yo-he-ho' theory*: As people worked together, communal and rhythmical grunts emerged, which duly evolved into language. Again, obviously limited.

5   *The 'la-la' or the 'hey-nonny-nonny' theory*: This view of Jespersen's was that language began with 'emotional, song-like outpourings of primitive man, which were gradually canalized into speech'.[7]

This list of theories is not exhaustive, and others are yet more fanciful. Still, despite the obvious limitations, each theory may represent some contribution to language development and, in so doing, may suggest that any single-factor approach is likely to be deficient.

With the nineteenth-century Darwinian revelations, and with all the subsequent theorizing which combines principles of natural selection with those of genetics (in what has been termed the 'modern synthesis'), it is not surprising that, now, language origins and development are embedded in a larger evolutionary picture. Speech developed because it had survival value, and this value must have been considerable, given that the evolutionary alterations, especially in the larynx, which enable human language also mean increased risk of choking.[8]

A very recent theory holds that the survival value of language was originally linked to social bonding.[9] Gossip, the banal exchange of social experiences, is thus seen as central, for it represents the human equivalent of mutual grooming in baboons and chimpanzees. This has been related to a linkage between the size of the neocortex and the optimal size of a social group. If the latter, for human beings, is roughly three times that of baboons and chimps (about 150 individuals, as opposed to 50) then human grooming as social lubricant would have had to increase commensurately. It was at this point, so the theory goes, that language as a bonding instrument arrived. Those most proficient could then positively affect their survival chances by being more informed and more manipulative. The theory is of course quite controversial, but the universality of gossip –

constituting as much as 70 per cent of everyday talk, by one reckoning – is indisputable. Whether it is the basis of further language functions and refinements, or whether it developed from previous linguistic capacities, is an open question.

The linguist Charles Hockett – perhaps the most prominent of Chomsky's critics, by the way – has provided us with a set of 'design features' of animal communication, including human language, in which the evolutionary value of speech is central. Those features which distinguish human speech from other communication systems are:

1   *displacement*: the ability to talk about things remote in space and/or time;
2   *productivity*: the capacity to say things never before said or heard which are yet understandable and acceptable by others;
3   *traditional transmission*: by which linguistic conventions are carried on through teaching and learning (*perhaps* shared by other species);
4   *pattern duality*: the enormous store of words is represented by small combinations of a still smaller stock of distinguishable sounds, themselves meaningless (thus the words *tack, cat* and *act* are semantically distinct yet are composed of only three of the basic, meaningless sounds).

Other design features, though shared with other animals, are none the less much more refined in human language (semantics, for example, or the arbitrariness of the linkage between meaning and sound: the word *salt* is not, itself, either salty or granular; *whale* is a little word for a huge object, while *micro-organism* is the reverse).

Hockett's discussion includes the central issue of how human speech 'left' the others; how the uniquely human features developed. In general, the answer is clear: the survival value just mentioned. Specifically, Hockett gives some speculative consideration to just how initial, perhaps accidental, uses of these features might have occurred; positive consequences would then be 'reinforced' in an evolutionary sense. Throughout, the story of language development is inextricably tied to larger social evolution: 'Man's own remote ancestors, then, must have come to live in circumstances where a slightly more flexible system of communication ... made just the difference between surviving ... and dying out.'[10]

However language originally developed, it is clear that all known languages are of considerable complexity. There are no 'primitive' languages, and although different varieties can be very divergent indeed, in the way they interpret and codify the world, none has been found which is deficient for its speakers' purposes and environment. In 1921, the linguist Edward Sapir (1884–1939) observed that:

The lowliest South African Bushman speaks in the forms of a rich symbolic system that is in essence perfectly comparable to the speech of the cultivated Frenchman.... When it comes to linguistic form, Plato walks with the Macedonian swineherd, Confucius with the head-hunting savage of Assam.[11]

Well, the phrasing here is no longer, perhaps, *comme il faut* – and there is more head-hunting now in corporate jungles than in those of Assam – but Sapir's words continue to be endorsed by virtually all linguists.

Finally here, to end with a definition, we might say that the essence of human language is a communication system composed of arbitrary symbols which possess an agreed-upon significance within a community.[12] Further, these symbols are independent of immediate context, and are connected in rule-governed ways. The existence of *rules* (or grammar) is of course essential for infinite creativity based upon a finite number of elements (*productivity*, in Hockett's scheme).

LANGUAGES AND LANGUAGE FAMILIES

It seems sensible to me to begin a discussion of multilingualism by considering how many languages there are in the world, which are the most widespread, which have the greatest number of speakers, and so on. This turns out to be a more difficult task than might first be imagined.

In 1929, the Académie Française identified some 2,800 different languages and a German estimate of 1931 was about 3,000.[13] Yet between these two (in 1930) John Firth, the first person to hold a chair in linguistics in Britain, had said that there were approximately 1,500 languages in the world.[14] Current estimates are higher than any of these – around 4,500 languages. What accounts for this large variability? There are four main factors of importance: inadequate basic knowledge, the 'dead or alive' distinction, the 'naming' problem and, perhaps most salient, the language–dialect dimension (the last three are all specific instances of the first general point).

The world may be much smaller now than it once was, but there are still areas which remain little known. In parts of Africa, South America and Oceania, for example, the linguistic jigsaw still lacks some pieces and has others that do not seem to fit. In New Guinea, we find an incredibly rich and complicated linguistic scene; indeed, some have claimed it is the most complex area in the world. Yet, because there are groups uncontacted and languages unknown, estimates of language numbers range from about 600 to about 1,000 and population estimates range from 3 to 5 million. Basic language surveys are non-existent or incomplete in many parts of the world; even in 'developed' societies, census information – especially that touching upon language abilities and use – is notoriously unreliable, subject to a wide variety of hindrances (geographical, political, psychological, and so on).[15]

Table 2.1 Gaelic speakers[16]

Census year	Canada	Nova Scotia
1931	32,000	25,000
1941	32,700	12,000
1951	14,000	6,800
1961	7,500	3,700
1971	21,400	1,400

Sometimes this means that languages are 'missed' altogether and sometimes – more commonly today – it confuses our understanding of the
distribution of known varieties. For example, in table 2.1 are the findings
of five Canadian censuses on Scots Gaelic speakers, in the country as a
whole and in the province of Nova Scotia specifically. On the face of it,
something remarkable happened between 1961 and 1971: the pattern of
decline, country-wide, was dramatically altered. In fact, for the 1971 census,
Celtic languages other than Welsh were lumped in with the Gaelic figures.
Anyone who looked at the forty-year pattern, and who knew anything about
immigration flows, might well have thought that something was amiss in the
1971 reporting, but a less well-informed reader who checked only the most
recent survey could be widely misled.

If we do not always have accurate basic information, it follows that we
cannot be sure if a language once recorded continues to be spoken.
Languages are clearly vulnerable to social, political and economic changes
affecting their users, and physical disease can often rapidly decimate a
speech community. These factors take their greatest toll, of course, among
'small' or 'endangered' languages and these, in turn, are often the ones we
knew least about to begin with. It is interesting to note, in this connection,
that many scholars who *have* shown interest in threatened varieties have
been animated largely by antiquarian and literary motives; that is, they have
not always cared very much about the language as a living oral medium.
The 'last' Cornish speaker, for example, Dolly Pentreath of Mousehole,[17]
died in 1777; formal concern for the language took another century to gear
up. More pointedly, consider Matthew Arnold's deep interest in Celtic
literature, a concern which co-existed with a desire for the rapid disappearance of spoken Welsh and the assimilation of all the Celtic peoples.[18]
The study of languages safely dead, or on the way to extinction, is an
altogether neater scholastic exercise than is coming to grips with breathing
speakers. One recalls, here, the formidable Miss Blimber in *Dombey and Son*:
'She was dry and sandy with working in the graves of deceased languages.
None of your live languages for Miss Blimber. They must be dead – stone
dead – and then Miss Blimber dug them up like a Ghoul.' Dickens's
characterization of philology in the 1840s (*Dombey and Son* was written

between 1846 and 1848) retains some degree of accuracy today.

It may also be quite difficult to ascertain just when a language is dead, since the process of decline may be a gradual one in which speakers' competence and language functions shrink.[19] The death of the last speaker is one thing; a progressively debilitating illness is another – but it might well be that at some point in a lingering decline, a point at which a competing variety's power seems overwhelming, we might for some purposes at least consider the first language gone. Practically speaking, this point might be reached when a language – perhaps already greatly restricted in form or function – becomes only a passive competence and is no longer used.

There is of course considerable drama attaching to a last speaker's death, and it may be a bit deflating to learn that the legendary Dolly Pentreath – whose house in Mousehole is marked with a plaque, and whose stone memorial stands in the churchyard in Paul, just above Mousehole – was *not* the last person who could speak Cornish. We may be on firmer ground in assuming that Ned Maddrell was the last native speaker of Manx when he died in 1974. Still more confident were French researchers, who reported in 1985 that 82-year-old Tevfik Esenc was the last speaker of Oubykh, a language of the Caucasus.[20] It would be fair to say, incidentally, that it was not only an impending language death which fascinated the researchers; more important was Oubykh's virtually unparalleled phonological richness – eighty-two consonants, but only three vowels.

With improved communications we can, nowadays, track the fortunes of languages more accurately, providing the interest and opportunity are there. Heightened attention does not ensure, unfortunately, that we can stem linguistic decline. A good example of this – and one which also reflects the complex interweaving of language with all other aspects of social life and intergroup contact – is found in the current status of aboriginal varieties in Canada.[21] It was recently estimated ('as nearly as can be determined') that there are fifty-three distinct indigenous languages, in eleven language groups, in the country. Some of these are not unique to Canada: in the Eskimo-Aleut family, for example, there are three times as many speakers (47,000) of Inuktitut outside Canada (mostly in Greenland) as within, and this proportion is about the same for Tlingit (a total of 2,000 speakers in northern British Columbia, Alaska and the Yukon) and Dakota (15,000 speakers in central Canada and the United States). Few of the fifty-three languages are healthy, as table 2.2 indicates.

Han, an Athapaskan language spoken in Alaska and the Yukon, is one of those eight in the final category. A population of several hundred at the turn of the century was reduced by smallpox, typhus and other diseases, so that by the 1930s only about 60 people were left. Since then, the population has recovered to perhaps 400, but the language has not. Even more serious is the state of Tagish, another language in the same area, where Angela Sidney was described in 1988 as the last 'fluent' speaker. The demise of

Table 2.2   The indigenous languages of Canada

State of health	Number of speakers (Canada)	Number of languages
Excellent chance of survival	More than 5,000	3
Moderately endangered	1,000–5,000	13
Endangered	500–1,000	11
Quite endangered	100–500	13
Extremely endangered	10–100	5
Verging on extinction	fewer than 10	8

Tagish cannot be laid entirely at the feet of English, as it suffered heavily – through trade and intermarriage – from Tlingit, which is itself now on the endangered list.[22]

Whatever the reasons, it is surely a sad day when any language becomes extinct as an ordinary communicative medium. To the degree that different languages represent and transmit different perspectives of the world, we are all diminished when one is lost. Dr Johnson may not have been entirely accurate when he equated the loss of language with that of national pedigrees,[23] but clearly something momentous has happened when a Dolly Pentreath or an Angela Sidney dies.

The 'naming' problem arises simply because a language is often given different designations. The Oubykh language I mentioned above, for example, is often referred to as Ubykh by non-francophone writers, and it has also been called Ubyx and Pekhi. Multiple names are of course particularly likely to occur for remote, 'small' varieties, but even better-known languages may have several, and it is not at all the case that the various names are similar (as with Oubykh–Ubykh–Ubyx). Here are some examples:[24]

Principal area	Names for the same variety
South Africa	Fanagolo, Isikula, Silunguboi, Cilololo
Congo	Kituba, Ikeleve, Fiote, Monokutuba
Cameroon	Nso, Lamnso, Bansaw
Sudan	Otoro, Kawama, Dhitoro
Zaire	Zande, Badjande, Niam-Niam
Turkey	Circassian, Adygey, Cherkes
Bhutan	Dzongkha, Bhutanese, Lhoke, Bhotia
Indonesia	Ambonese, Nusulaut, Haruku
New Guinea	Ikobi-Mena, Kasere, Wailemi, Meni
Colombia	Desano, Wina, Boleka, Kusibi
Brazil	Atruahi, Jawaperi, Waimiri

| North America | Gwichin, Loucheux, Tukudh, Kutchin |
| Mexico | Matlatzinca, Ocuilteco, Tlahura |

Multiple names arise for a number of reasons. The names of different subgroups, tribes or clans may all become attached to the language they share. Different groups of 'foreigners' – whether adjacent language communities, explorers or invaders, or scholars of different nationalities – may have their own names for the same people and language. Different writing systems and conventions will also, of course, complicate matters: just a small variation (as between Ubykh and Oubykh) may lead to problems of indexing and categorization. One of the greatest contributors to multiple naming, however, is the confusion between language and dialect; I am sure, for example, that some of the names listed above for the 'same' language are, in fact, names for different dialects within one larger variety.

A dialect,[25] strictly speaking, is a variety of a language which differs from other varieties in its vocabulary, grammar and pronunciation (accent); because, however, dialects are forms of the same language, they are ostensibly mutually intelligible – French speakers cannot understand Fanagolo speakers, but Texans can understand Cockneys (theoretically). If you *brew* your tea, pronounce it *tay* and say *Come here till I pour you a cup*, your friend should know what is happening, even if she *mashes* her tea and would invite you to the table *so that* she can pour you a cup. However, we have all heard some dialects that are almost impossible to comprehend because of the extreme variation in one or another of the three components – so mutual intelligibility can certainly be problematic. Indeed, there are degrees of distinction within dialects themselves. Within a Norfolk dialect we could identify East and South varieties; we could talk, on different occasions, about Yorkshire dialect or the dialect of Dentdale. Whether we describe such smaller varieties as dialects themselves, or subdialects, the important point is that continuing subdivisions are theoretically possible (if of diminishing general use) all the way down to *idiolect* – the speech of one person.

Mutual intelligibility as a criterion of dialects (and not languages) falters at another level. Suppose we observe a *dialect continuum*, along which lie varieties A, B, C and D. Speakers of dialect A can easily understand B, can barely follow C, but cannot comprehend D. Are A and D then different languages, even though C and D speakers understand one another, even though a chain of intelligibility exists from A through to D? Such continua are in fact quite common: dialects of German and Dutch form such a chain, as do varieties of Slovak, Czech, Ukrainian, Polish and Russian, or western Romance dialects of Italian, French, Catalan, Spanish and Portuguese. This is not just an old-world feature, of course; consider, for example, the long Spanish–Portuguese frontier in South America.

We must also bear in mind here issues of political allegiance and national identity (and power: 'A language,' said Max Weinreich (1894–1969) 'is a dialect that has an army and navy'). Cantonese and Mandarin speakers may have considerable difficulty understanding one another but they are considered to speak dialects of Chinese, not only because they use the same written form, but also because of the overarching state of which they are members. On the other hand, Norwegian and Danish speakers can understand each other well, but the demands of national and political identity require that they have different languages. Norwegians and Swedes may thus claim that they can hardly understand Danish, or 'that the Danes cannot differentiate between Norwegian and Swedish and therefore have to ask Scandinavian tourists what nationality they are before they decide how to treat them'.[26] On the basis of intelligibility alone, there are two Scandinavian languages: a continental variety which comprises Norwegian, Danish and also Swedish, and an insular language (Icelandic and Faroese). There are other examples, too, of the dominance of political concerns over purely linguistic ones, concerns which dictate that Serbian and Croatian, Hindi and Urdu, Flemish and Dutch, and so on, are to be seen as separate languages. It can be appreciated that these important matters of pride and status are changeable over time, as groups redefine themselves *vis-à-vis* others. Among the Urhobo dialects of Nigeria, mutual intelligibility was generally considered quite high until Isoko speakers began to claim that their 'language' was different from the rest, a claim coinciding with their demands for increased political autonomy. Speakers of the Okpe dialect – linguistically very close to Isoko – were not making such nationalistic claims, and *they* continued to perceive mutual intelligibility. It is possible that, given sufficient time, Isoko and Okpe could diverge to such an extent that mutual intelligibility would truly be lost.[27] Besides time, some group volition would help, too, and Isoko speakers' nationalism is central here; if, as well, decreasing group contact could be contrived, then elements would be in place similar to those which created a transition from dialect to language status for French, Italian, Romanian, Portuguese and Spanish – the Romance languages which began life as dialects of the vulgar Latin of the Roman empire (the word 'romance' comes from the vulgar Latin *romanice* – meaning 'in the local variety (descended from Latin)', and contrasted with *latine* (i.e., 'in Latin itself').

It is when all these factors are taken into account that we arrive at a current total of some 4,500 living languages.[28] These are arranged in *families* of related varieties, although in many cases the classification is unclear or debatable. The idea of interrelationships among languages, of family trees and lineages is, of course, hardly new. Giraldus Cambrensis[29] (Gerallt Gymro, or Gerald of Wales: 1147–1223) noted in his *Descriptio Cambriae* that Welsh, Cornish and Breton had a common source, which itself had connections with Latin and Greek. Centuries ago, it was well understood in Europe, for example, that French, Spanish, Portuguese and other Romance varieties were all related; indeed the parent language, Latin, continued to exist. *Padre, père, pai* and *pare* all have some obvious resemblance to the Latin *pater*. By the sixteenth century, the Italic, Germanic and Slavic clusters were all, in fact, recognized (in Europe) because of well-trodden trade paths. The growth of knowledge about the Indo-European languages in particular can serve here as a convenient illustration of language-family matters.[30]

Developments in commerce, and the linguistic contacts they established, were accompanied by more and more adventurous scholarly excursions. Joseph Scaliger (1549–1609), for example, attempted to order European languages into four major and seven minor classes. The first set corresponds to the Greek, Germanic, Slavic and Italic groups we know today, and the second also has recognizable divisions. Sixteenth- and seventeenth-century linguists generally approached the task of organizing languages as if they were studying minerals, flowers or animals; thus, language classifications resembled the more traditional herbals and bestiaries. The Swiss naturalist, Gesner, published a dictionary of languages in 1555 (*Mithridates*) as one of a series of taxonomic volumes. Along with language locations and histories, Gesner set out the Lord's Prayer in twenty-two languages. By the end of the century, Heironymus Mesiger could reproduce forty versions of it, including an Amerindian and a Chinese form. This sort of effort culminated in the 500-language collection of Adelung (1732–1806), published in 1806 (and also called *Mithridates*).[31] The choice of the Lord's Prayer as a cross-language comparison is understandable, given the tenor of the times, the familiarity with the Bible, and the particular appeal of the Babel myth. As a useful scholarly text, of course, it provided limited opportunities for theorizing. Still, the sixteenth-century interest in language varieties signalled an important change: no longer was the global confusion of tongues seen as a regrettable divine punishment, unworthy of scholarly attention. From these first rough attempts at classification grew more sustained and scientific efforts.[32]

In 1643, Salmasius (Claude de Saumaise: 1588–1653) published his *De hellenistica*, in which Latin, Greek, Persian and the Germanic languages were seen to descend from a (lost) common ancestor.[33] Thirty years later, the list of descendants was extended to include the Italic, Slavic and Celtic groups. Progress was not smooth, however, for by the end of the century Leibniz (1646–1716: the famous mathematician influenced the work of Pallas and Hervas – see notes) was reverting to the view that the relationships between languages were largely dependent upon geographical proximity.

It is only from the beginning of the nineteenth century that the 'common-ancestor' approach has been put on a firm footing. Central here was the increased access to Sanskrit – again, a development allied to trade and colonial expansion – and the realization of its importance. In 1786, Sir

William Jones (1746–94) presented a paper to the Asiatick Society of Bengal (which he had founded two years earlier) in which the British orientalist and jurist noted that:

> The Sanskrit language, whatever be its antiquity, is of a wonderful structure; more perfect than the Greek, more copious than the Latin, and more exquisitely refined than either; yet bearing to both of them a stronger affinity, both in the roots of verbs, and in the forms of grammar, than could possibly have been produced by accident; so strong indeed, that no philologer could examine them all three without believing them to have sprung from some common source which, perhaps, no longer exists.[34]

Jones's proposition, in fact, was that an Indo-European family included the Sanskrit, Greek, Latin, German and Celtic languages.

The basic idea had been current for some time – and the term Indo-European had been proposed in 1760 – but now the insistence on a source variety linking geographically widespread languages, and on roots and grammar, was clearly stated. In just over a century, Salmasius's Indo-Scythian theory had become an Indo-European one. An historical approach to language classification, with its evolutionary tenor, was not novel in the century of Darwin's *Origin of Species* – so, as with the earlier linguistic analogues to herbals and bestiaries, language families were now viewed as products and reflections of evolutionary development. August Schleicher (1821–68), the philologist chiefly responsible for the idea of language 'family trees' thought, indeed, that language dynamics could be best understood from a natural-science, organismic perspective. In response to Darwin's famous volume, he wrote a pamphlet called *Darwinism Tested by the Science of Language* (1863). Here he noted that linguistics had long recognized that species variation over time, that development of modern forms from earlier ancestors, which the evolutionists now presented with some novelty and controversy. The strength of the organic metaphor in language matters, in which Schleicher believed, is shown in this statement from his booklet:

> The kinship of the different languages may consequently serve ... as a paradigmatic illustration of the origin of species, for those fields of inquiry which lack, for the present at least, any similar opportunities of observation.[35]

Important figures in the nineteenth-century efforts to understand Indo-European language relationships in particular, and to establish rules for language comparison generally, include August (1767–1845) and Friedrich von Schlegel (1772–1829), Rasmus Rask (1787–1832), Jacob Grimm (1785–1863) and Wilhelm von Humboldt (1762–1835) – brother of Alexander, the explorer – who appointed the great Sanskrit scholar Franz

Bopp (1791–1867) to his post in Berlin. In 1818 Rask had published his findings on the relationship among Germanic, Slavic, Baltic, Greek and Latin.[36] And, in 1822, Jacob Grimm (of fairy-tale fame) demonstrated regular relationships among Indo-European consonants – e.g., the 'p' in Latin words like *pater* becomes an 'f' in Germanic varieties (*father*). These sound shifts – nine main sets of correspondences – were covered by 'Grimm's Law' (as it was termed by the Oxford scholar, Max Müller (1823–1900)) though Rask had earlier noted sound correspondences.

Bopp it was who, in 1816, had published a grammar comparing verbs in Indo-European languages[37] and who, between 1833 and 1854 produced a larger work, the first full comprehensive grammar of Indo-European languages, comparing the grammars of the Sanskrit, Greek, Latin, Lithuanian and Germanic languages.[38] In it, he outlined the scope of comparative description, leaving 'untouched only the secret of roots and the reasons behind the naming of the original concepts'.[39] By the third edition in 1868, Bopp had extended his scope to include Slavic, Celtic and Albanian. The famous Swiss linguist, Ferdinand de Saussure (1857–1913), also published on Indo-European (in 1879). At the end of the century, Karl Brugmann (1849–1919) produced his summary outline (*Grundriss*) of Indo-European grammatical studies.[40] Of course, the work continues; a recent effort is Jerzy Kuryłowicz's Indo-European grammar.

In the last few paragraphs, I have touched upon the two main methods of language classification: genealogical/historical and typological.[41] The former, of course, is the attempt to relate languages through family descent; the latter aims to demonstrate similarities of phonology, lexicon and grammar. While the first approach is better developed it can be appreciated that it works best where written records exist. An optimum outcome is one in which typological and historical approaches are complementary. The seminal figures in the area of typological classification are the Schlegels and von Humboldt, whose work was mainly in the field of morphology, the division of grammar concerned with word structure. In 1818 August Schlegel proposed a three-part division, which was later expanded by von Humboldt into a four-part one. The names given by von Humboldt to the four types of languages thus morphologically classified have remained: isolating, agglutinating, flectional (inflecting) and incorporating.

In isolating varieties, all words are invariable – that is, the basic roots are without grammatical modifications and it is the order of words which determines meanings. Chinese is an example of such a language, as the following sentences demonstrate:

Tā   qù zhōngguó xué   zhōngguó huà.
He/she go China   learn China   painting
He/she went to China to learn Chinese painting.

Here, the pronoun *tā* is invariant and does not change with gender, the

Table 2.3 Language families of the world

Language family	Some important sub-groups	Geographical area	Some languages of the family	Estimated number of speakers (millions)
Afro-Asiatic (Hamito-Semitic)	Berber, Cushitic, Semitic	North Africa, Saudi Arabia	Amharic, Arabic, Hausa, Hebrew, Riff, Somali	230
Altaic	Manchu-Tungus, Mongolian, Turkic	Central and North-East Asia	Azerbaijani, Japanese, Kazakh, Korean, Tatar, Turkish, Uzbek	270
Andean-Equatorial	Arawakan, Quechumaran, Tupian	South America	Aymará, Goajiro, Guaraní, Quechua	
Australian Aboriginal	Pama-Nyungan, Tiwi	Australia	Pitjanjatjara, Warlpiri	0.05
Austro-Asiatic	Mon-Khmer, Munda, Nicobarese	South-East Asia, Nicobar Islands	Khmer, Santali, Vietnamese	60
Austronesian	Eastern Austronesian, Western Austronesian	Hawaii, Madagascar, New Zealand	Javanese, Malagasy, Malay, Maori, Tagalog, Tahitian	200
Aztec-Tanoan		Mexico, South-West U.S.A.	Comanche, Hopi, Nahuatl	
Caucasian	Abkhazo-Adyghian, Kartvelian, Nakho-Dagestanian	Caucasus	Chechen, Circassian, Georgian	6
Dravidian		South-East India	Kannada, Malayalam, Tamil, Telugu	140
Eskimo-Aleut		Alaska, Canada, Greenland	Inuktitut, Yupik	
Ge-Pano-Carib	Carib, Macro-Panoan	Eastern South America	Carib, Mataco	
Hokan		North-East Mexico, South-West U.S.A.	Tlapenec	
Indo-European	Celtic, Germanic, Indo-Aryan, Italic	Europe, North India	Armenian, English, Icelandic, Irish, Sanskrit, Spanish	2000

Family	Region	Subgroups	Example languages	Speakers (millions)
Indo-Pacific	New Guinea		Chimbu, Enga, Medlpa	3
Khoisan	South-West Africa		Khoikhoin, San	0.05
Macro-Algonquian	North America		Cree, Micmac, Mohican, Ojibwa	
Macro-Chibchan	Central America		Cuna, Guaymi	
Macro-Siouan	Central North America		Crow, Dakota, Mohawk	
Na-Dené	North-West Canada	Athapaskan	Chipewyan, Dogrib, Slave	
Niger-Congo (Niger-Kordofanian)	Sub-Saharan Africa	Benue-Congo, Kwa, Mande, West Atlantic	Bambara, Fulani, Igbo, Rwanda, Swahili, Xhosa, Yoruba	260
Nilo-Saharan (Sudanic)	Upper Nile, Central Africa	Nilotic, Saharan	Dinka, Kanuri, Luo	30
Oto-Manguean	Mexico		Mixtec, Zapotec	
Palaeosiberian	North-East Siberia	Luorawetlan, Yeniseian, Yukaghir	Chukchi, Gilyak, Koryak	0.025
Penutian	Western U.S.A., Central America, South-West South America	Mayan	Araucanian, Maya, Quiché	
Sino-Tibetan	China, Tibet	Miao-Yao, Tibeto-Burman	Burmese, Chinese, Tibetan	1050
Tai	South-East Asia	Kadai, Kam-Sui, Tai	Laotian, Shan, Thai	50
Uralic	Estonia, Finland, The Urals, Hungary	Finno-Ugric, Samoyedic	Estonian, Finnish, Hungarian, Yurak	23

Nota: The numbers of speakers are rough estimates from the 1980s. All Amerindian languages together are estimated to have about 25 million speakers. The status of Japanese and Korean, shown here as members of the Altaic family, is disputed; they may be language isolates. Similarly, Vietnamese may be a Tai language and not an Austro-Asiatic one (as shown here). Macro-Panoan (Ge-Pano-Carib family), Miao-Yao and Tibeto-Burman (Sino-Tibetan) and Kadai and Kam-Sui (Tai) are sometimes considered to be separate families themselves. The Khoisan group comprises the so-called 'click' languages; here, sharp sounds made by the tongue and lips are used as consonants. Rwanda, Swahili and Xhosa – members of the Niger-Congo family – are languages of the powerful Bantu group within the Benue-Congo division.

verbs *qù* and *xué* show no tense distinctions, and the noun *zhōngguó* remains the same even when (in its second occurrence) it has adjectival force. Another example:

Wŏ māi júzi   chū.
I   buy orange eat
I bought some oranges to eat.

In agglutinating languages, words represent a gluing together of a number of endings or affixes to a root, where all these elements are invariant. Thus 'I love you' in Swahili is 'Mimi ninakupenda wewe', in which *mimi* means *me* and *wewe* means *you* and *ninakupenda* is a combination of these elements: *ni* (I) and *na* (marker of present tense) and *ku* (you) and *penda* (love).

Inflecting languages allow roots themselves to be modified to express different grammatical relationships. Latin is a well-known instance here; the inflection, the *o* ending of the word *amo*, tells us that the meaning is 'I love' – first person, singular, present tense, active voice, indicative mood.

Finally, the category of incorporating languages involves those in which a single word stands for a whole sentence. Within such words may be found both agglutinative and inflectional features. In the Australian aboriginal language, Tiwi, *ngirruunthingapukani* means 'I kept on eating'. Here, the analysis is: *ngi* (I) and *rru* (past tense marker) and *unthing* (for some time) and *apu* (eat) and *kani* (repeatedly).

These classifications are far from perfect and many varieties cannot be uniquely placed in one category. English, for example, shows agglutinating characteristics (antidisestablishmentarianism), inflecting ones (big-bigger-biggest) and isolating ones (the boy kisses the girl – the girl kisses the boy). Most languages, in fact, show similar patterns of morphological 'mixing'. And, of course, morphological classification is not the only way to order languages; syntactic and phonological typing is also possible. Allowing for the very real difficulties that dog efforts to accurately categorize languages, from both typological and genealogical perspectives, there has none the less emerged a rough consensus, and this is reflected in table 2.3 and the following map.

It has proved impossible, for some languages, to give anything like an accurate classification. These are the varieties known as 'language isolates'. In some instances we can hope that further study will eventually permit placement; this may occur, for example, for some South American Indian forms, or for Japanese and Korean (see table 2.3). In other cases, we know so little about historically-remote languages that no firm categorization will ever likely emerge. Here we could mention ancient varieties known only because of references in classical literature – Bithynian, Cappadocian and Pontic were languages in Asia Minor about which we know next to nothing. Although we have thousands of inscriptions of Etruscan – the language of

Map 2.1 Language Families

Table 2.4 Numbers of speakers of major world languages

Language	Language family	Speakers (millions)
Arabic	Afro-Asiatic	175
Bengali	Indo-European	150
Bihari	Indo-European	65
Chinese	Sino-Tibetan	1000
English	Indo-European	1400
French	Indo-European	220
German	Indo-European	100
Gujerati	Indo-European	35
Hausa	Afro-Asiatic	40
Hindi	Indo-European	700
Italian	Indo-European	60
Japanese	Altaic/Isolate	120
Javanese	Austronesian	65
Korean	Altaic/Isolate	60
Malay	Austronesian	160
Marathi	Indo-European	50
Persian	Indo-European	55
Punjabi	Indo-European	70
Polish	Indo-European	40
Portuguese	Indo-European	160
Russian	Indo-European	270
Spanish	Indo-European	280
Swahili	Niger-Congo	30
Tagalog	Austronesian	50
Tamil	Dravidian	55
Telugu	Dravidian	55
Thai	Tai	50
Turkish	Altaic	50
Ukrainian	Indo-European	45
Urdu	Indo-European	85
Vietnamese	Austro-Asiatic	60

Notes: The figures shown here are generally upper estimates, and include speakers for whom the language is not the mother tongue.

a pre-Christian society in what is now Tuscany – little deciphering has been achieved and Etruscan is an isolate. So too is Sumerian, even though the written record here, some 5,000 years old, has been decoded. Modern Basque is also an isolate, thought to be a relic of pre-Indo-European Europe. Ainu, the language of a group in Japan who are physically unlike the Japanese, is another variety which cannot be connected. In North America, the languages of the Salish and Kootenay Indians of British Columbia are isolates and, across the continent, so is the now-extinct language of the Beothuks in Newfoundland. This last society was ruthlessly slaughtered by whites – sometimes with the assistance of Indian merce-naries from the mainland – and the last speaker died of disease in St John's in 1829. It is ironic that this tribe should have been the one to prompt the generic term 'Red Indian'; when John Cabot first encountered them he observed, and in due course reported, their custom of rubbing themselves with red ochre.

Finally here, it is appropriate to present some approximate figures concerning major languages and their speakers. The numbers on table 2.4 largely speak for themselves, but I would draw attention to two important points: the first is that, collectively, the Indo-European varieties can claim some 3,800 million speakers; the second is that English is by far the most numerically dominant force, both within and without the Indo-European family (once we go beyond the ranks of mother-tongue speakers only). How this numerical force is aligned with other types of dominance is a subject I shall take up later.

THE RISE AND ACKNOWLEDGEMENT OF MULTILINGUALISM

Although I shall have to say more below of purely definitional matters, it is apparent that multilingualism – the ability to speak, at some level, more than one language – is a widespread global phenomenon.[42] Simple observation of the number of existing languages, and of the degree of their spread and contact, reveals that at least a bilingual competence is commonly required. It is not difficult to understand how such a situation arises, at least in broad terms. First, there is the simple movement of people. Immigrants to a new country bring their languages into contact with each other, and with those of existing populations. This is a common experience in all the new-world 'receiving' societies. Territorial expansion is another type of migration, with similar results. Sometimes, as with imperialist and colonial expansion, it is not necessary for large numbers of people to physically move; they may 'move' their language into contact with others through military and economic pressures which require but a handful of soldiers, merchants and bureaucrats. A few thousand people ruling the Indian sub-continent brought about a massively expanded base for English among a (current) population of some 800 million. Now, about 75 million of these people can speak English – in addition, of course, to at least one other variety.

Another common context in which multilingual competence arises is political union among different linguistic groups. Peoples who may have existed in sufficient isolation as not to need a broadened language ability may find themselves more closely united, with obvious linguistic consequences. Switzerland unites four official-language groups – the German, Italian, Romansch and French; Belgium is a country of French and Flemish speakers;

Canada has English and French 'charter' groups. In addition to these unions, there are federations based upon more arbitrary, and often involuntary, amalgamations. These often result from colonial boundary-marking and country-creation; modern examples are found in Africa and Asia.

Multilingualism (as well as those dialect continua I have already mentioned) is also commonly observed in border areas. Such areas are to be found world-wide, often arising because of the arbitrary boundary-making just noted. Two North American examples can be found along the Mexican–American border in the south, and on that between New England and Quebec in the north. The latter instance also illustrates an interesting but unsurprising extension of the usual border multilingualism (i.e., where French speakers, originally from Quebec, and continuing to have ties with it, have come to require English competence because of American residence). Historically monolingual speakers who have no cross-border connections (American shopkeepers in northern Vermont) may begin to develop a halting ability in French in order to more effectively and profitably deal with Quebec shoppers. This, incidentally, is on the increase as American prices become even more attractive to tax-beleaguered Canadians.

These are the most obvious reasons for the growth of multilingual competence; they are not, of course, the only ones – cultural and educational motivations will also expand linguistic repertoires, for example, even if there is no desire or possibility to use the new ability in ordinary conversational ways. It can be seen, however, that through the examples cited here – perhaps even those where purely educational factors are at work – runs a thread of necessity. A moral, then, which could be drawn is that multilingualism is largely a practical affair, that few people become or remain multilingual on a whim. A corollary, which I mentioned in the introduction, is that we should expect that, in most instances, an individual's abilities in his or her two, three or four languages will not be equal. On the contrary, we might predict that they will extend just about as far as circumstances demand.

Sometimes circumstances interact with individual talents and opportunities in remarkable ways; there are prodigies in language just as there are in music and mathematics. The chief curator in the Vatican Library, Giuseppe Mezzofanti (1774–1849) reportedly spoke 60 languages fluently, and could translate more than 150 languages and dialects. A more modern example is Georges Schmidt, who was head of the Terminology Section at the United Nations between 1965 and 1971. In 1975 he reported fluency in 19 languages and a less-than-fluent capability in a dozen more. The occupations of these men are noteworthy, surely, as is that of James Murray – he was the editor of the *Oxford English Dictionary*. In 1866, at the age of twenty-nine, he described his linguistic abilities in a letter applying for a post in the British Museum Library:

I possess a general acquaintance with the languages and literature of the Aryan and Syro-Arabic classes ... with several [languages] I have a more intimate acquaintance as with the Romance tongues, Italian, French, Catalan, Spanish, Latin and in a less degree Portuguese, Vaudois, Provençal and various dialects. In the Teutonic branch I am tolerably familiar with Dutch ... Flemish, German, Danish. In Anglo-Saxon and Moeso-Gothic my studies have been much closer.... I know a little of the Celtic, and am at present engaged with the Sclavonic [sic], having obtained a useful knowledge of Russian. In the Persian, Achaemenian Cuneiform and Sanscrit [sic] branches, I know for the purposes of Comparative Philology. I have sufficient knowledge of Hebrew and Syriac to read at sight the O.T. ... to a less degree I know Aramaic Arabic, Coptic and Phenician [sic].[43]

No wonder an observer regarded the remarkable Murray as 'a natural curiosity', no wonder his breadth of linguistic knowledge seemed suspiciously great in some quarters. (He did not get the job, incidentally; perhaps, with hindsight and with appreciation of his lexicographical contributions, we might think this fortunate).

While few have the extraordinary competence of a Mezzofanti or a Murray, more mundane levels of multilingualism are sufficiently common that societies may have to make formal responses. As I have already noted, only about one-quarter of the world's states currently recognize more than one official language – although it is perfectly clear that virtually none of the remaining three-quarters are anything like monolingual. Furthermore, among those countries that do grant official status to more than one language, the vast majority (again about three-quarters) are bilingual only. Switzerland, Singapore and India (where 15 languages have state sanction) are among a handful giving legal recognition to three or more languages. There are some obvious reasons, having to do with numbers and efficiency, why countries cannot officially acknowledge all the varieties spoken by their inhabitants but, as might be expected, there are other reasons too; as the discussion develops we will confront some of them. We must also deal with those varieties which, although lacking an official imprimatur, have considerable de facto importance.

Whether or not a language is in some way or other recognized in legislation, many societies try to assess regularly the type and extent of multilingualism within their borders. This is most obviously done by census, although census information is often limited in important ways. An initial difficulty arises in the phrasing of questions. Should we ask, 'What is your mother tongue?' If so, how do we know that all informants will interpret 'mother tongue' in the same way? And what of those who feel they have more than one mother tongue or of those who have forgotten their maternal variety? In Canada, censuses up to 1941 defined mother tongue as the language first learned and still spoken.[44] From 1941 to 1976 it was the language first spoken and still understood. In 1981 informants were asked about the language first learned and still understood. In other national censuses, mother tongue is essentially defined as the language spoken in the informant's home when he or she was a child; in this case, a 'mother tongue' might never have been actually learned by the informant.

Should we ask the question in simpler form, such as 'What is the first language you spoke?' But perhaps this will not provide us with the up-to-date information required. Perhaps, then, a useful question might be something like, 'What language do you most often speak now?' Apart from altering the thrust of the enquiry, this type of probe also raises difficulties; how, for example, will it be answered by those who speak two or more varieties to more or less equal degree? Such problems are compounded by usual census practice which, for ease of data coding, often permits one response only and which offers the respondent little or no room for elaboration, explanation or qualification. There are of course inherent problems here with the whole questionnaire approach, especially when it exists in tightly structured or 'closed' format. However, a format which permitted 'open-ended' responding would create huge difficulties of summary. In short, census questionnaires cannot ask about language matters with sufficient scope and breadth to illuminate details which language planners and policy-makers might really require for accurate assessment and action. An illustrative example is provided by the Canadian census for 1986.[45] One question was, 'Can you speak English or French well enough to conduct a conversation?' This is obviously open to a huge degree of interpretation by the informants. Another asked, 'What language do you yourself speak at home now (if more than one language, which language do you speak most often)?' Again, problems.

It has been suggested that there are, in fact, three main kinds of language questions usually found in censuses:[46]

1   those asking about the informant's main language (here, the emphasis is on the present);
2   those asking about mother tongue (with a stress on the past);
3   those probing abilities in specific languages of interest to the census authorities.

We have already noted the difficulties with mother-tongue questions. Those of type 3 are also open to possible problems with informants' abilities and language 'claiming'. It is interesting, for example, that in Ireland, where Irish competence clearly declined dramatically in the nineteenth century, 25 per cent of the population reported themselves as Irish speakers in 1861, and 28 per cent said they were in 1971.[47] To interpret this as a rise in the fortunes of the language would be quite inaccurate; a majority of the 1861 informants were no doubt fluent, while by 1971 hardly anyone was. Consequently the latter percentage actually refers, in the main, to those who, through the schools, have acquired a very thin wash of Irish competence. So, the interpretation of Irish-speaking ability clearly altered over a century; also, the 1971 results may have built into them a desire to see Irish regain some lost ground, a desire to have oneself counted as 'fully Irish' (or some such sentiment). Similar difficulties attach to type 2 questions which are sometimes further confused by being phrased as some variant of 'What is the language most often spoken in your home?' It is apparent, generally, that large grey areas emerge because of the phrasing of questions and the consequent varieties of interpretation open to respondents.

The type of answer given may also vary with the way in which the question is administered; in Canada, the 1961 census employed enumerators, while in 1971 it was purely a self-reported effort. And this omits entirely variation due to informants' conscious distortions. At one time, for example, there was considerable under-reporting of Gaelic competence in Nova Scotia; this was probably due to the desire to deny possession of a stigmatized variety and to avert the attentions of 'impertinent, inquisitive and romantic' outsiders.[48] So, there may be both over-claiming and under-claiming (as the Irish and Gaelic examples show). Questions may, as well, vary from one census to another; this hinders comparisons – of patterns of language shift, for example. In 1960, informants born in the United States were not asked at all about their mother tongue. In 1970,[49] a question *was* asked: 'What language, other than English, was spoken in this person's home when he was a child?' (which, in any event, is quite over-inclusive: one grandparent in the home speaking German (for example) would add all family members to the German mother-tongue group).

It was realized, in fact, that the 1970 American census question may have created particular problems. The Census Bureau re-interviewed a sample of 11,000 people who had answered the question, of whom 15 per cent had indeed said that a non-English variety had been used at home. Three-quarters of these *now* said that *they* spoke this variety. Now, of *this* last group, it was further discovered that about 12 per cent had, in answer to *another* census question, reported that *only English* was in use in their childhood home! The remaining quarter (of the 15 per cent above) said that they themselves *did not* speak the non-English language used at home. Almost half had said on the other question that only English had existed at home. If one cares to work back through this rather confusing affair, one will realize that about one-quarter of the original 15 per cent who said yes, a language other than English was used at home, *also* said (in response to the other query) that only English was spoken!

In other cases, questions about *ethnicity* have been asked on one census, questions about *language* on another; and the former term is, if anything, more elastic than the latter. We have already seen, as well, the changes in the Canadian census in the way mother tongue was to be interpreted in different decades. In Belgium, *all* language-related questions were abolished in censuses after 1947 because of the possible political, ethnic and social ramifications in that linguistically-riven state.

It follows, from all these factors, that those who collate and interpret census data have almost insoluble difficulties. Earlier in this chapter, the consequences of lumping Celtic languages together (in Canada) were discussed. In some cases there are social and political motives behind census practices and, since these motives can alter with changes in society, the practices themselves change too. In the 1980 American census,[50] a possible response to a question about ethnic origins was 'Spanish–Hispanic', a label which could be seen to serve as a unification for all the varied groups that speak Spanish (or are reputed to, or who would like to, or who want increased funding for Spanish-language education, and so on).

Sometimes, census reflections of official policy – and the distortions they may occasion – are quite obvious. In Singapore, there are four official languages – Tamil, Malay, Mandarin and English – and all Singaporeans are placed in one of these groupings, all have 'mother tongues' assigned on the basis of this categorization.[51] Thus, even though Indians in Singapore may speak Malayalam or Gujerati, the policy selects Tamil as 'their' language. Very few Chinese have Mandarin as a true mother tongue (Hokkien, Teochew and Cantonese are the major variants), but it is 'theirs'. The centralist policy is one of promoting English and Mandarin and it is hoped that, in time, the other Chinese 'dialects' (for example) will disappear. In the Singaporean case, then, census statistics may indicate a wide variety of mother tongues, and of language use, but the implications of the data will be interpreted in quite a specific light. The official policy has certainly caused some distress, particularly among elements of the Chinese population. In 1991, the Singapore *Straits Times* reported the plight of Mrs Chionh Soo Chin, a Teochew speaker who feels bewildered by the English–Mandarin policy; almost completely ignorant of English, she also has only a limited understanding of Mandarin. This causes her great distress: for example, in following signs and announcements in public places. She also complains of a generation gap between Chinese of her age and the younger ones fluent in Mandarin. The newspaper report goes on to observe that, although perhaps part of a vanishing generation, Mrs Chionh is one of almost 200,000 'dialect' speakers aged sixty and over. The policy has also led to some confusing situations. A case was reported in 1980, for example, of a civil servant who was ethnically Chinese but who had Malay as a mother tongue and English as a second language. Permission was refused for this person to sit an examination in Malay because it was deemed 'only natural' that one should be competent in one's mother tongue – designated here, on the ethnic principles of Singapore, as Mandarin.

A similar situation existed in the Soviet Union, where one's national origin (*narodnost'* or *natsional' nost'*) did not necessarily coincide with one's language.[52] In such a case, the language–ethnicity difference was recognized at census level but not in official documents like identity papers. While *narodnost'* was officially inalienable, census declarations of mother tongue were variable over generations. A Soviet citizen whose mother was ethnically Jewish and whose father was ethnically Ukrainian, and who was a monolingual Russian speaker, would be deemed ethnically Ukrainian (actually, children of parents of different ethnicities were generally classified the same as the mother; however, where one parent was Jewish, classification could be in the non-Jewish parent's ethnic group).

One obvious implication of all these actual and potential confusions is that, when accurate language data are needed, specialized surveys usually must be conducted. These may build upon census information and, in some contexts, it is possible to have custom-made tabulations prepared by central statistical authorities (in Canada, for example). Usually, though, special field work is required. For a comprehensive understanding of non-official languages in Canada (that is, those other than English and French) a detailed survey of ten ethnic groups in five metropolitan areas was carried out in 1973.[53] A similar project (1979–83) surveyed the 'other languages' of England.[54] Apart from these (and many other) country-wide approaches, the technical literature is full of specialized studies of particular groups, regions, languages and social settings. Serious students of multilingualism may begin by looking at census information, but they must inevitably go well beyond it, and this means turning to these studies. However, it cannot be assumed that, even in the scholarly literature, one will always find disinterested assessment, for even scholars (should one say, especially scholars?) have esoteric axes to grind.

THE CONSEQUENCES OF BABEL

In most instances, multilingualism arises, and is maintained, through contact and necessity. Equally, however, multilingualism imposes another necessity, that of crossing language barriers. It is obvious, in other words, that despite widespread multilingual competence, there arise many occasions when some means of bridging a language gap is required. There are two main methods here: the first, the use of some sort of lingua franca, is either part of the existing multilingual picture, or necessitates an extension of it; the second is translation. If we consider lingua francas[55] first, we can conveniently divide them into three varieties: (i) existing languages which have achieved some position of power in a region (or globally) – these varieties have been referred to as 'languages of wider communication'; (ii) restricted or limited forms of existing languages, whose diminished scope is at once easy to master and sufficient for communicative purposes which are, themselves, quite circumscribed; (iii) constructed or 'artificial' languages meant, again, to be easy to learn.

Languages of wider communication

It is clear to even the most casual student of history that there have always existed powerful languages which served as bridges between national groups and language communities. It is equally clear, to the modern linguist at any rate, that these varieties achieved widespread power and status because of the heightened fortunes of their users, and not because of any intrinsic linguistic qualities of the languages themselves. The most common elements here have to do with military, political and economic might, although there are also examples in which a more purely cultural status supports the lingua franca function. However, in this latter case, the cultural clout which lingers has generally grown from earlier associations with those more blatant features just mentioned. The muscle, in any case, which these languages have derives from the fact that their original users control important commodities – wealth, dominance, learning – which others see as necessary for their own aspirations. The aphorism, 'all roads lead to Rome', has linguistic meaning, too.

Greek and Latin, of course, are examples of classical lingua francas.[56] By the fourth century BC, the former had spread throughout the Near and Middle East. The Romans, more ardent imperialists, ensured that Latin had an even greater sway. Indeed, even after the emergence of the Romance varieties which it spawned, Latin remained as an instrument of religion and scholarship, weakening finally (in Europe) with the rise of 'Protestant mercantilism'. It held out longest in German universities, where, in the late seventeenth century, Christian Thomasius (1655–1728) – one of the seminal figures of the Enlightenment – was expelled from Leipzig for lecturing in German and not Latin. The last major English philosophical work to be published in Latin was Bacon's *Novum organum* (1623), and the last important scientific work was Newton's *Philosophiae naturalis principia mathematica* (usually known more simply as the *Principia*: 1687). Latin has not entirely lost its hold, however; the Vatican still makes pronouncements in that language and has, in fact, recently updated a dictionary last published in the reign of Pius XII. In *Latinitas nova et vetera* we will now find, for example:

Societas internationalis ab amnestia (Amnesty International);
exterioris pagine puella (cover girl);
escarorium lavator (washing machine);
sphaerludium electricum numismate actum (slot machine);
serpentinus cursus (dribbling: football, not oral).

The simple fact that these terms make their greatest impact as oddities is a comment on the status of Latin as a lingua franca nowadays. Of course, Latin 'oddities' have been popular for a long time. When Sir Charles Napier conquered Scinde in the 1840s, a contributor to *Punch* (18 May 1844) suggested that his despatch to Lord Ellenborough, the Governor-General, must surely have read, simply, 'Peccavi' ('I have sinned').[57]

After Latin, several other languages have achieved lingua franca status. French, for example, was a powerful link language throughout Europe and beyond by the eighteenth century. It had particular influence at the higher levels of society. Thus, when Voltaire (1694–1778) went as philosopher and poet to the Prussian court of Frederick II in 1750, he was able to make the remark about the utility of French which I reproduced in the introductory chapter. Italian, as a component of the 'original' lingua franca, is clearly important here, as is Arabic after the Islamic conquests. Today there is no doubt that English is the most important global variety and thus has the greatest status as a world lingua franca.[58] As some indication of its breadth, we can recall that, across all levels of proficiency and 'native-ness', English is probably spoken by more people than any other language; indeed, were we to ignore the runner-up, Chinese, we would see that the next most numerically powerful language, Hindi, has only half the speakers that English does. As noted earlier, there are now more English-speaking Indians – perhaps 75 million – than there are English speakers in Britain. Of course, number of speakers is not the whole story. Consider, as well, that 75 per cent of all letters, cables and telexes are in English, that more than half the world's learned journals are in English, that 80 per cent of all computer information is stored in English, that the language of most multinational companies is English, that English is formally studied as a second language more than any other variety, that English is the medium of international popular music and entertainment. When the space probe *Voyager One* was launched in 1977 it carried brief recorded greetings in fifty-five languages – but the chief message was from the Secretary-General of the United Nations (Kurt Waldheim), speaking for all the countries of the world, in English. It is a sobering thought that if intelligent beings were to listen to this, their conception of the global lingua franca would be based upon Austrian-accented British English.

Pidgins and creoles

The second major type of lingua franca is that of a restricted or simplified language mixture (indeed, as indicated in the notes to this chapter, the very term *lingua franca* first had this connotation exclusively). Such a mixture is referred to as a *pidgin*. In his *Voyage to China*, published in 1850, Julius Berncastle observed that: 'The Chinese not being able to pronounce the word "business", called it "bigeon", which has degenerated into "pigeon", so that this word is in constant use.'[59] Pidgin (or *pigeon, pidjin, pidjun, pidgeon*) is a mixture, then, of languages – in Berncastle's case, an amalgam of mainly English words with some Chinese forms – which is no one's maternal variety.[60] However, the etymology of this interesting word remains debatable. Apart from the putative connection with *business*, it has also been seen to derive from the Portuguese *ocupacāo* (business), from the Amerindian *pidian* (meaning 'people'), from *pequeno* (Portuguese for 'baby': hence, baby-talk), from the Hebrew *pidjom* (barter) or even from *pigeon* (a bird which can carry simple messages; perhaps there is also some sense here of the bird-like, and rather superficial, repetitions associated with trade communication).

In any event, there are many pidgins in use, most involving a European colonial language. Their vocabulary and grammar are restricted, yet allow simple communication and, since this is their purpose, the very existence of pidgins shows linguistic creativity. Although some pidgins have considerable longevity, many do not last long; if the communities in contact (traders' settlements and indigenous populations, for example) drift apart, then clearly the pidgin is no longer needed. In other cases, where prolonged contact exists, one group may learn the other's language. In Papua New Guinea, with hundreds of languages and a relatively small population, *Tok Pisin* ('talk pidgin', New Guinea Pidgin) is in fact officially recognized and is the most important 'native' variety, spoken by more than a million people. Here is an example of Tok Pisin, taken from Luke XV:31, in the New Testament (*Nupela Testamen*):

Na papa i tokim em, i spik, 'Pikinini, oltaim oltaim yumi tupela i save stap wantaim. Na olgeta samting bilong mi em bilong yu'. [and he said unto him, Son, thou art ever with me, and all that I have is thine].

Here is another example, this time in Cameroon Pidgin English, which is an important variety retaining lingua franca status; readers can work this one out for themselves:

Dis smol swain i bin go fo maket,
Dis smol swain i bin stei fo haus,
Dis smol swain i bin chop sup witi fufu,
Dis smol swain i no bin chop no noting,
An dis smol swain i bin go wi, wi sotei fo haus.[61]

It should be obvious that a variety of language which, however limited relative to others, can deal with a spectrum of communicative needs anchored by the Bible at one end and children's rhymes at the other, can certainly handle most ordinary exchanges.

Closely related to pidgins are *koinēs*,[62] where the latter term also indicates a mixing of varieties and some linguistic simplification; here, however, the varieties are either mutually intelligible or, at least, much more similar than are those involved in the formation of pidgins. Also, 'koineization' is a much slower and more gradual process, requiring sustained contact and, indeed, integration. The term itself comes from the Greek *koinē* (common) and was first applied to the type of Greek that became an eastern Mediterranean lingua franca. It was mainly Attic Greek which had mixed into it elements from other dialects. A harsher view was provided by Arnold Toynbee: 'the exquisite parochial Attic of Sophocles and Plato degenerates into the vulgar [*koinē*] of the Septuagint and Polybius and the new Testament'.[63]

A pidgin may evolve into a *creole*; this happens when a pidgin becomes a mother tongue, when children born in pidgin-speaking communities begin to develop (or 'creolize') their linguistic inheritance. The developing language becomes, then, richer and more expressive than the parent variety. Nobody's mother tongue becomes somebody's mother tongue. A national language of Sierra Leone is Krio (creole); it is the maternal variety of about 10 per cent of the population and is a second language for many others. Krio, in combination with other languages, now spawns pidgin varieties.

Creole itself is generally thought to derive from the Portuguese *crioulo*, via the French *créole*. The meaning is one of European descent born and reared in a colonial setting. In 1590, Joseph de Acosta, in his *Historia natural y moral de las Indias*, thus referred to 'algunos criollos, como alla llaman los nacidos de las Españoles en Indias'.[64] The meaning gradually shifted to include Africans born in the (non-African) colonies and, further, to encompass the social and linguistic practices of such creole persons. Now, as noted, creole in its linguistic sense means an expanded pidgin. Here is part of Antony's famous speech in *Julius Caesar* (III:ii):

> Padi dem, kohntri, una ohl wey dey na Rom. Meyk una ohl kak una yeys. A kam ber Siza, a noh kam preyz am. Dem kin memba bad wey pohsin kin du lohng tem afta di pohsin kin dohn dai. Boht plenti tem di gud wey pohsin du kin ber wit im bon dem.[65]

Constructed languages

The third category of lingua franca is the 'artificial' or constructed language.[66] The example most readers will know is Esperanto but in fact the idea of a constructed language – those connected with such varieties obviously dislike the term 'artificial' – is not at all new. Going back no farther than the seventeenth century, we find that Comenius (1592–1670), Descartes (1596–1650) and Leibniz (1646–1716) were all interested in a universal auxiliary language that could cross boundaries. Since that time there have been hundreds of constructed languages.

In most cases, the initial desire has been to produce a *neutral* auxiliary that would facilitate global communication, although the rhetoric surrounding constructed languages has often been very grandiose indeed. The desire for neutrality has meant that powerful 'natural' languages cannot serve (in the eyes of the language makers) for they are tinged, as it were, by history and 'imperial prestige'. Thus the way has been seen as theoretically clear for a constructed language to fill a yawning and bothersome gap.

Among the more successful language schemes that have appeared in the last hundred years are *Volapük* (created by J.M. Schleyer in 1880), *Latino Sine Flexione* (G. Peano, 1903), *Ido* (L. de Beaufront, 1907), *Occidental* (E. de Wahl, 1922) and *Novial* (O. Jespersen, 1928). Perhaps to this list one should also add C. Ogden's *Basic English* (a simplified English, 1930). None of them, however, proved as successful as *Esperanto*, published by Ludwig Zamenhof in 1887. It has, without doubt, stood the test of time better than any of the others. The core of Esperanto lies in its famous 'Sixteen Rules' of grammar, and the guiding force behind these is simplicity and regularity. Thus, all nouns end in *o* (nominative case), with an *n* added for the accusative; the definite article *la* serves for all cases, numbers and sexes; all adjectives end in *a*; verb forms are the same, regardless of person or number; accent is always on the penultimate syllable; and so forth.

Zamenhof, a Polish oculist, had already interested himself in constructed languages – particularly Schleyer's Volapük – when he published his own scheme on *Lingvo Internacia* under the pseudonym of Dr Esperanto (the hoping one). Encouraged by the initial response, Zamenhof published a second book on the language in the same year (1887); further publications followed and the first international congress on Esperanto took place in Boulogne in 1905.

It is clear that Zamenhof, like most other makers and supporters of constructed language, hoped that Esperanto would provide more than a universal second language to supplement, but not supplant, mother tongues. He believed it could contribute greatly to some 'trans-national identity',[67] an apt goal for one who observed that 'if the nationalism of the strong is ignoble, the nationalism of the weak is imprudent'.[68] To dilute the former and to obviate the latter must have seemed a pressing need when Zamenhof said this – in 1914.

It is very difficult to gauge accurately the current status and scope of Esperanto;[69] one problem, for example, is the many Esperantists who are unaffiliated with formal organizations. We can note, however, that in 1979 the Universal Esperanto Association (UEA) based in Rotterdam had 30,000 members, of which over 80 per cent were European. As of 1975 there were associations in sixty-four countries, although not all national bodies are associated with the UEA. Conferences of the UEA, held annually, can attract 5,000 people from fifty countries. Politically, Esperanto almost succeeded in obtaining official recognition from the League of Nations in the 1920s, and has had some success with UNESCO (that body noted, in 1954, that the universalist goals of Esperanto accorded with its own). In 1966 the UEA proposed to the United Nations that it encourage and support Esperanto; this proposal was 'signed by 920,954 people in 74 countries, and by 3,843 organisations with a combined membership of 71,165,500'. The proposal, however, was not adopted. Proponents of constructed languages have also naturally been interested in the educational dissemination of their variety. It has been estimated that, during the 1970s, Esperanto was taught in some 600 schools and thirty universities around the world. Non-European educational support was particularly strong in China in the 1980s.

There is little doubt that, foremost among constructed languages though it is, Esperanto has not – particularly in recent times – captured a sufficient amount of general attention to become the functioning worldwide auxiliary its proponents wish. One rough distinction seems to be between those who, while not necessarily wholly unsympathetic to the idea of constructed languages, nevertheless perceive fatal flaws, and those who see Esperantists (and other constructed-language apologists) more or less as cranks and faddists. One linguist in the 1930s referred to 'language cranks and language maniacs'.[70] Bertrand Russell, in his famous exchange with Louis Couturat (1868–1914: philosopher and logician, and proponent of universal language), revealed his feelings about constructed languages generally when he suggested 'idiot' as a word to signify an adherent to Ido, Couturat's offshoot from Esperanto.[71] Bernard Shaw, who was himself interested in the simplification of English, wrote to a correspondent that 'toothpicks like universal language cannot move the world . . . damn your Esperanto'.[72]

More moderate but still unenthusiastic views have been expressed by other well-known figures. Thus, H.L. Mencken noted that 'the trouble with all the "universal" languages . . . is that the juices of life are simply not in them'.[73] George Steiner felt that '[among constructed languages] only Esperanto continues to lead a somewhat Utopian, vestigial existence'[74] and that 'it is the absence from them of any natural semantics of remembrance [what a lovely phrase] which disqualifies artificial languages from any but trivial or *ad hoc* usage'. Tolkien, the philologist and author of *Lord of the Rings*, observed that Esperanto and other similar attempts are 'far deader than ancient unused languages, because their authors never invented any Esperanto legends'.[76] I.A. Richards, himself keen on the idea of modified natural language as a lingua franca, noted that 'the immediate incentive which would make enough people learn and use one [a constructed language] is lacking . . . the feeling that you are contributing in your small way to an idealistic but doubtful future is an inadequate motive'.[77] This, I think, is a very telling observation. Finally, a modern feminist critique[78] has it that Esperanto is a sexist, male-orientated language (e.g., *patro* 'father';

patrino 'mother'), which thus missed its opportunity of becoming a truly universal medium meeting the needs of *all* human beings. This last criticism is an example of a broader problem: constructed languages are *not* neutral – most recent examples have been based upon western European languages and thus are more accessible (and appealing) to some than to others.

Of course, these and other criticisms have been dismissed by Esperantists, but the fact remains that all constructed languages have suffered, on the one hand, from suspicions of naive idealism, lack of intellectual rigour and even presumption (how can you 'invent' a language?) and, on the other, from impracticality.[79] That is, even if what might be called the symbolism of constructed languages could be set aside, the apparently logical desire to have everyone learn the same auxiliary language, or lingua franca, flounders on a paradox. These varieties might be seen as more appealing if there were a community of speakers in which one's acquired competence could be set to use. However, since this is not the case, many are unwilling to learn them. To construct adequate motivations for people to begin, to take the plunge as it were, has always been the central difficulty dogging proponents of constructed languages. This is particularly so in societies in which powerful languages already hold sway, and still more so when these other languages are, like English, contenders for global lingua franca status.

Perhaps I have given more attention to constructed lingua francas than might have been expected but I have done so intentionally since they represent, superficially at least, a logical and 'neutral' solution to communication problems, but are widely misunderstood (if known about at all). Indeed, it could be said that the scholarly community, too, has ignored an interesting, if somewhat peripheral, phenomenon. Sociolinguists have in general neglected, prejudged or seen as taboo the whole area even though, as one writer put it, there are 'facts, texts, and living subjects readily available'.[80] Constructed-language activists might also merit some psychological study of their motivations and concerns.

While it is true that some well-known figures have interested themselves in constructed languages (including the linguists Jespersen, Sapir and Firth), these interests have not translated into research. The little research that *has* been done has been largely of the opinion-poll variety and has not generally shown much rigour in either sampling or analysis. An interesting, but hardly scientific, study was the theoretical and psychoanalytic interpretation of Flugel, an early British follower of Freud.[81] A recent sociological study has, however, given statistical information and 'profiles' of the Esperanto movement and its adherents.[82] Some important observations that can be culled from this are that the movement has always swung on the twin hinges of *practicality* and *idealism* (and there has sometimes been tension here), that the movement has been mainly European, from non-

English-speaking countries, that there has always been a 'quasi-religious' element to the Esperanto movement – Zamenhof himself moved markedly in this direction in his later years, and Esperantists have often rejected other constructed-language adherents as heretics from the true cause – and that there have been close links between socialism and Esperanto ideals.[83]

Translation

The three previous sections all deal with varieties of lingua francas, but a second broad approach to bridging language gaps is that of translation. It is perfectly obvious that using a translator or interpreter has practical benefits; it is perhaps less obvious that psychological disadvantages may present themselves. The translator is one whose linguistic competence gives entry to (at least) two language communities, and there may be apprehension. As George Steiner has pointed out, 'there is in every act of translation – and specially where it succeeds – a touch of treason. Hoarded dreams, patents of life are being taken across the frontier'.[84] The old Italian proverb is blunter: 'traduttori, traditori'. This suggests that concealment is as much a feature of language as is communication and this, too, has been expressed in many ways and for a long time.[85] Privacy, the construction of fictionalized myths, legends and stories, and outright dissimulation are at once important and threatened by translation and translators; one modern theme is the 'appropriation' of native stories by outsiders, for in many cultures – particularly ones with powerful and rich oral traditions – stories *belong* to the group or, indeed, to some designated story-teller.

In any event, we can note Talleyrand's (1754–1838) view that 'la parole a été donnée à l'homme pour déguiser sa pensée'.[86] More recently, Ortega y Gasset observed that 'al conversar vivimos en sociedad, al pensar nos quedamos solos',[87] Wittgenstein that 'die Sprache verkleidet den Gedanken'[88] and Popper that 'what is most characteristic of the human language is the possibility of story telling'.[89] They all refer to that aspect of language Steiner calls 'enclosure and willed opaqueness',[90] an aspect which is of great historical (and psychological) interest. The power of the word – spoken or written – has often attained mythic or religious significance and, in this sense, Popper, Wittgenstein and the others have simply extended a religious metaphor. In the Christian tradition this is expressed, in St John's Gospel, in the most forthright way: 'In the beginning was the Word, and the Word was with God, and the Word was God ... and the Word was made flesh, and dwelt among us.' The Word, the scriptures, are divinely incarnate in Christ (as the *logos*)[91] and it is this intimate connection between revealed knowledge and religious truth which is at the heart of the matter; needless to say, this is not a uniquely Christian equation. It follows that any tampering with the Word is of the utmost gravity. Indeed, there are clear meanings – in Judaism and Christianity, to give but two examples – that translation is blasphemy. To hear the *arcana verba*[92] is a sacred revelation and cannot be stained by mortal utterance. The translation of the Jewish Law into Greek led to three days of darkness on the world.

On a more terrestrial plane, however, translation – with all its difficulties – is a fact of multilingual life. It is not, however, a simple or technical one. Apart from an almost useless word-for-word exercise, every act of translation involves interpretation and judgement. For this reason, it has sometimes been supposed that 'true' translation is impossible; however, although a perfect version which captures *every* nuance and allusion is rather unlikely – and becomes more so as the material to be translated becomes less prosaic – we have none the less translated, for practical purposes, throughout history. Steiner notes: 'to dismiss the validity of translation because it is not always possible and never perfect is absurd. . . . The defence of translation has the immense advantage of abundant, vulgar fact.'[93]

Seeing translation as interpretation also links, incidentally, cross-language exercises with communications within the same language. That is, even the simplest of conversations between two speakers of the same language involves interpretation, and is analogous to 'reading between the lines' in written language.[94] The contextualization of messages and the necessity, for fuller understanding, for at least some degree of familiarity with the appropriate cultural background and underpinnings lie at the heart of the difficulties experienced by those who know a language only at the technical level of lexicon and grammar. We need only look over our 'own' literature to realize that, as the centuries roll back, we are in more and more unfamiliar territory. Indeed, we will soon arrive at a place where even lexicon and grammar change. Even Dickens is now sufficiently linguistically alien to be off-putting to many. It is through a constant process of translation that we continue to possess our 'own' literature and, indeed, our own culture. Similar feelings exist for second-language learners: the fluent technical English sufficient for a Japanese engineer is hardly going to fit him or her for an appreciation of Shakespeare. In summary, even omitting the mythic relevance of translation, one is yet faced with an act heavy with subjectivity and nuance, an act in which mistakes are common, and where one slip can break a chain of understanding.

It is, historically, an act in four scenes.[95] The first extends from Cicero's admonition not simply to translate *verbum pro verbo* (in his *Libellus de optimo genere oratorum* of 46 BC) up to the end of the eighteenth century. In this long first period we observe, above all, a concern for practical problems of the translation exercise, and it is marked by statements and theories largely driven by the difficulties of rendering the classics into English (for example). In 1549, Joachim du Bellay (1523–60) wrote a little chapter entitled 'Of bad translators, and of not translating the poets'. Here it is:

But what shall I say of some truly more worthy to be called traducers than translators [*traducteurs/traditeurs*]? For they traduce those whom they undertook to explain, robbing them of their glory, and by the same means seduce ignorant readers, showing them white for black; and, to acquire the name of savants, they translate on credit those languages of which they never understood the first elements, like Hebrew and Greek; and again, to make themselves the better known, tackle the poets – a race of authors certainly to which if I were able or wished to translate I would so little address myself, because of that excellence of invention which they have more than others, that grandeur of style, magnificence of words, gravity of sentences, audacity and variety of figures, and countless other lights of poetry: in short, that energy, and I know not what of spirit which is in their writings, which the Latins would call genius. All which things can as much be expressed in translating, as a painter can represent the soul with the body of him whom he undertakes to draw from nature. What I say is not addressed to those who by command of princes and great lords translate the most famous Greek and Latin poets, because the obedience one owes to such personages admits of no excuse in this place, but indeed I mean to speak to those who from blitheness of heart (as we say) undertake such things lightly and in the same way acquit themselves thereof. O Apollo! O muses! Thus to profane the sacred relics of antiquity! But I will say no more thereof. He then who would make a work worthy of price in his own tongue, let him leave this labour of translating, principally the poets, to those who from a laborious and little profitable thing, I would even say useless, nay, harmful, to the enrichment of their language, rightly get more of vexation than of glory.[96]

In the preface to his translations from Virgil in 1697, John Dryden (1631–1700) noted that:

On the whole matter, I thought fit to steer betwixt the two extremes of paraphrase and literal translation; to keep as near my author as I could without losing all his graces, the most eminent of which are in the beauty of his words; and those words, I must add, are always figurative. Such of these as would retain their elegance in our tongue, l have endeavoured to graft on it; but most of them are of necessity to be lost, because they will not shine in any but their own. . . . I have endeavoured to make Virgil speak such English as he would himself have spoken, if he had been born in England, and in this present age.[97]

These sorts of concerns have not, of course, faded away over the last two centuries. In fact they remain the most immediately pressing for the day-to-day enterprise of the translator. The last point Dryden notes, for example – to cast the original in the language of the 'present age' – remains central; it is perhaps most difficult when the translator is faced with the problem of reflecting social-class distinctions of speech. Between 1871 and 1893, Emile Zola wrote twenty novels meant to follow 'scientifically' the effects of heredity and environment on one family: *Les Rougon-Macquart* ('Histoire naturelle et sociale d'une famille sous le Second Empire'). These include *L'Assommoir* and *Germinal* and, in his introduction to each, the translator, Leonard Tancock, makes some apposite remarks. The former, Tancock notes:

> is for Paris what a rich novel of Cockney life would be for London ... the nicknames Bec-Salé, Bibi-la-Grillade, Mes Bottes, Gueule d'or (called Goldie in this translation) ... have as authentic a ring as, say, Nobby Clark or Ally Sloper or for that matter Fanny Adams might have to a Londoner.[98]

The problem, of course, is how best to indicate to English readers the sense of slum life and language intended by Zola in his *style indirect libre*, and Tancock saw it as a formidable one:

> The translation of slang and swearing in general is self-defeating in that the more exactly it hits off the tone of the original in the slang of the moment ... the less durable it is likely to be ... on the other hand, a translation must speak the language of its own time, and any attempt to reproduce 'period' slang or popular language is bound to produce effects as grotesque as 'Marry, thou art a scurvy knave.' In the case of *L'Assommoir* nobody could in any case hope to reproduce the idiom of, say, the east end of London in 1870, but on the other hand contemporary slang is bound to introduce an element of TV and Americanism.[99]

One might interject here that, if a translation ought to 'speak the language of its own time', and if that time is heavily influenced by television and by America, then these elements should – for best effect – be reflected. The only solution to this aspect of the translator's problem is retranslation as necessary; 'new' translations of the classics have always been seen as vital to their continued popular existence. Tancock's more immediate solution was:

> to use popular speech as timeless as I could make it, sprinkled fairly freely with the obvious and equally timeless swear-words and obscenities ... my rendering is therefore unavoidably 'free' in this respect, since one can only hope to reproduce the sort of language comparable people might use in pubs or off their guard.[100]

Tancock echoes these concerns in his preface to *Germinal*:

> Some of the strongest French oaths used in this novel are more or less blasphemous variations and elaborations on the *Nom de Dieu!* theme. I have frequently substituted for this sort of thing language more likely to be used by Englishmen of a similar type in similar circumstances.[101]

Tancock here also discusses his more general intent which is, of course, to remain faithful to the *tone* of the original, to what Rieu (the founder editor of the series of which Tancock's renderings of Zola are a part) called the 'law of equivalent effect'. Since *Germinal* is a 'brutal and angry book' (it deals with a violent clash between owners and workers in northern French collieries), a translation which attempted to make it more 'refined' or 'literary' would have been ludicrous, and a travesty of Zola's intent.

I think it is interesting, by the way, that the greatest threats to good translation appear at opposite ends of the literary continuum. On one hand, rough and slang-laden speech poses the sorts of difficulties Tancock discusses; on the other, poetic or philosophical productions also lay traps in their use of metaphor, allusion or dense, abstract reasoning. It is in fact a greater awareness of this latter issue – roughly the need to 'understand' an original work in a hermeneutic way – that characterizes the second historical thrust in translation theory, which is embedded in a larger concern with the relationship between language and mind. In the contemporary world, both 'practical' and 'philosophical' matters inform serious translation; indeed, they have always co-existed and it is perhaps more accurate only to say that the relative weightings have altered over time.

The most modern current, dating from the 1940s, comprises the last two 'scenes' in the translation production, which supplement (without replacing) the two earlier dimensions. First here, we have the advent of machine translation, more formal linguistic enquiry and statistical manipulation. There are now bodies of professional translators and interpreters, and scholarly journals devoted to the subject. But – and this is the final aspect – there has arisen most recently a renewed concern for a more philosophical, 'almost metaphysical' approach to translation. Taken all in all, we can see that the difficulties in the area have remained quite stable, and this is surely not to be wondered at. The essential questions remain the same, from Cicero's day to our own: does the literal version or the literary one come first, and how much freedom should the translator exercise? These are the oversimplified statements upon which rest all matters of translation. If we remember Cicero's precept not to translate word for word, and then consider Vladimir Nabokov's declaration that, in the translation of poetry, anything but the 'clumsiest literalism' is a fraud, we see that we have come full circle. Somewhere between a literalism which reflects the view that any translation freedom means a sea change from the original – that translation means loss and that, therefore, we had better eschew interpretation – and the opposing view that Nabokov's idea is itself unworkable in any satisfactory sense – that for better or worse we must depart from literalness – we find both an animating tension and most actual production.

Translation may be blasphemous, insensitive or inaccurate but, in a multilingual world, we need it. Furthermore, notwithstanding the difficulties, there is much of a relatively prosaic nature that can be translated at generally acceptable levels. Josef Skvorecky, the Czech-Canadian writer, observed that Theodore Dreiser is not as threatened by translators as is Emily Dickinson, and we might take comfort from this, given the needs and inclinations of most people.[102] Shakespeare, because of the richness and density of his language, has always presented problems, and is a good example of the 'Emily Dickinson' end of the continuum. For his Paris production of *The Tempest*, Peter Brooks observed that, whereas in English a word is often marvellously used because of its many meanings to the audience, a French listener might respond best to a clear and single significance. Perhaps he had in mind Rivarol's famous statement (in the eighteenth century) that 'ce qui n'est pas clair n'est pas français' (it is less well known that Rivarol went on to add that 'ce qui n'est pas clair est encore anglais, italien, grec ou latin'). Equally, however, a good translation can bring fresh urgency to Shakespeare and, it is claimed, can unlock new layers of meaning.[103] In line with the hermeneutic approach, noted above, the essential Shakespearean 'message' – of love, freedom, evil and so on – can be endlessly reinterpreted. In Azerbaijani, 'to be' is *alom* and 'not to be' is the same word pronounced slightly differently; it is easy to see that this might give a quite moving freshness to Hamlet's soliloquy. It is interesting to consider, then, that the very poetic richness of an original might engender, through sensitive translation, new and provocative insights.[104]

However, even an author as apparently prosaic as Agatha Christie can create problems. Skvorecky recounts the story of a translation into Czech. Previous attempts were thought to fail because they made Hercule Poirot talk like the other characters whereas, in Christie's English original, the clever Belgian detective speaks a very 'Frenchified' English. The result of the new translation was, in the eyes of some, to make Poirot sound like a Sudeten German. More interesting still are the efforts to translate Christie into French, to render Poirot's Frenchified English into French itself. Poirot's statement that 'Stamboul, it is a city I have never visited. It would be a pity to pass through – *comme ca* [he snaps his fingers]. Nothing presses – I shall remain there as a tourist for a few days', comes out, in Postif's translation for the Librairie des Champs-Elysées, as: 'Ne connaissant pas Stamboul, je ne voudrai pas y passer sans m'arrêter. Rien ne me presse. Je visiterai la ville en touriste.' M. Bouc, a director of the Compagnie Internationale des Wagon Lits is made to say in the original, 'C'est rigolo.' In the French translation he says 'Dites plutôt que c'est inconcevable.' And so on (or, if you prefer, *und so weiter*).[105]

PAROCHIALISM AND INTERCOURSE

Three important aspects of language in society have been described here: they are (i) the existence of many different varieties; (ii) the necessity for overcoming this for intercommunity and interpersonal communication; (iii) the strong desires to maintain one's 'own' language, one's own perspective and interpretation of the world. There is undoubtedly a tension here, which we saw most clearly in the discussion of translation.[106] At the broadest level it is a tension between a globalization of culture which, in the realm of language, manifests itself in the dominance of a small number of 'large' languages, and a desire, which has always existed but which is also fuelled by this globalization, to maintain and defend one's own culture and language.

An interesting discussion of this was provided by the Swiss linguist, Ferdinand de Saussure (1857–1913) in his *Cours de linguistique générale*, a book published by his students, largely on the basis of his lectures, after his death. Saussure, in describing the spread of language – 'la propagation des ondes linguistiques' – referred to two conflicting tendencies, 'la force d'intercourse et l'esprit de clocher':

> The laws that govern the spread of linguistic phenomena are the same as those that govern any custom whatsoever, e.g., fashion. In every human collectivity two forces are always working simultaneously and in opposing directions: individualism or *provincialism* [*esprit de clocher*] on the one hand and *intercourse* – communications among men – on the other.[107]

In his lectures, Saussure used the English term *intercourse* which his students retained in their publication as apt, if rather *pittoresque*.[108] Provincialism keeps small communities faithful to their own, original habits; but, while provincialism makes people 'sedentary, intercourse obliges them to move about ... [it] spreads language ... prevents dialectal splintering by wiping out an innovation ... [but may also] promote unity by adopting and spreading an innovation'.[109] Now, while it is true that Saussure intended his remarks to apply specifically to linguistic changes such as consonantal mutation, diphthongization and so on, his introductory comment (above) clearly places provincialism and intercourse in a more general framework. Furthermore, it seems particularly timely now to reflect on this very human tension, not only for language *tout court*, but also for those larger political and nationalistic convulsions with which it is often so closely associated.

Thus we observe today the operation of the two 'axial principles of our age – tribalism and globalism'.[110] Opposing centrifugal and centripetal forces are, as Saussure implied seventy years ago, at work simultaneously in many settings: consider the break-up of the Soviet Union and the inter-republic (and intra-republic) strife which seems a necessary precursor to some new federal arrangement; or, the similar events in that fragile creation, the former Yugoslavia, where the unravelling following Tito's death has latterly become dismemberment; or, the ongoing efforts to accommodate local desires in an ever more tightly-knit European federation; or, the constitutional crisis in Canada, as francophone and anglophone communities (and others) attempt to renegotiate their partnership.

These are matters to which I shall return in greater detail. Let me conclude here by recalling (for analogy only, for I am not a devout analytical psychologist) Jung's notion that a sense of personal unity, a fusion of all our disparate attitudes and functions, is impossible without a thoroughgoing self-awareness at an elemental level. All the bits and pieces of the psyche have to be closely examined and understood before they can meaningfully be combined; a process of *individuation*, as Jung styled it, must precede psychological nirvana. At a descriptive level this makes some sense: how can you build a sturdy house without knowing well your materials? How can you engage in *intercourse* without being fully cognizant of your provincialism? The difference between Jung and Saussure, the difference between social tendencies towards unity and individual ones, is that (in Jung's eyes, at least) once fusion of the elements has occurred, the psyche has substantively altered – Jung speaks of *transcendence*; in social life, on the other hand, 'provincial' elements are just as likely to be dealt with by accommodation (whose own configuration will change with time) as they are by assimilation.

3

BILINGUALISM

Competence in more than one language can, as we have seen, be approached at either an individual or a social level. Furthermore, these two levels need not be as neatly connected as might first be thought. While it is true that a country full of multilingual people is itself multilingual in an obvious sense, it may nevertheless recognize only one or two varieties and thus, in another sense, be something less than multilingual. Conversely, a country may be officially bilingual or multilingual and yet most of its citizens may have only a single-language competence. Many states in Africa, for example, have two official languages – usually a strong indigenous variety and an important European one – for a highly heterogeneous and multilingual population. On the other hand, a country like Switzerland, with recognition granted to four languages or, better, Canada, which officially sanctions two, hardly resembles the linguistically rich and varied countries of Africa. It will be necessary in this chapter, then, to consider both individual and social manifestations of bilingualism, but it is also necessary to point out from the beginning that the emphases are quite different; a thoroughgoing discussion of individual bilingualism involves, for example, linguistic and psycholinguistic dimensions which figure much less prominently, if at all, at the social level where other dimensions – historical, educational, political and so on – arise for consideration.

CONCEPTS AND CONFUSIONS

Everyone is bilingual. In saying this, I make the assumption that there is no one in the world (no adult, anyway) who does not know at least a few words in languages other than the maternal variety. If, as an English speaker, you can say *c'est la vie* or *gracias* or *guten Tag* or *tovarisch* – or even if you only understand them – you clearly have some 'command' of a foreign tongue. Such competence, however, does not lead many to think of bilingualism. If, on the other hand, you are like George Steiner, who claims equal fluency in English, French and German, and who further claims that, after rigorous self-examination – of which language emerges spontaneously in times of emergency or elevated emotion, which variety is dreamt in, which is associated with the earliest memories – no one of the three seems dominant, then bilingualism (actually trilingualism in this case) does seem a rather more apt designation. The question, of course, is one of degree, and it is a question that not only continues to exercise the imagination but also, as we shall see, has importance in research studies.[1]

As may be imagined, it is easy to find definitions of bilingualism that reflect widely divergent responses to this question of degree. In 1933, for example, Leonard Bloomfield (1887–1949) observed, in his seminal *Language*, that bilingualism resulted from the addition of a perfectly learned foreign language to one's own, undiminished native tongue; he did rather confuse the issue, however, by admitting that the definition of 'perfection' was a relative one.[2] With this admission, Bloomfield did not remove the question of *degree*, but he did imply that any division between monolingualism and bilingualism should occur nearer to the Steiner end of the continuum than to the *c'est la vie* one. Others have been purposely vaguer. Uriel Weinreich, a central figure in sociolinguistics, simply defined bilingualism (in 1953) as the alternate use of two languages.[3] At about the same time, Einar Haugen, in his study of Norwegian in America, suggested that bilingualism began with the ability to produce complete and meaningful utterances in the second language.[4] This suggests that even members of the *c'est la vie* camp *are* bilingual. Generally speaking, earlier definitions tended to restrict bilingualism to equal mastery of two languages, while later ones have allowed much greater variation in competence. But since this relaxation proves in practice to be as unsatisfactory as an argument from perfection – at least for the purpose of defining bilingualism in any generally applicable fashion – most modern treatments acknowledge that any meaningful discussion must be attempted within a specific context, and for specific purposes.

Further complicating this matter of degree, this question of where bilingualism starts, is the fact that any line drawn must cross not just one general language dimension, but many more specific threads of ability. Consider, first, that there are four basic language skills: listening, speaking, reading and writing.[5] Consider further the possible subdivisions: speaking skill, for example, includes what may be quite divergent levels of expression in vocabulary, grammar and accent. There is, thus, a substantial number of elements here, all of which figure in the assessment of bilingualism; it does not follow that strength in one means strength in another:

> A pupil may be able to understand spoken English and Welsh, speak English fluently but Welsh only haltingly, read in Welsh with a reading age of six and in English with a reading age of eight, write poorly in English and not at all in Welsh. Is that pupil bilingual?[6]

In general, given both the basic skills, and their subdivisions, there are at least twenty dimensions of language which could or should be assessed in order to determine bilingual proficiency.[7] It may be, as Weinreich observed many years ago, that a rough gauge of relative proficiency may be easily accomplished, that in many cases we can with some certainty say which language is dominant, but these matters are not *always* simple, and a rough reckoning may be quite inadequate if we wish, say, to compare groups of bilingual individuals, or if we wish to study the relationship between bilingualism and other personality traits.

A number of tests are commonly employed to measure bilingualism; these include rating scales and fluency, flexibility and dominance tests.[8] The first of these can involve interviews, language usage measures and self-assessment procedures. In some ways, relying upon self-ratings has a lot to recommend it, but the strengths here rest upon the capacity of an individual to be *able* to self-report accurately, a roughly equivalent sense across individuals of what competence means, and a disinterested and unbiased willingness to communicate proficiency levels. None of these can be taken for granted, and the inaccuracies of census information about languages (discussed in Chapter 2) often rest upon self-assessment difficulties. Indeed, some of the problems here can also affect the apparently more objective tests of fluency and flexibility. We might, for example, ask people to respond to instructions in two languages, measure their response times and, on this basis, try to ascertain dominance. Or we could present picture-naming or word-completion tasks, we could ask subjects to read aloud, or we might present a word which occurs in both languages (*pipe*, for example, occurs in both French and English) and see how it is pronounced. We could simply test for extent of vocabulary, or see how many synonyms for a given word a person can come up with. Yet, although the results of such tests often intercorrelate, they are clearly far from perfect.

Apart from the hazards already noted, it can easily be seen that factors such as attitude, age, sex, intelligence, memory, linguistic distance between the two languages, and context of testing are all potentially confounding. Furthermore, even if we were able to gauge with some accuracy, there would remain problems of adequate labelling; that is, it is hardly to be expected that measured individuals would neatly fall into one, or two, or four neat categories of ability, or degrees of bilingualism. There even remains confusion as to what term ought to be applied to those much sought-after individuals whose bilingual capacities are great: are they to be known as 'balanced bilinguals', 'ambilinguals' or 'equilinguals'?[9] One author has described the ambilingual as a person who, in all contexts, can function equally well in either language, and who shows no trace of language A when using B, and vice versa. But, given that such individuals constitute a 'rare if not non-existent species'[10] the term 'balanced bilingual' (or 'equilingual') is reserved for those whose mastery of both varieties is more roughly equivalent. What we see here, in effect, is a continuation of those difficulties and hazards, of those confounding factors, to the very highest levels of ability. What *is* clear, however, is that the vast number of those to whom the term 'bilingual' can be at all reasonably applied fall into the category of 'non-fluent' bilingualism.

There are some other matters, too, which must be briefly mentioned here, and which cut across the larger topic of degree of fluency. For instance, a useful distinction can be made between *receptive* (or passive) bilingualism, and *productive* (or active) competence; the difference here is between those who understand a language – either spoken or written – but cannot produce it themselves, and those who can do both. A receptive competence only has been referred to as *semibilingualism*.

This latter term should not be confused with another, *semilingualism*, which refers to a lack of complete fluency in either language. In 1927, Bloomfield characterized this in his description of a North American Indian:

> White Thunder, a man around 40, speaks less English than Menomini, and that is a strong indictment, for his Menomini is atrocious. His vocabulary is small, his inflections are often barbarous, he constructs sentences of a few threadbare models. He may be said to speak no language tolerably.[11]

More recently, the idea of knowing neither of two languages well has been advanced in connection with ethnic minority-group speakers (for example Hansegård's notion of the *halvspråkighet* affecting Finnish–Swedish bilinguals), and this has meant that semilingualism has become extended from a solely linguistic description to a catchword with political and ideological overtones relating to majorities and minorities, domination and subordination, oppression and victimization. This is so because of the conditions – particularly of minority-group children at school – which allegedly produce semilingualism. In fact, we see here a return to the confusion surrounding 'balanced bilingualism', where complete monolingualism anchors the argument at one end, and 'full competence' in two languages is at the other. Thus, for example, one could imagine a person who was both a semilingual and a balanced bilingual, if one allowed that two *incomplete* fluencies were matched.

Added to all this is the common metaphor of some finite 'containerized' competence which has bedeviled the literature for some time, and which continues. At its simplest, it suggests that what you gain on the swings of one language you lose on the roundabouts of the other. But using such a container metaphor for language acquisition and skills may be quite mistaken. It has reminded more than one writer of the old craniometry axioms that linked brain size to intelligence. It seems to me, that these sorts of attempts are psychologically understandable, however, because they represent the hope that something rather intangible can be better grasped by linking it – directly, or by analogy – with something observable. There have been many examples throughout history: the bodily 'humours', phrenology, physiognomy, 'constitutional' psychology, and so on. It need hardly be said, however, that an understandable effort to come to grips with complexity may do more harm than good. And a final point here: even if we were to admit the likelihood of some finite-capacity model, all that we know of intellectual structures and functions would suggest that the capacity – for languages, among other things – is quite large enough that we need not worry about exceeding our limits.

Early in his partnership with Watson, Sherlock Holmes explained his ignorance of many things by saying that the brain was like an attic, that one should fill it wisely according to one's needs, and that 'it is a mistake to think that that little room has elastic walls and can distend to any extent'.[12] But while there *are* limits, Holmes grievously underestimated them; he could easily have remedied his ignorance of literature and astronomy without displacing his knowledge of poisons or the many varieties of cigarette ash. If there *is* any credibility to the idea of semilingualism, it must rest upon a rather rare complex of social deprivations and should not particularly be seen as any sort of looming danger attaching to linguistic duality – for which it represents only 'a half-baked theory of communicative competence',[13] and the view that the usual goal of the bilingual speaker is to have each language container hold not only equal but 'full' amounts. In short, semilingualism is another species of the argument from perfection[14] – and in any event, we have seen how thorny are all issues of measurement of linguistic competence. We should remember, finally, that for all 'non-fluent' bilinguals (i.e., the overwhelming majority; perhaps all), the second language may be weaker than the first which, itself, will never reach perfection, and that all language matters here interact strongly with demands of function and context.

Not to be confused with all of this is another distinction, that between *additive* and *subtractive* bilingualism. In some circumstances the learning of another language represents an expansion of the linguistic repertoire; in others, it may lead to a replacement of the first. The different outcomes here reflect different social pressures and needs, and will necessitate some further discussion of languages in conflict. Here we could simply note that additive bilingualism occurs principally where both languages continue to be useful and valued; a classic example is found in the bilingualism of aristocracies and social élites in systems in which it was considered natural and proper that every educated person know more than one variety. Subtractive bilingualism, on the other hand, reflects a society where one language is valued more than the other, where one dominates the other, where one is on the ascendant and the other is waning.

Yet another common distinction is between *primary* and *secondary* bilingualism; between a dual competence acquired naturally, through contextual demands, and one where systematic and formal instruction has occurred. These are not watertight compartments, of course: one might, for example, pick up a conversational (and quite fluent) grasp of a language in a relatively informal way, and then feel the need later to add some grammatical skills, for reading and writing, in a more rigorous fashion. This would, incidentally, recapture the process by which a mother tongue is developed, and it is noteworthy that more enlightened school language curricula have tried to reflect this in their second-language programmes. Still, it is not difficult to appreciate that there are some interesting and broadly-based differences between primary and secondary bilingualism, some of which go beyond language itself and touch upon the interweaving of language with culture. As a contemporary example, compare those English–Gaelic bilinguals, in the west of Ireland or in the Highlands and islands of Scotland, whose fluencies result from growing up in a particular location, with those who, in Dublin, Glasgow or Edinburgh, have more self-consciously set themselves to become bilingual. Consider further the ways in which lumping these two groups together, under a single 'bilingual' rubric might, for example, give a rather inaccurate picture of the state of health of Irish and Scots Gaelic.

While the foregoing discussion does not exhaust the list of terminological, definitional and other complexities, it does suggest the breadth that any full-scale study of bilingualism must have – and this only at some initial level of ground clearing. Given that the exercise so far has been less than complete, I now want to turn to some other central matters.

SECOND-LANGUAGE LEARNING

The fact that a majority of the global population has at least some level of multilingual competence surely indicates that adding a second language need not be some superhuman or unnatural feat. Indeed, the experiences of the Mezzofantis, Murrays and Burtons of the world – as well as those of many lesser lights – suggest that the more languages you have, the easier it is to add still more. And yet, especially within powerful linguistic groups, it is common to find references to the difficulties involved or to the peculiar lack of language talents supposedly possessed. Thus, in the modern world English and American monolinguals, for example, often complain that they have no aptitude for foreign-language learning. This is usually accompanied by expressions of envy for those multilingual Europeans, and sometimes (more subtly) by a linguistic smugness reflecting a deeply-held conviction that, after all, those clever 'others' who do not already know English will have to accommodate in a world made increasingly safe for anglophones. These attitudes are not new, however, and some historical expressions of them are both amusing and inventive. In 1644, John Milton (1608–74) observed that: 'We Englishmen, being far northerly, do not open our mouths in the cold air wide enough to grace a southern tongue.'[15] What, then, of the Inuit (Eskimos), the Saami (Laplanders) or even the Scandinavians, Dutch and Germans – all condemned, no doubt, to a physiologically and climatically-determined monolingualism?[16]

In point of fact, all such prejudices reveal more about social convention than about anything else. Vocal organs have little to do with it – notwithstanding the real difficulties of accurate pronunciation experienced by many otherwise fluent adult language learners – and, although there are doubtless *degrees* of language aptitude, relatively low levels here are neither fatal for language-learning efforts (if motivation is sufficient) nor more characteristic of one group than of another.

It may be useful to divide second-language acquisition here into two broad categories, *simultaneous* and *successive*. The first describes exposure to more than one variety from the onset of speech or, at least, from a very young age (some commentators have suggested age three or four as a rather arbitrary cut-off), and the second the addition, at a later age, of a new variety to an existing maternal one.

A few years ago, I visited some friends who were living outside Paris. The mother was American, the father was German, and they were on a two-year secondment from Stuttgart. They had a daughter, aged four, who had become bilingual through talking to her mother in English and to her father in German. By the time of my visit to Le Vésinet the child had become quite fluent in French, to the extent that she was a useful interpreter for her parents. It was interesting to see her playing, in French, in the garden and, upon running into the kitchen, switching effortlessly into either German or English. This lack of effort was almost certainly accompanied by an ignorance of her ability, perhaps of the very concept of three different languages. Many readers will no doubt have experienced similar situations, which can be generally seen as examples of the 'one person, one language' (or, 'one environment, one language') principle.

In 1913, Jules Ronjat published a formal account of the principle at work, describing his son's acquisition of German (from his mother) and French (from his father).[17] Over the course of the child's first five years, Ronjat's observations included the following:

1 initially, pronunciation was the same in both French and German, reflecting a unified, cross-language phonology;
2 parallel development occurred in phonetics, morphology and syntax;
3 there was an early awareness of bilingual ability and, consequently, of translation skills.

In later life, some functional allocation of languages occurred, with French being preferred for technical expression, and German for more personal purposes. This was considered a reflection of schooling (and one might also speculate here about the mother's German influence).

Another well-known documentary effort was that of Werner Leopold who, between 1939 and 1949, published four volumes describing the acquisition of English and German by his daughter.[18] Leopold spoke German to his wife and daughter at home, while his wife spoke English only. As with Ronjat's child, no negative effects were found in general linguistic and mental development, and language choice became increasingly dependent upon situational and personal context. There are a number of other such studies which, generally, demonstrate both a lack of any retardation attributable to bilingual upbringing and the increasing dominance of one variety because of extra-domestic constraints. Most recently, several books have appeared which build upon such work and provide parents with encouragement and information about simultaneous bilingualism.[19]

A very useful typology of bilingual-acquisition possibilities has recently been provided by Suzanne Romaine, as follows:

Type 1: one person – one language
Parents have different native languages, but each has some competence in the other's variety, the *community* language is one of the parental varieties, and the *strategy* is for parents to each speak their own language to the child (example: English-speaking mother, German-speaking father, each using their own language, bringing up the child in the United States).

Type 2: non-dominant home language
The same as above except that the *strategy* here is for *both* parents to speak to the child in the language *not* dominant in the community. The assumption is that the child will (at nursery school, for example) acquire the dominant community language because of extra-domestic pressure (example: English-speaking mother, German-speaking father, both using German, in the United States).

Type 3: non-dominant home language without community support
Here the two parents have the same language which is *not*, however, dominant in the community. The strategy is obviously for both to use this variety with the child (example: French spoken by both parents in the United States).

Type 4: double non-dominant home language without community support
Each parent has a different native language, neither of which is dominant outside the home. Each speaks their own variety to the child (example: French spoken by the mother, German by the father, each using their own, in the United States).

Type 5: non-native parents
Parents have the same native language, which is also dominant in the

community. However, one parent (perhaps a professional linguist!) always talks to the child in a non-native variety (example: the father and mother are both native English speakers, but father speaks German to the child, in Australia).

Type 6: mixed languages
Parents are bilingual, the community may also be bilingual, and each parent switches and mixes languages with the child (example: French/English bilingual parents in Montreal).

There is evidence, for all these scenarios, that bringing up children bilingually need involve few risks. Furthermore, where negative consequences or unhappiness have been observed it is almost always due, not to the bilingualism process itself, but rather to social, personal, cultural or other factors. Indeed, most observers point to the advantages of an early-acquired bilingual competence; these tend to reflect, above all, the relative ease of early learning and the higher levels of fluency, vocabulary and so on. There are some controversies as to *when* in early life bilingualism is best set in train – from birth, from the age of three? – but, generally, early childhood is better than anything later (particularly, perhaps, for native-like pronunciation ability).

There is also the argument that the young brain is more plastic and flexible than the older one.[20] On the other hand, an overemphasis upon early acquisition and brain malleability, and the idea that there is some ethological 'critical period' for adding another variety are open to criticism. Older learners obviously have cognitive experience lacking in small children and, provided the motivation is sufficient, can often prove to be better learners. If one could combine the maturity and articulated necessity of the older with the impressionability, imitativeness, spontaneity and unselfconsciousness of the younger, we would surely have a recipe for rapid and proficient bilingual acquisition.

We have moved here, of course, from more or less simultaneous bilingualism to early successive and later successive forms. What links and fuels them all is necessity. This clearly drives the older or adult learner, but it also informs the home situation of the young 'simultaneous' learner, even if the latter cannot articulate it. In the process of becoming bilingual, native aptitude, age and intelligence are less important than a supportive context of necessity. With the right social conditions, then, bilingualism becomes just as 'natural' as monolingualism in others, and is a capacity available to anyone of normal talents.

There is a large literature on the specifics of second-language acquisition, both 'natural' learning and that which occurs formally, at school. It should be stressed again here that, with sufficient motivation and opportunity, all normally intelligent people can learn another variety; those who claim they are 'no good' at foreign languages are usually lacking in one or both of these. This is not to deny that there may exist individuals who have a greater innate or acquired aptitude – a 'good ear' may be helpful, as well as a good memory and a capacity for self-initiated application. Beyond these, adaptability and genuine interest in other cultures are no doubt important. It can be seen, though, that virtually all of these qualities are of *general* value and do not form a package specifically directed at language learning. It is often claimed (see above) that children learn more quickly and effortlessly than do adults and, provided that formal instruction is carefully and appropriately presented, or that informal context-based learning occurs in a supportive psychological atmosphere, this can be true. On the other hand, adults have a broad experience to draw upon and this can be of very great value if coupled with desire and necessity.

The formal methods used to teach language are many, and they range from well-researched techniques to schemes advertised by fly-by-night charlatans. One might say, very generally, that older methods tended to emphasize memorization of grammatical rules and lexicon in the service of literary study; little attention was given to spoken language. In more contemporary school settings this has changed but one need not go back very far to find remnants of the grammar translation approach. My own school career, for example, included the study of French from about the age of ten to the end of secondary level. Seven or eight years of lessons gave me a fairly good vocabulary and some limited speaking skills but it was on the whole much easier to rhyme off the pluperfect subjunctive than to order a glass of wine and a *croque-monsieur*. Worse, there was always a great air of artificiality about the language class. We were repeatedly told that this was not a subject like the others but was rather a tool to be used in a way that we might not expect a knowledge of the Napoleonic campaign to be applicable; in fact, the whole exercise *did* remain disembodied. It was hard for us to create a motivation here that was not naturally generated and most, especially during the hyperconscious teenage years, would have agreed with (and extended) Orwell's observation that 'nearly every Englishman of working-class origin considers it effeminate to pronounce foreign words correctly'.[21] Attempts were made to immerse us more fully in French and latterly we had exercises in a language laboratory, but this tended more to individualize what had gone on previously than to change course for more conversational competence.

Now, variants of the 'direct method' (the oral approach) are much more common and although it is still hard to change the classroom into a representation of the street, the tendency is for more and more conversation. Students are encouraged to speak before learning formal grammar, and the use of the maternal variety is kept to a minimum; in short, second-language acquisition is meant to resemble first-language learning.

There are, as well, a number of theories about the process by which a second language is acquired. Most modern varieties reject a simplistic behaviourist approach – which has, besides, been shown as woefully inadequate for understanding mother-tongue learning – and endorse a cognitive conception in which rules are formulated and tested. Learning occurs in a series of non-random stages, each of which is characterized by a sort of *interlanguage*. It can easily be seen here that the analysis of errors made at different points in the progression is very important, since they can reveal a misapplied rule. If someone says 'sheeps', for example, it is clear that the 's-forms-the-plural' rule has been learned but overgeneralized (this sort of error is also common in children working out the refinements of the mother tongue).

Theories within social psychology have paid particular attention to the motivational features already discussed, and this makes a good deal of sense.[22] If we agree that language is a social activity, and if we accept that almost everyone is cognitively capable of learning second (and subsequent) varieties, then it follows that the force of the situation, and the attitudes it provokes in potential learners, are central.

A distinction first made in the 1960s was that between *instrumental* and *integrative* motivation for second-language learning. The former refers to a desire to learn for utilitarian purposes, the latter to language learning as part of a wish to know more about, to interact with, and perhaps ultimately to immerse oneself in, another culture. Perhaps, however, a well-fleshed instrumental attitude must include at least some integrative motivation, and one can also imagine a development of the former into the latter. In any event, a well-known framework for second-language learning is that of Robert Gardner, who attempts to link the social context, and the cultural beliefs within it, to individual learner capacities – including, of course, motivational levels – and the formal/informal settings in which the language is to be learned. Throughout, Gardner stresses the influence of integrative motivation upon positive outcomes (he also, incidentally, distinguishes between attitudes and motivation – a useful point, as we can imagine an individual with positive attitudes but poor motivation, whereas the opposite is unlikely to occur). Another model, that of Richard Clément, aims to embed individual motivations still more deeply in the social setting. In particular, he notes that a tension exists between an integrative motivation and fear of assimilation; hence his model has particular relevance for those language learners who are also minority-group members, and whose first language is threatened by the forces of those speaking the second. Clément's emphasis upon collective forces and outcomes is carried further in the formulation of Howard Giles and his colleagues. Here language learning is seen, centrally, as an intergroup process. Much more consideration is thus given to assimilative tendencies and apprehensions, to the preservation of ethnic-group boundaries and identities; this is tied closely to Giles's conception of *ethnolinguistic vitality* (an idea to be treated later), in both an objective and a perceived sense, and its ramifications for language-learning motivation.

A very recent 'general theory' of second-language learning has been proposed by Bernard Spolsky.[23] It aims to synthesize earlier and more particularized efforts and, indeed, also touches in important ways upon *first*-language acquisition. Spolsky's approach has five pivotal features: it attempts to bring *all* aspects of language learning under the one roof; it aims for precision and clarity so that the broad coverage does not blur details of varying contexts, goals and outcomes; it assumes that all aspects of learning are interactive – although they need not be operative in all contexts, they all interpenetrate (on the subject of motivation, for example, Spolsky wants to detail types and strengths); it argues that all language learning must be seen within a social setting; and it holds that some conditions for learning are 'graded' (i.e., the more intense or favourable they are, the more likely a linguistic consequence becomes) while others are 'typicality' states (i.e., they occur usually but not necessarily).

Of course, in all these models, application and prediction are the acid test, and some might suggest that they do little more than codify and formalize what has been known for a long time. None the less I think it is important to see that they all scotch the myth that some people, or some groups, have no 'head' for languages and that second-language aptitude is a rare commodity usually best seen in non-anglophones. Instead, they stress the power of the setting and, within it, the desires, needs, attitudes and motivations of ordinary people. It should be apparent that the social factors impinging upon language learning are, quite simply, the most important ones. Finally, we might recall that, for those millions of people who pick up bilingual or multilingual competence in the informal realm of daily life, simple necessity is the great motivator and the great determiner of how far this competence develops. It can dwarf all other features (barring internal intellectual ability) and, in particular, can ride roughshod over personal attitudes and motivation. Most historical changes in language use have a bilingual component, and most owe much more to socioeconomic and political exigencies than they do to attitude. The adoption of English by the Irish population, for example, was not accompanied – for the masses – by favourable attitudes, much less integrative ones. There may have been a grudging instrumentality at work, but it certainly was not of the type which pushes students to study French or German in the hopes of joining the diplomatic service.

BILINGUALISM AND INTELLIGENCE

I have already cited the view of the emperor Charles V that one's personality broadens with extra languages, and this has always been a common observation – particularly among those already bilingual and, more particularly still, among the social élite for whom an additional language or two was always an integral part of civilized life. Yet, if there have been many who have seen bilinguals as having an extra arrow in their quiver, there have also been those who demurred; here, I have cited Milton and Butler. But, on a more professional linguistic level, consider the opinion of Firth, who, in 1930, said:

> The average bilingual speaker, it is true, has two strings to his bow – one rather slacker than the other.... Every cultured man needs a second and perhaps a third foreign language – but he need not be bilingual. The unilingual have the advantage, and the bigger the cultural community in that language the bigger the advantage. As a first principle, pin your faith to the mother tongue.[24]

From the current standpoint, Firth's view looks quite misinformed, even if his second sentence does encourage a capacity which most would, in fact, admit as bilingual.

Weinreich, in his classic *Languages in Contact*, was able to quote many expressions of the problems allegedly faced by bilinguals; these included split national loyalties and problems of 'marginalization' (or *anomie*, to use Durkheim's famous term), emotional difficulties, moral depravity (through receiving inadequate religious instruction in their mother tongue), stuttering, left-handedness, excessive materialism, laziness and detrimental consequences for intelligence.[25] All these ideas seem dated, to say the least, and Weinreich himself was generally dismissive, preferring experimental evidence – which is always, of course, in shorter supply than the speculation underpinning most of these assertions. He cites with approval, for example, a study done in 1946 which demonstrated that the problems of bilinguals are much more likely to stem from social factors in bilingual households than from linguistically driven 'mental conflict'.[26] This is much more in line with modern thinking, although if it were true that bilingual families have a heightened level of social tension this could be taken as an indirect discouragement of bilingualism. No such evidence is available. One can imagine, of course, families applying the 'one-parent-one-language' principle to children in a unduly rigid or harsh way; no doubt this occurs, and no doubt this can create problems associated with the growth and use of bilingualism. But again, there is no reason to believe that such practices are anything more than aberrations of an unsystematic kind.

Of all of the connections made between bilingualism and other features of individual life, none is more central or contentious than the presumed link between bilingualism and intelligence.[27] Many prominent linguists in the past felt there was a negative trade-off. Jespersen observed in 1922, for example, that:

> It is, of course, an advantage for a child to be familiar with two languages: but without doubt the advantage may be, and generally is,

purchased too dear. First of all the child in question hardly learns either of the two languages as perfectly as he would have done if he had limited himself to one.... Secondly, the brain effort required to master the two languages instead of one certainly diminishes the child's power of learning other things.[28]

Two general points are of interest here: first, Jespersen raises the possibility of a sort of semilingualism (see above); second, he invokes – as did Firth – a limited-capacity model of human intellectual functioning (again, see above).

Early studies tended to associate bilingualism with lowered intelligence, and it is unsurprising that many of them were conducted, in America, at a time of great concern with the flood of immigrants from Europe (roughly, 1900–20). The story of the intelligence-testing movement itself, which flourished at this time, is a fascinating and detailed one, as well as an example of the misuse of 'science' allied to ignorance and prejudice. Suffice it to say here that the 'objective' intelligence tests of the time reflected a very culture-bound ideal and, consequently, immigrants – especially those who were non-white, non-English-speaking, non-northern-European, non-educated and so on – did not fare well. In such a climate it is easy to see that the 'feeble-minded' immigrants (or hopefuls) were especially mentally handicapped by their languages, and that the greater their use of English, the higher their measured intelligence. One well-known study concluded, for example, that 'the use of a foreign language in the home is one of the chief factors in producing mental retardation'.[29] Incredible assertions like this are understandable only in their context but even so, even allowing for general intolerance and nativism, even understanding the feelings of those concerned to protect the social *status quo* from a horde of barbarians (in the Greek sense of that word), it is still chastening to think that such comments could appear in respected academic journals. This is not just a new-world disease either: recall that, at about the same time, famous scientists in the old world were gearing up for a full-scale denunciation of 'Jewish science'.[30]

In addition to negative associations between bilingualism and intelligence which stemmed, somewhat indirectly, from social fears of immigrants, there were more disinterested studies which pointed to problems.[31] They are, however, flawed by inadequate controls in their experimental procedures. One study of Welsh/English bilingualism, for example, showed no IQ difference between urban monolinguals and bilinguals, but a substantial one for rural children – and yet it did not take into account obvious social-contact differences between the city and country dwellers, nor occupational and social-class variation among the parents. There is also, in all such work, a problem of statistical inference: if one observes a correlation between low intelligence and bilingualism, then has the first caused the second, or vice versa (or is there a third factor, perhaps unknown or unmeasured, which influences both and thus accounts for their relationship)? If you see more storks in Denmark around houses with new babies, it does not necessarily mean the two are directly connected; it may have rather more to do with people keeping their houses warmer for their new-borns, and with the understandable preference storks have for nesting on warmer, not colder, chimneys. Correlation need not imply causation.

Later research tended to show essentially no relationship between intelligence and bilingualism, and this work was generally more carefully done than the earlier studies. Controlling sex, age and social-class differences became common procedure, and the lack of such control was increasingly seen to have produced the negative associations found in previous work.

What some have seen as a turning-point came in the early 1960s, when findings showing a *positive* relationship between intelligence and bilingualism began to appear. A study in Montreal in 1962, for example (by Elizabeth Peal and Wallace Lambert), more carefully controlled the relevant variables in an examination of ten-year-old bilingual and monolingual children.[32] In particular, all the subjects were from middle-class backgrounds and all the bilingual youngsters had equal proficiency in French and English. The bilinguals were found to outperform their monolingual counterparts on both verbal and non-verbal intelligence tests and the authors concluded that the bilingual child had 'mental flexibility, a superiority in concept formation and a more diversified set of mental abilities'.[33] However, they also noted that 'it is not possible to state from the present study whether the more intelligent child became bilingual or whether bilingualism aided his intellectual development'.

Following Peal and Lambert's study many others have appeared which support a positive linkage between bilingualism and intelligence. There have also been some dissenting views, as well as cogent criticism of the 1962 study itself. The latter centres upon the limitation just cited from Peal and Lambert themselves and upon the generalizability of the results. Important here are the restriction, in their study, to only 'balanced' bilinguals, and questions about the representativeness of the sample of children and the difficulty of equating home backgrounds simply by holding socioeconomic status constant. On this last point, an appositive example has recently been provided:

Two children of the same sex and age living in the same village may have fathers who work side by side as underground miners. One family regularly attends Welsh chapel, eisteddfodau, and competes in penillion singing and poetry competitions at local and national eisteddfodau. The miner and his wife send their bilingual child to a designated bilingual secondary school. The culture of the second family concerns bingo, the Club, discos and pigeon racing. Their monolingual child attends a non-Welsh-speaking school. For the quantitative researcher, the children are matched on socio-economic class. In reality the differences are great.[34]

By way of summary, some of the difficulties involved in attempting to show a relationship – positive or negative – between bilingualism and cognitive development, mental flexibility, intelligence and so on involve these questions:

1   How do we adequately define bilingualism itself; do we require perfectly balanced bilinguals for the 'best' contrast with monolinguals, and how do we measure bilingualism, balanced or otherwise?
2   How do we define intelligence; relatedly, how do we know that IQ tests adequately assess this quantity? This is obviously an important matter which I cannot go into here; it has a large literature.
3   How do we ensure comparability between groups of bilinguals and monolinguals; controlling for age, sex and some other variables may not be difficult, but what about socioeconomic status? Most measures of this may not come to grips well enough with home differences of vital importance.
4   How do we interpret any relationship found between bilingualism and intelligence? Is it a causal one, and, if so, in which direction? Does bilingualism lead to increased IQ, for example, or does a higher IQ increase the likelihood of functional bilingualism?

These and other factors mean that strong conclusions about bilingualism and cognition are not warranted. Some feel that there *may* be some link between the two, but that any cognitive advantages attaching to bilingualism are rather slight. Others have been mainly concerned to show that there is not a cognitive *price* to be paid for bilingualism. One author noted that:

> In short, almost no general statements are warranted by research on the effects of bilingualism. It has not been demonstrated that bilingualism has positive or negative consequences for intelligence, linguistic skills, educational attainment, emotional adjustment, or cognitive functioning. In almost every case, the findings of research are either contradicted by other research or can be questioned on methodological grounds.[35]

We should understand that social factors are virtually always of great importance in accounting for contradictory reports about bilingualism and cognition. Most positive findings come from studies of immersion children (where language attitudes are favourable), most negative ones from those 'submersed' in second-language education (leading to so-called 'subtractive' bilingualism); on these matters, see Chapter 7.

My own view is that being bilingual (or multilingual, for that matter) is unlikely to mean any significant increase in cognitive and intellectual skills, although it would also seem that bilingualism need not lead to decreased or weakened capacities. It would be perverse, however, to deny that bilingualism can represent another *dimension* of one's capacities, and in that sense a repertoire expansion. I see nothing controversial about this, just as I would see nothing controversial in the statement that a number of years' devotion to the study of great literature can lead to a heightened or, at least, altered sensitivity to the human condition.

If we have moved historically from a period in which detrimental effects of bilingualism were alleged, to a 'neutral' period, and then on to a positive one, perhaps now we should cautiously step back a bit.

THE BILINGUAL BRAIN

I have already mentioned George Steiner's self-description as a balanced trilingual.[36] He describes his 'natural condition' as a polyglot one and, when asking if a 'polyglot mentality' might operate intrinsically differently from a unilingual one, he implies the possibility of neurologically-based and deep-seated variation. Forty years ago, Weinreich discussed a distinction between *co-ordinate* and *compound* bilingualism. If one's first language was English, and if French were acquired later, then different conceptual systems might operate for each language. *Book* would have its own meaning, and so would *livre*. But if French and English were learned more or less concurrently, then the neurological representation of the two languages could be somehow fused or joined; in such a *compound* system a common meaning, a single conceptualization, would underlie both *book* and *livre*. Steiner mentions the 'co-existence' of *chestnut tree, marronnier* and *Kastanienbaum.*

Studies of bilingual production and access have been, as one might expect, inconclusive. There seems little support for the idea that different languages are stored in the brain in essentially separate compartments, but the possibility remains that, within some overarching linguistic-storage unit, there may be subsystems associated with separate languages.

There is clearly much more to be discovered here. For example, studies of aphasia, strokes and other disabilities continue to suggest interesting neurological underpinnings of bilingualism. Consider the following cases:[37]

1 A 44-year-old man whose maternal language was Swiss-German, and who had subsequently acquired German and French, suffered a stroke. Within a couple of days he was able to understand all three varieties, but his speech was severely impaired. He first recovered productive

power in French, then German, then Swiss-German (i.e., in reverse order in which they were learned). Later, the French faded, and Swiss-German re-emerged as dominant.

2   A 75-year-old man, a native German speaker with competence in French and English, suffered a brain injury which caused him to mix these varieties (saying, for example, 'I vil home kommen' for 'I want to go home').

3   A Chinese–English bilingual who suffered a brain tumour lost the ability to read and write in Chinese (his maternal tongue) but retained it for English.

4   My mother-in-law, a native French speaker who latterly used English to a great extent, suffered a stroke. Her first words afterwards were those of standard French prayers she had learned as a child. When a nurse, thinking to assist in her recovery, heard this she began speaking to her in French. This indeed elicited more speech from my *belle-mère* – but in English!

These and many other similar occurrences (as well as experimental work on 'normals') have led researchers to believe that bilingual or multilingual capacities may have anatomical consequences which, in turn, may lead to different ways of processing and producing different varieties. But to say that there are many unanswered questions here is a large understatement indeed.

BORROWING, INTERFERENCE AND CODE-SWITCHING

Outright language choice is obviously available to bilingual individuals, and an illustrative example is found in Paraguay. Here, more than 90 per cent are bilingual in Guaraní and Spanish. Language choice is non-random, and heavily influenced by external constraints, as figure 3.1 shows.[38]

It is also common to find linguistic alteration occurring within one unit of speech directed to one listener. In his classic volume on the subject, Weinreich stated that all such 'deviation from the norms of either language' may be referred to as *interference*.[39] It seems evident, however, that not every switch from one language to another results from the unwelcome intrusion which the term *interference* suggests; speakers may often switch for emphasis, because they feel that the *mot juste* is found more readily in one of their languages than in another, or because of their perceptions of the speech situation, changes in content, the linguistic skills of their inter-locutors, degrees of intimacy and so on. Some writers have thus opted for the more neutral term *transference* which implies, among other things, a greater element of volition. There is certainly a wide range of possibilities, as the following examples suggest:[40]

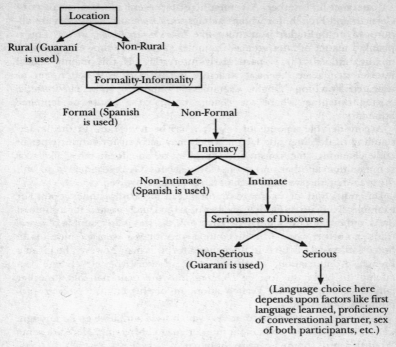

Figure 3.1 Factors influencing language choice in Paraguay

Source: after Rubin, 1968

(1) The proceedings went smoothly, ba? (Tagalog)
(2) This morning I hantar my baby tu dekat babysitter tu lah ('This morning I took my baby to the babysitter'). (Malay–English)
(3) De pompier militaire van de staat ... loop partout me ne vitesse zoo rapide as de chemin de fer ('The state military fireman ... runs everywhere with the speed of a railway'). (French–Dutch)
(4) Sano että tulla tänne että I'm very sick ('Tell them to come here that I'm very sick'). (Finnish–English)
(5) Sometimes I'll start a sentence in English y terminó en español ('Sometimes I'll start a sentence in English and end it in Spanish').

These examples of code-switching (some refer to it as code-*mixing*; these and other terms have yet to reach agreed-upon definition) illustrate changes of various types. Example (1) shows 'tag-switching', where a stock element in one language (often interrogatory or exclamatory) is joined to an utterance in another. A common related event is when speakers of German and French, for whom the tags *nicht wahr* and *n'est-ce pas* are all-purpose say, in English, something like **She's a nice person, isn't it?* This is plainly a matter of interference. Examples (2) and (3) show *intrasentential* mixing; indeed, (3) is particularly interesting. Is this mainly lexical interference, since the basic structure is Dutch, or is it better seen as repeated switching? Finally, examples (4) and (5) show *intersentential* mixing/switching, where the change occurs at a clause or sentence boundary.

A considerable amount of research has been devoted to the understanding of the linguistic factors which may account for various types of code changing, the constraints which make one form more likely or common than another, and so on. Obviously this has a great deal to do with the grammar and syntax of each of the languages involved.

Different *types* of language transfer can be easily understood. For example, if a Brussels French speaker uses the Dutch *vogelpik* for a game of darts, rather than the standard French *fléchettes*, this is an example of *lexical* transfer. Further, *vogelpik* in this context constitutes a *loanword* since it is an 'intrusion' regularly used in unchanged form. It may, however, be given a French pronunciation, which indicates another type of 'change', an attempt to bring the foreign element into the maternal fold (another familiar example is the French adoption of the English *pullover,* pronounced 'poolovaire').

Sometimes loanwords become very widely used and, if we go far enough, we reach the level of permanent interlanguage borrowing. Here are some 'English' words showing eastern influence:[41]

ALCOHOL (Arabic *al-koh'l*): powdered antimony, then any quintessence (e.g., 'alcohol of wine' via distillation), then just the intoxicating ingredient.

ALGEBRA (Arabic *al-jebr*): the reuniting of broken parts, first used in English to refer to the setting of bones.

ASSASSIN (*hash-shashin*): hashish-eaters, a sect who killed under the influence of cannabis.

BUCKRAM: first meant a high-quality fabric from Bokhara then, later, coarse cloth.

EUNUCH (Greek *eunoukhos*): 'bed-guard'.

GAZETTE (Italian *gazeta* or *gazzetta*): name of a small Venetian copper coin.

ONYX (Greek *onux*): 'claw, fingernail' (pink, with white streaks).

PUNCH (Hindi *panch*, Sanskrit *panchan*): 'five' (i.e., the five basic ingredients: wine/spirit, water/milk, sugar, lemon and spice).

TABBY: from *Al-'at-tabiya*, a suburb of Baghdad named for Prince Attab where a cloth was made known as *attabi*; this was usually striped. Later applied to cats.

A modern example of words beginning to enter a foreign vocabulary is found in the English of Quebec, where a speaker might now say something like:

> I took the autoroute to the dépanneur [convenience store], stopped at the caisse populaire [credit union] ... crossed [met] the representative of my syndicate [union], who has been seized with [informed of] my dossier.[42]

It is interesting to note, though, that not all languages can incorporate borrowed elements equally easily. The grammatical constraints may be such – say, between two languages widely removed from one another typologically – that borrowing may be less frequent than it is between closely-related languages. More simply, borrowings from language A may not fit as easily into B as into C. This may have important consequences for B and C if A, for example, is the variety of a 'developed' society and they are not.

Another variety of lexical transfer occurs when loan *translation* occurs: for example, the adoption of the English *skyscraper* into Dutch (as *wolkenkrabber*), German (*wolkenkratzer*), French (*gratte-ciel*) and Spanish (*rascacielos*). Such words are called *calques* (literally, 'copies'). *Morphological* transfers occur when a word in language A is more fully embraced by language B: the Dutch *kluts* (dollop) becomes, in Brussels French, *une clouche*, and *heilbot* (halibut) becomes *un elbot. Syntactic* transfer occurs in such examples as *Tu prends ton plus haut chiffre* ('You take your highest figure') – said by a native Dutch speaker, who makes his adjectives precede the noun, as they would in Dutch (*Je neemt je hoogste cijfer*) but not as they would in French. *Phonological* transfer is very common, of course, and is a most difficult area in which to avoid interference (consider fluent adult speakers with 'horrible' accents). Equally, *prosodic* transfer – subtle differences in stress and intonation between languages, such that one's dominant variety influences the other – is also difficult to avoid. In Standard French the appropriate emphasis would be *il faut pas dire ça!* ('You mustn't say that!') but in Brussels French the emphasized word is *dire*, on the model of the Dutch *Ge moogt dat niet zeggen*.

This brief discussion of interference and code-switching only scratches the surface, but it does reveal something of the variety of transference and, more importantly, the variability in terms of conscious intent. That is, bilingual speakers may *choose* to use *vogelpik*, and their choice may be determined by non-linguistic, social factors; syntactic and phonological interference, on the other hand, is presumably less subject to such factors or, more accurately perhaps, is less easily or directly influenced by them, necessitating more effort to remove it. In general one might roughly view interference phenomena as those determined by internal factors, and code-switching as more influenced by extralinguistic constraints; however this *is* only general, as even the few examples given here suggest.

However we divide the subject up, and whatever labels we apply – interference, code-switching, mixing, transference, etc. – it is clear that in all cases something is 'borrowed' from another language. Further, the degree to which the borrowed element is integrated (or can be integrated) into the other code may be of considerable interest for studies of group contact, of relative linguistic prestige, of the perceived or actual ease with which different languages deal with given topics, and so on. Borrowings may be on a 'nonce' basis or may represent more established practice, but the latter grows from the former and presumably reflects stronger and more widespread need. However, a further subdivision has been suggested for these established borrowings; some are indeed necessary – words filling lexical gaps in the other language, for example – but some are 'gratuitous' – there already exists the equivalent item. Why, then, the borrowing? The motivation here is most often perceived status and prestige. Common examples include the use of foreign words or phrases. To say that something is a *sine qua non* or, *mutatis mutandis*, might become *la crème de la crème* (*sensu bono*, of course) in terms of representing the *Zeitgeist*, is perhaps to reach the *Ultima Thule*, *poco a poco*, of prestige – but it can be overdone, *non è vero*? Four hundred years ago, du Bellay also had reservations:

> Among other things, let our poet take care not to use the Latin and Greek proper names, a thing as absurd really as if thou shouldst apply a piece of green velvet to a dress of red velvet. But would it not be an absurd thing to use in a Latin work the proper name of a man or other thing in French, as *Jan currit, Loyre fluit*, and other like words? Suit, then, such proper names, of whatever language they be, to the use of thy vulgar tongue . . . say in French *Hercule, Thésée, Achille, Ulysse, Virgile, Ciceron, Horace*. Thou shouldst, however, in this use judgment and discretion, for there are many such names which cannot be appropriated into French: . . . I refer you to the judgment of your ear. As for the rest, use words purely French, not, however, too common, nor yet too rarely used.[43]

At another level, one can observe the trendy status of English which seems to be growing around the world, even among those ignorant of it. It has been reported, for example, that shops in the re-emerging eastern European countries often find it easier to sell their products (when they have any) if they are labelled in English. No English competence is implied or required in either seller or buyer; simple recognition and cachet apparently do the trick. English is the international language, too, of pop music and culture (the coca-colonialism factor). As Michael Luszynski, a Polish singer, wryly noted recently, a phrase like *Słysze warkot pociagu nadjedzie na torze* does not have the same oomph as 'I hear the train a-coming, it's rolling down the line' – even to Polish speakers with no English. In Germany, teenagers wear *die Jeans*, in Moscow you can attend a *dzhazz-saission*, you can say *baj-baj* in many countries, and even the French grudgingly acknowledge the appeal of *le drugstore* and *le weekend*. In Japan, English has a social clout which, again, is underpinned by neither knowledge nor grammaticality. Tomato juice may be sold as 'red mix for city actives', a coffee-shop motto is 'world smell in cup, full', a soft drink is called 'Pocari sweat' and one can get advice on 'how to sex'.[44] This omits the use of English words more fully integrated into Japanese, often in abbreviated form (e.g., *hamu tosuto* for a 'toasted ham sandwich', *apaato* for 'apartment' and many others in regular use).

Under the heading 'Pretentious diction', Orwell excoriated the use of many foreign words and expressions – *Weltanschauung, status quo, ancien régime* and all the rest – which he said are used to 'give an air of culture and elegance'. Some abbreviations – *e.g. i.e.*, and *etc.* – are useful, and Orwell thought that a few other terms might be necessary. He noted, though, that 'if we really need the word *café* ... it should either be spelled "caffay" or pronounced "cayfe"'. He went on to say that 'bad writers, and especially scientific, political and sociological writers, are nearly always haunted by the notion that Latin or Greek words are grander than Saxon ones'; thus he also saw as unnecessary such terms as *ameliorate, deracinated* and *clandestine*. The avoidance of perfectly good English words, he felt, led to 'slovenliness and vagueness'. Finally, Orwell criticized phrases like *a not unjust final assumption* – which he thought should be laughed out of existence: 'One can cure oneself of the *not un-* formation by memorizing this sentence: *A not unblack dog was chasing a not unsmall rabbit across a not ungreen field.*' Well, there is a lot to all of this but, as elsewhere, Orwell's passion and generalization obliterate some useful elements along with many bad ones.[45] I would not like to lose *clandestine*, for example, and phrases like *ancien régime* have resonances which one may quite appropriately wish to summon, and are not easily replaceable with concision.

In still other cases, borrowing may occur for what Weinreich lightly termed 'cacophemistic purposes'. Citing a study done in the 1930s, he observed that:

> the patois of French Switzerland have no morally favorable terms of German origin, but they swarm with German words for disreputable or badly dressed women, rudeness, coarseness, indolence, sloth [and] avarice, corresponding to the stereotyped ridicule with which the French Swiss regards the German Swiss, his culture, and above all his language, of whose inferiority the former is deeply convinced.[46]

This sort of borrowing is often, too, allied to the desire to produce a comic effect and both this and its unilingual counterpart – alteration of accents, say, within a joke – are well-understood and frequently used devices available to virtually all speakers.

It is interesting, in all of this, to recognize that attitudes towards code-switching are often negative, particularly on the part of monolinguals who are sometimes inclined to dismiss it as gibberish.[47] Terms like *Tex-Mex, Franglais, Japlish* (and many others) are often used, and often meant pejoratively. Bilinguals, too, are wont to see their behaviour here as 'embarrassing', 'impure', 'lazy', even 'dangerous', but the reasons they give for the practice – fitting the word to the topic, finding a word with a nuance unavailable in the other variety, helping out a listener, strengthening intimacy, and so on – make a great deal of sense. If you have two languages to draw upon, why not maximize this happy circumstance as appropriate? The chimeras of impurity and laziness are exposed when we realize that, very often, switching involves the *repetition* – for emphasis, for intimacy – of the same idea in both languages. We see, then, speakers whose twin bow-strings allow them not only the style-shifting available to monolinguals (see below) but also full language-shifting. It is hard to imagine that this is anything but a valuable addition.[48]

VARIATION WITHIN ONE LANGUAGE

I have already noted that everyone is bilingual, and we have now seen how, with sufficient fluency, switching and mixing between varieties occur. One could, with equal accuracy, say that we are all bidialectal, multi-accented, and have available a range of speaking *styles*. Just as bilingualism can range from extremely halting to very proficient, so bidialectalism (and multi-accentedness) varies widely. At one extreme we find those who know only a few words in another dialect, or who can only adopt a rather caricatured non-maternal accent (jokes provide a common illustration here, especially those of the Scotsman–Irishman–Englishman kind). At the other we find those individuals who can assume native coloration, and here actors are a good example. However, the most widely available variation for mono-lingual speakers is at the level of *style*. In a sociolinguistic context, this term refers to speech variations which reflect one's perception of the social context and what is or is not 'appropriate'. The most common influence and product is the degree of formality. There is quite a difference, for example, among the statements, *I am extremely fatigued, I'm very tired* and *I'm bloody knackered*, yet one speaker could easily utter them all, in different settings. This sort of variation is so effortless that we usually do it without much thought, and normal members of speech communities adapt all the time. In fact, most are so good at this that we notice the variation only when it seems 'odd'. A doctor who looked over her glasses and said 'Well, it's the high jump for you, squire' would seem frivolous and unfeeling; and a mechanic who reported that 'Your conveyance is, I regret to inform you, in a most sadly dilapidated state' would invite both wonder and laughter.

Of course, some people seem more 'monostylistic' than others, less willing or able to alter their speech with situations, or quite unaware of their rigidity. Inflexibility itself clearly has an effect; perhaps this accounts for the appeal of the exchange between a don and T.E. Lawrence, recounted by Robert Graves in his autobiography:

> Professor Edgeworth, of All Souls', avoided conversational English, persistently using words and phrases that one expects to meet only in books. One evening, Lawrence returned from a visit to London, and Edgeworth met him at the gate. 'Was it very caliginous in the Metropolis?' 'Somewhat caliginous, but not altogether inspissated,' Lawrence replied gravely.[49]

On the other hand, the following response by Gladstone to a drunken heckler may fall more in the 'unaware' category:

> May I request the gentleman who has, not once but repeatedly, interrupted my observations by his interjections, to extend to me that large measure of courtesy which, were I in his place and he in mine, I should most unhesitatingly extend to him.[50]

It is reported, in any event, that the man 'was sobered by the shock' of Gladstone's eloquence – no doubt the rest of the audience was stunned, too.

A highly readable account of stylistic variation is found in Martin Joos's little book *The Five Clocks*, so titled because the author held there to be five distinct styles of English usage.[51] The five are *frozen, formal, consultative, casual* and *intimate*. Although not all would agree that Joos's divisions are the most accurate or have universal applicability (and, furthermore, in inexact sciences, whenever anyone tells us there are exactly five of this or seven of that, or eleven of the other, we ought to be wary), they remain useful and provocative.

Joos starts by discussing the *consultative* style, 'because the readers of this report are presumably best at home there'.[52] Its defining characteristics are the provision of necessary background information, without which the listener cannot make sense of the message, and the participation of the listener in the conversation. With friends and 'in-group' members – as the social psychologist would have it – we tend to switch to the *casual* style; here we can dispense with contextual grounding and listener participation. Within this format we can expect to find examples of slang and ellipsis. Confusion is common in consultative and casual speech, because we sometimes err in estimating the degree to which an interlocutor actually *does* have the information we possess; sometimes we tell him or her things already known (or unnecessary for the present purposes: 'Last Thursday I went to see the doctor . . . wait, perhaps it was Wednesday . . . no, Wednesday

I was at Auntie Hilda's, so it must have been Thursday ... hang on, though, Auntie was out when I rang for our usual meeting last week, so perhaps I *did* go to Dr Fell on Wednesday') and sometimes we omit information which *is not* common. If someone rattles on about Auntie Hilda and her family, assuming incorrectly that we know who she is – well, it is clear enough that a bit more background was needed.

In both consultative and casual styles, information is important (even if it need not be spelled out). In *intimate* style, however, information and its exchange become much less central; in fact 'an intimate utterance pointedly avoids giving the addressee information from outside of the speaker's skin'.[53] If someone simply says *cold* or *ready*, the meaning can be quite clear to an intimate. Joos also includes here the use of jargon – a permanent in-group code – but not slang, which he views as 'ephemeral' and therefore casual rather than intimate. Many professional groups have their own jargon, of course, but an example of a highly restricted and intimate form might be those special 'family' words known and used only under the domestic roof.

To move in the other direction, from consultative to *formal* style, is to delete listener participation. Perhaps the group has grown too large – Joos suggests that consultation is difficult among more than half-a-dozen people – or perhaps the listener is unfamiliar. Formal style is for transmitting information and this is 'its dominating character, something which is necessarily ancillary in consultation, incidental in casual discourse, absent in intimacy'.[54] It requires advance planning and is defined by detachment and cohesion. Most university lectures are delivered in formal style, and it may also be commonly observed among 'urbane strangers'. The fifth 'clock' – *frozen* style – is used for declamation and, most commonly, is the form enshrined in print. It lacks participation and intonational clues and requires no social exchange between speaker (or writer) and listener (or reader). It necessitates care and planning, for one of its great advantages is that, when written, it can be reconsulted at will. A good frozen style lures us on, and this reminds us that not all written language has the same force, not every attempt to transmit formal knowledge is equally successful. The best frozen language can be thus equated with timeless literature.

Joos also provides some of the guidelines regulating the use and shifting of the styles. For example, between strangers, formal usage is largely ceremonial introduction in which no real information is exchanged; it is short-lived and soon displaced by consultation. Formality can return, however, when embarrassment (for example) arises or is imminent, and it may also signal the end of a conversation. Another rule is that, while there is generally no requirement to confine oneself to a single style on any given occasion, 'normally only two neighboring styles are used alternatively, and it is anti-social to shift two or more steps in a single jump'.[55]

Joos's work hardly qualifies as a technical, detailed study (and there are

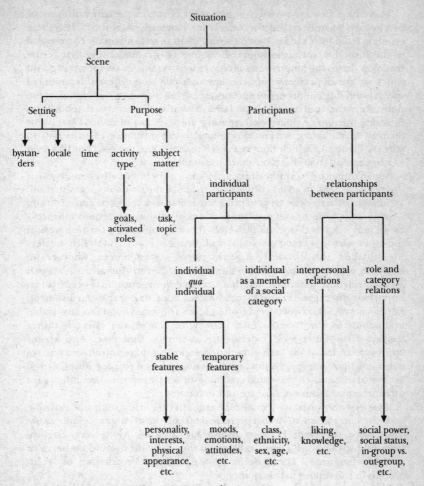

Figure 3.2 Situational influences on speech

other influences on style beside formality) but its basic message is sound: all ordinary speakers have a range of possibilities in their linguistic repertoire, from which they pick and choose according to their sense of the occasion. This is code-switching, and its ubiquity and frequency are worth noting – not only because they illustrate a powerful and virtually automatic grasp of linguistic and sociolinguistic subtleties, but also because they link monolingual performances to the more apparent juggling of the bilingual.

There have been some interesting recent efforts, especially within social psychology, to understand the *reasons* for language variation.[56] It is clear enough, from Joos's study, that different levels of style normally correspond to the formality, the seriousness, the intent of an interaction; that is, the situation drives the language to a large extent. Again, this is something with which we are all perfectly familiar – we 'naturally' use different manners of speech with our children, our spouses, the bank manager, our chums in the pub, the vicar, and so on. In a fashion similar to that used (above) to illustrate the choice points determining the selection of either Guaraní or Spanish in Paraguay, we could schematize the influence of situation on speech. Figure 3.2 which does not, itself, exhaust the details, could be seen as a formalization and expansion of Joos's ideas.[57]

But if context determines linguistic choice then, equally, language (or dialect, or accent, or style) choice can influence the psychological situation. We may, in other words, wish to put a particular stamp on our conversation; we may want to approach our listener (out of existing or desired intimacy) or we may want to dissociate ourselves (because of dislike, because we feel the other person is being psychologically invasive, etc.). This desire to affect the situation will obviously have linguistic consequences, whether we explicitly intend these or not. Some early studies in this area of 'speech accommodation' demonstrated that 'accent convergence' may occur (in an important interview, for instance, when we hope to impress our listener). Furthermore, such convergence often leads (unsurprisingly) to favourable evaluations by the listener. Like flattery, of course, the effect is rather spoiled if the latter feels a deliberate attempt is underway. And accent convergence is not the only linguistic weapon we have in our arsenal: we may also adjust our speech rate, utterance length and pausing times, as well as manipulate such essential paralinguistic features as smiling, gaze directness and duration, posture and so on.

If we can converge, we can also diverge. In one interesting study people strongly committed to Welsh were learning it in a language laboratory. They were surveyed, in their individual cubicles, by 'a very English-sounding speaker' who caustically asked them why they would bother with a 'dying language'. There occurred a noticeable broadening of Welsh accents in the replies to this challenge!

There are many subtleties underlying the operation of accommodation: it can be upward or downward (i.e., towards or away from high-status speech variants); full or partial (in fact, it is probably never completely full – too difficult, too obvious, too self-denigrating) in terms of all the possible points on which convergence/divergence *could* occur; large or moderate (again, too large can be risky: maybe I should shift my accent *somewhat* towards the manager's, but not aim to clone it); symmetrical or asymmetrical (one or both parties may accommodate: I wish to impress my boss, but he wants to put me more at ease). Running through all these specificities is the group–individual distinction – that is, is convergence/divergence in the service of facilitating or hindering a purely personal exchange, or is it a component of one in which one (or more) of the participants is acting in some sense as a representative of a group (see the Welsh example, above)? Neither of these exists in pure form outside the mind of the experimental manipulator, but there certainly is a range of possibilities here.

BILINGUALISM AND SOCIETY

If we recognize that bilingualism, switching and other dual-language phenomena are still seen as suspicious by some and arcane marks of erudition by others, we should also recall their global nature. Expanded linguistic competence is usually driven by necessity but it has also historically reflected and supported upper-class boundaries. There is a distinction, in other words, between élite and folk bilingualism. In different ages, not to have known Latin or Greek or French in addition to one's mother tongue would have been simply unthinkable for educated people.[58] At other levels and for other reasons more humble citizens have also been bilingual from earliest times: we know it was necessary under the Ptolemies to acquire Greek, even for quite minor posts, and Athenian slaves – representatives of the lowest class of all – were often bilingual as they were pressed into domestic service and teaching.

There are important differences between individual bilingualism and collective or social bilingualism, regardless of whether the latter is officially endorsed (as in Canada) or simply a fact of ordinary life (as in Taiwan, where Mandarin is official but where most speak Fukienese as a mother tongue). Collective bilingualism in many settings, ancient and modern, is an enduring quantity, unlike the impermanent, transitional variety common in many immigrant contexts in which, in fact, bilingualism is a generational way-station on the road between two unilingualisms. The classic pattern for newcomers to the United States, for example, was bilingualism (mother tongue and English) by the second generation and English monolingualism by the third. The more permanent collective bilingualism remains, of course, largely because of a continuing necessity which is absent among most immigrant populations, and this necessity usually rests upon different social functions and different domains of use for each language. This situation is now commonly referred to as *diglossia*. This word is simply the Greek version of *bilingualism* and, on the face of it, would not seem to be a useful innovation; it does not, for example, logically encompass the social, collective aspect that, in practice, it refers to. However, 'la logique n'est pas maître de la terminologie'.[59]

Near the end of the last century, hellenists wishing to describe the roles of dialects in Greek society introduced the idea of *diglossie*. Psichari, for example, saw as diglossic the contemporary use of both *demotic* Greek and *katharévusa*, that is, the ordinary spoken variety and the 'purer', more classic form. It soon became apparent that modern Greece was not the only setting where a functional differentiation existed between 'higher' and 'lower' varieties of the same language. In North Africa, for example, a similar situation obtained for classical and vernacular Arabic. In 1930, Marçais looked more closely at *la diglossie arabe* and, in doing so, raised the question of whether diglossia was restricted to two dialects, or whether it could be extended to different *languages* having separate social functions.

Diglossia was brought into modern perspective in 1959, in a germinal article by Charles Ferguson.[60] He noted four 'defining' instances, two of which were the Greek and Arab, the other two being Swiss-German and Haitian Creole; all had both high ('superposed') and low (regional) forms, as follows:

	High	*Low*
Arabic	'al-fusha	'al-ammiyyah
Swiss-German	Schriftsprache (standard German)	Schweizerdeutsch
Haitian	français (standard French)	créole
Greek	katharévusa	dhimotiki

Ferguson stressed from the outset the functional differences, the high variety (H) reigning in formal and printed contexts, and the low (L) serving more mundane purposes; he also observed that 'the importance of using the right variety in the right situation can hardly be overestimated'.[61] The interweaving of the functions is illustrated by the common practice of reading a newspaper written in H and then discussing it in L. The H variety, of course, is the more prestigious, and some may even feel that a knowledge of L alone is insufficient qualification as a speaker of the language itself. Many educated speakers may deny that they even use the L form at all, although this is belied by observation. The H variety is, unsurprisingly, held to be more logical, more aesthetically appealing and better able to carry serious messages; it is often preferred in formal contexts (like political speeches or poetry readings) even when the use of L would be more widely intelligible. The H form is usually associated with religious and literary heritage, and is acquired through formal education which ensures, incidentally, that it is almost never as intimate a medium as is L.

At more technical levels, it is the H variety which is grammatically and orthographically standardized, which is linguistically more complex than L. It also has lexical items which have no L equivalents, although the reverse is also the case (a religious abstraction spoken about in H, or a car part discussed in L). In addition, there are many concepts common to *both* H and L which have quite different labels in each format. In Haiti, the créole term for donkey is *bourik* while *âne* is the Standard French equivalent. In Greece the word on the menu for wine is *inos* but the customer asks for *krasi*. Ferguson observes that English 'parallels' – like *purchase–buy*, or *children–kids* – do not capture the degree of difference existing in his 'defining' examples of diglossia. Perhaps we could (roughly) say that this sort of variation in English is more at the level of style.

The musings of Marçais were revived when, following Ferguson's discussion, several writers did extend the scope of diglossia from two dialects of the same language to separate languages altogether (or, indeed, to styles and registers as well). The important matter remains functional differentiation. Joshua Fishman in particular attempted to relate bilingualism and diglossia in a systematic way, outlining four possible interactions:[62]

1 *Speech communities with both bilingualism and diglossia*: In Paraguay, for example, not only are most of the people bilingual in Spanish and Guaraní, the two languages are (as we have already seen) functionally separated; Spanish here is the H variety, Guaraní the L. Another example is found in nineteenth-century eastern Europe, where Hebrew was H and Yiddish L for Jewish males. Ferguson's Arabic case is also found under this heading.

2 *Diglossia without bilingualism*: In many European states it was traditionally the case that the élite spoke a 'fashionable' language (French, say) while the masses used a local variety. Here we really see *two* speech communities, in the larger of which (at least) monolingualism prevails, united in one political unit. A more recent example is Canada where, traditionally, few anglophones are bilingual and where mainly urbanized French-Canadians are, yet where an official place is made for both languages.

3 *Bilingualism without diglossia*: The classic example here is found among immigrants to a new society, which also emphasizes that bilingualism, as we have now come to see it, is essentially an individual phenomenon, while diglossia signifies social organization. Without some overarching diglossia, bilingualism tends to be temporary and transitional.

4 *Neither diglossia nor bilingualism*: This category is the rarest, but perhaps socially unstratified tribal or clan units provide examples – all members are monolingual and only one language is used across all domains. But, as Fishman remarks, even within such communities *some* role differentiation (between elders and others, between religious leaders and their congregation) and some accompanying linguistic diversity are often found. This category shrinks still more if we admit style-shifting under the rubric of diglossia. Finally, because small and tightly knit communities tend, eventually, to come into contact (or be forced into

contact) with others, Fishman is probably correct in saying that they are often 'self-liquidating'.

It will also be seen that, especially in the expanded sense of the terminology, there are examples of triglossia (in North Africa, for example, where classical and vernacular Arabic co-exist with French) or tetraglossia (again, in North Africa, where the three varieties just mentioned, as well as Berber, operate within Morocco). In fact, a 'polyglossic spectrum'[63] is the norm in many parts of the world. In the Malay speech community, for example, there is Royal Malay (*bahasa di raja*) and there is Common Malay; these two approximate the classical H–L dichotomy. But, within the latter there are Refined Malay (*bahasa halus*) and Educated Malay (*bahasa terpelajar*) and these two are not at all the same – an educated speaker may yet lack that background and 'breeding' characteristic of a Refined Malay speaker. As well, there is a colloquial and coarse variety (*bahasa kasar*) and one which is colloquial without being coarse (*bahasa basahan*). Or consider the Arabic situation, which provided Ferguson with one of his 'defining' instances. A five-point continuum has been suggested as follows:

fusha al-turath	Classical Arabic, Ferguson's H variety;
fusha al-casr	Modern Standard Arabic, the current literary medium, only written;
cammiyyat al-muthaqqafin	High Standard Colloquial, the usual spoken variety of educated people dealing with serious topics – part of Ferguson's L;
cammiyyat al-mutanawwirin	Middle Standard Colloquial, the everyday language of the literate – part of Ferguson's L;
cammiyyat al-ummiyyin	Low Colloquial, the everyday language of the illiterate – part of Ferguson's L.

Further, we must recognize that not all diglossias are the same: if virtually everyone in diglossic Paraguay speaks both varieties, the same cannot be said for Haiti – another of Ferguson's 'defining' cases – where only one or two in twenty have access to both varieties (the rest being monolingual in créole).

While diglossia, as collective bilingualism, is seen to be a stable condition, it should be remembered that even stability is relative.[64] The French–English diglossia that prevailed in England after the Norman conquest eventually broke down and the L variety (English) achieved dominance; an important watershed here was Chaucer's *Canterbury Tales* (started around 1386, but never completed), written in the East Midlands dialect of Middle English, the earliest records of which date from about 1100. Also, the stability of diglossia is apt to be interfered with by political pressure. When the 'colonels' overthrew a liberal Greek government in 1967, the previous programme of extending the use of *dhimotiki* was reversed – because of its leftist associations – and *katharévusa* was supported. In 1975, constitutional government returned and *dhimotiki* was declared the country's official language the following year; the Athenian variety is the model here, although in several formal sectors *katharévusa* persists.

There are many problems associated with the extension of the term (as well as with its original format, as Ferguson himself has recently acknowledged). Most generally, it has been argued that something has been lost in going from instances like the Greek and the Arabic to a very large variety of quite dissimilar situations. Part of Ferguson's original conception was that the H variety was used by no one conversationally, but this qualification is lost in the expansion. Thus, Ferguson's diglossia would exclude a combination of many standard-plus-regional-dialect scenarios, because some people normally use the standard, prestigious variant for all purposes; Fishman's expansion, on the other hand, *would* allow this under diglossia.[65] Also changed is the requirement that one of the forms be of the H variety – if Canada, for example, is seen as a diglossic community, which is the H language? We see, too, in this sort of expanded instance, that 'territorial compartmentalization' is now permissible which, again, was not a feature originally.

The territoriality just mentioned brings me to the final matter I want to discuss here, and it is one that is conveniently approached from a Canadian perspective. Prior to the Official Languages Act (1969), which legally underpins French and English in Canada, a Royal Commission on Bilingualism and Biculturalism was established to study and make recommendations. Paying special attention to the linguistic situations in Belgium, Finland, Switzerland and South Africa, the commissioners closely examined the so-called 'personality' and 'territorial' principles relating to bilingualism. In the first of these, rights are seen to inhere in *individuals*, wherever they live within a state. This operates most clearly in South Africa. According to the territorial principle, however (as in Belgium), rights vary from region to region and the linguistic arrangement is usually some sort of 'twinned' unilingualism. The distinction between these two approaches is not unlike that made by political scientists between 'consociation' and 'universalism'; if consociation is sometimes seen as the democratic alternative best suited to divided societies (as in Belgium and Switzerland), it is also often an elaborate and fragile system of checks and balances among ethnic groups. Universalism, with its first emphasis on individual rights, is the preferred approach in most modern democracies but it can be seen, here, that ruling 'group rights' out of court is not always possible nor desirable.

The Commission opted for the application of the personality principle in Canada even though official-language minorities were small in all provinces except Quebec and New Brunswick. Difficulties in following this South

African example were acknowledged (some 66 per cent of whites there claimed to be bilingual, for example, as opposed to only 12 per cent in Canada; and, official-language minorities in South African provinces ranged in strength from 23 to 39 per cent, whereas they were under 15 per cent in nine of the ten Canadian provinces), and the Commission recognized the advantages of territorialism. However, political factors (chiefly, the 'symbolic' importance of the Canadian francophone population) and a highly mobile Canadian society were seen to suggest the personality approach – this despite the fact that the Commission could have considered more 'mixed' possibilities (as in Switzerland, for example, where the personality principle operates only at the federal level).[66]

The recommendation, therefore, was for federal bilingualism and the provision of bilingual services at the provincial level; but only Quebec, Ontario and New Brunswick were to become 'officially' bilingual. As conditions became more viable for francophones outside Quebec, other provinces would adopt official bilingualism (roughly, whenever French speakers came to constitute 10 per cent of the population). In fact, at the time of the Commission's recommendations, Ontario was only about 7 per cent francophone (and, in Quebec, anglophones comprised about 13 per cent). Only New Brunswick is officially bilingual today.

Now it seems as if the Canadian bilingual dream has faded, at least from the 'personality' perspective. The country has moved steadily towards 'twinned' unilingualisms – French in Quebec and English elsewhere – with a 'bilingual belt' in parts of Ontario and, especially, New Brunswick. This process has been assisted by the continuing assimilation of francophones outside Quebec and the rejection, within that province, of bilingualism. 'Territorialism' seems to have emerged, in other words, and some have suggested making it legal by giving only *one* of the two 'charter' languages official status everywhere (except in New Brunswick). The current constitutional upheavals in Canada, which have had such a strong linguistic and cultural component (and to which I shall return) show, above all, how important are the political and social frameworks within which stable bilingualism occurs. A socially-engineered policy – which is how some have described the Canadian arrangement – must ultimately, it seems, be reconciled with widespread, popular perceptions of social reality and self-interest. When perceptions differ among powerful ethnic groups – in Canada, the anglophones, francophones, aboriginals and 'allophones' (i.e., all the 'others') are all central players, though none of these is itself monolithic – then centrally inspired arrangements for multiculturalism, bilingualism and 'extended' diglossia are seen to be quite delicate.

4

LANGUAGES IN CONFLICT

As language communities come into contact in a multilingual world, the need arises for bilingualism, translation and the use of lingua francas. Proximity, necessity and convenience also lead to borrowing and inter-penetration among languages. Also, however, it is quite apparent that languages in contact can become languages in conflict. The force of circumstance – 'natural' or contrived – can cause a group to abandon its original language for another; 'big' languages like English or French or Spanish can push smaller ones around and can contribute to their demise, and competition can exist among smaller varieties as they jostle for position, sometimes in the shade of an acknowledged and seemingly unassailable giant. If we are to study the contact, competition and conflict among languages and language varieties, and if we are, further, to consider the reasons behind these phenomena – and their relationships with, and influences upon, social life and group identity – it might be useful to begin by looking at evaluative reactions of a rather more decontextualized nature.

LINGUISTIC HIERARCHIES

In the introduction I noted that members of the élite have historically never shied away from saying which languages were the 'best' or the most appropriate in given circumstances; in so doing, I suggested, they were usually reflecting dominant linguistic attitudes derived from preferences and prejudices attaching to the *speakers* of various languages. When Richard Carew (1555–1620), for example, saw English as 'excellent', Italian 'without sinews', French 'delicate' and Dutch 'manlike', he was, in effect, giving us a picture of foreigners painted by an educated Englishman of the sixteenth century. When Antoine de Rivarol (1753–1801) observed that French was synonymous with clarity, and that English, Greek, Latin and Italian were mediums of ambiguity, he gave us the same picture, redrawn by a Frenchman two centuries later.[1] Language attitudes, then, are better understood as attitudes towards the members of language communities and, as in these two instances, are often allied with powerful protective sentiments for one's own group. I shall return later to this specific matter of protection and prescriptivism; I want to begin this chapter by asking more generally if evaluations can be fairly made of languages themselves, if 'better' or 'worse', 'stronger' or 'weaker', 'beautiful' or 'harsh' are linguistic labels that can be objectively placed.

Is it the case, for example, that one language can be seen, in some sense or other, as better, more logical or more expressive than another? Is this perhaps more reasonable to ask if the languages being compared are not relatively close to each other (e.g., French and German) but are, rather, somewhat farther apart (e.g., French and Yup'ik)? Is one somehow more primitive or less developed than the other? The idea has appealed to many in the past and has contemporary adherents too. However, as implied earlier, it is quite clear that no language can be described as better or worse than another on purely linguistic grounds. Given that language is an arbitrary system in which communication rests upon agreement among members of the speech community, it follows that the only 'logic' of language is to be found in its grammar (i.e., a logic of convention). What is grammatical in French (e.g., the use of two elements to express verbal negation) is not in English (where only one is used), but this surely says nothing about the relative quality of the two systems. And, even if we compare the language of a technologically advanced society with that of an 'undeveloped' one, we find the same different, but not deficient, relationship.

Linguists may not agree on much, but on this matter there *is* broad agreement. One writer put it as follows: 'Could it be that some languages require "less mature cognition" than others, perhaps because they are still more primitive? In recent years this notion has been thoroughly discredited by virtually all students of language.'[2] Languages are best seen as different systems reflecting different varieties of the human condition. Although they may be unequal in complexity at given points, this does not imply that some have, overall, greater expressive power. To put it another way, we could say that not all varieties have the same capabilities: different social, geographical and other conditions determine what elements will be needed and, therefore, developed. All are, however, potentially functionally equivalent. Languages differ in many aspects of complexity – lexical, grammatical, phonological – and bilingual speakers will often (as we have seen) prefer one language to another for specific purposes. But, the question of overall language 'goodness' is spurious, unless we were willing to define, compare and judge the goodness of situations, contexts and milieus.

Some *have* been willing, of course, but recent social-scientific tradition has more frequently rejected what is often labelled as simple ethnocentrism, in favour of a cultural and linguistic relativism. Cultural relativism has been a received notion within social science for some time and, it must be said, represents a welcome and logical change from the ethnocentrism which had been prominent, even in intellectual circles. Reading old anthropological accounts of the 'savage' mind, of 'debased' cultures, of 'primitive' languages, is to recapture something of a European world-view that was pervasive and respectable. Nowadays, cultures and languages only *differ* from one another and we realize that some universal yardstick against which all could be measured and ranked does not exist. At the same time, a thoroughgoing relativism, with its blatantly non-judgemental stance, does present problems. Are we to accept such things as rigid caste systems, brutal treatment of women, religious intolerance, cannibalism, slavery and prostitution as merely alternative ways of ordering societies?

Ernest Gellner maintains that, although cultural relativism cannot be logically refuted, it nevertheless can be questioned: 'It is worth noting that it is intuitively repellent to pretend that the Zande belief in witchcraft is as valid as our rejection of it, and that to suppose it such is a philosophical affectation which cannot be maintained outside the study.'[3] He holds that some cultures are better than others in terms of any common-sense evaluation of the broad satisfaction of human needs; one simply has more freedom and less trauma in some societies than in others. For Gellner, the most important argument against relativism is that, while it holds that cultures cannot be judged one with the other, or against themselves at different times, societies have always, in fact, engaged in such evaluation. Social evolution involves judgement, repudiation and change. Implicit in progress is the notion that change is for the better, that the society of a later time is superior to itself at an earlier one. The scientific society is pre-eminent here because it is the product of such evolution and because it permits (though by no means ensures) greater individual freedom. It is also generally the only one which regularly criticizes itself for being ethno-centric and supports a culturally relativistic view of other cultures – which, themselves, are often more closed and intolerant.

These sorts of critical observations on out-and-out relativism seem to me very well founded. They do not, however, apply to all features of societies, and the rejection made here of the 'primitive-language' thesis still stands.[4] The general point, I suppose, is that cultural relativism is itself a relative matter. While a fully-scaled yardstick is impossible, a rougher instrument which points to extremes is possessed by many. I take it for granted that a society which condones female circumcision and believes in witchcraft is inferior, *in these respects*, to one which does not. I do not see that this constrains me to accept, as well, that language A is superior to language B, even if B-speakers eat their enemies while A-speakers turn the other cheek. It is a very large and vexing question as to why some societies do not 'develop' as much as others, why 'cultures are extremely unequal in their cognitive power'. Physical environment is doubtless the most important distinguishing feature here, promoting or retarding social evolution. But we must recall that although cognitive capacities are differently developed, the same underlying potentials are found in all cultures. My conclusion is that linguistic relativity is unshaken as a basis for understanding language variation precisely because – whatever the degree of development of other cognitive skills in other areas – the development of adequate *language* is a universal.

The particular matter of linguistic relativity received further attention in the work of Edward Sapir and his pupil, Benjamin Whorf (1897–1941), and it goes hand-in-hand with a linguistic determinism. The 'Sapir–Whorf hypothesis',[5] bluntly stated, is that different languages carve up, and allow perception of, reality in different ways and that, therefore, the language one speaks determines the way one thinks. This hypothesis is not generally accepted. Although languages do differ in their grammar and lexicon, we can obviously translate (imperfectly perhaps) among them, and speakers of one variety whose circumstances change can learn another.

If we find that the Inuit talk and think about snow in a much more fine-grained and engrossing way than do Italians, we should simply accept that important features of the environment are very different for the two groups. If we discover a desert tribe whose colour vocabulary is much more limited than our own there is no reason to expect some permanent cognitive inability to perceive and talk about 'green' once they have all struck oil and moved to Surrey. What we do note here is that a 'weak' form of the Sapir–Whorf hypothesis – that language influences our *customary* ways of thinking – is both reasonable and unsurprising.

A little end-note here: Geoffrey Pullum's recent book *The Great Eskimo Vocabulary Hoax* makes it clear that the shop-worn example of the Inuit having many different words for what we refer to simply as *snow* is not simply tired, it is false.[6] They do not, after all, have distinct words for 'snow on the ground', 'fallen snow', 'slushy snow', 'snow drift', etc. In fact, Pullum shows how the list of such words has grown, in some writer's minds, to as many as 400! He also notes that the whole idea, though it would be trivial even if it were true, has captured hearts both within and without linguistics. The truth? According to an authoritative Inuit dictionary there are only two relevant roots – *ganik* (snow in the air) and *aput* (snow on the ground) – although many words can be derived from these, much as the English *snow* can lead to *snow-fall*, *snowflake*, *snowstorm*, etc.

It is, thus, a common observation among linguists, anthropologists and others that languages are always sufficient for the needs of their speakers. This was formally stated by von Humboldt in the eighteenth century and by Joachim du Bellay in the sixteenth. 'All languages are of a like value ... to each man his language can completely communicate every doctrine';[7] it is not true that 'diverse tongues are fitted to signify diverse conceptions, some the conceptions of the learned, others those of the unlearned'. A recent attack on this stance has, however, asked how speakers in 'primitive' groups can cope with higher mathematics, or Wittgenstein, or biochemistry; further, if all varieties are adequate for group needs, could we not claim that groups lacking the necessary vocabulary do not *need*, for example, modern technology or medicine?[8]

In both cases there is confusion between concepts and words. If a group, for example, begins to take an interest in simple arithmetic and, 500 years later, develops a theory of quantum mechanics it is surely reasonable to expect that words will grow with increasing sophistication. This is, in fact, what happens. There is, as well, no need to look at 'primitive' societies (in whatever sense 'primitive' is construed) here: consider our own intellectual and linguistic development. Second, and relatedly, it is the lack of the prerequisite conceptual understanding which prevents a group from possessing modern medical procedures. Words themselves are only indicators. Thus, the real meaning of a statement like 'language is adequate for its speakers' needs' refers to the fact that language keeps pace with conceptual advancement, which in turn determines the very needs of which speakers can even be aware.

While there must obviously be a finite lag between new ideas and new terms, this lag varies inversely with the general importance of the idea. How long did it take for *astronaut* to catch on? And, even while it was still to make its entrance, there were all sorts of other descriptive terms to fill the temporary void (we no longer hear *spaceman* very much). Description, albeit rough, is always possible. Thus, while the scientist searches for the word *laser*, he or she is perfectly able to convey the *idea* of what the word represents to others; in fact, if this were not possible, the new word itself would be empty. All of this rests upon accumulated conceptual advancement, and we have not, so far at least, had an instance of such a gigantic leap forward that description has proved impossible.

If popular attitudes about the superiority–inferiority of *languages* are resistant to change, despite the weight of linguistic evidence, then those concerning styles, accents and dialects are even more deeply ingrained.[9] *Ain't* is always wrong, as is a double negative (in English); saying *dese*, *dat* and *dose* is uneducated (at best) and slovenly; a Cockney or Joual variety departs from both accuracy and propriety; and so on. Vocabulary, pronunciation and grammar which are at variance with a received 'standard' are regularly dismissed, and a great divide is thus perceived between such a standard and all other 'substandard' forms. In fact, however:

> just as there is no linguistic reason for arguing that Gaelic is superior to Chinese, so no English dialect can be claimed to be linguistically superior or inferior to any other.... There is no linguistic evidence whatsoever for suggesting that one dialect is more 'expressive' or 'logical' than any other, or for postulating that there are any

'primitive', 'inadequate' or 'debased' English dialects.[10]

A very good demonstration of this was provided by William Labov. He studied Black English in the United States, which makes an excellent 'test case' for dialect validity since it had for so long been rejected by the white middle class, and since its speakers were victims of a prejudice that went well beyond language alone. If it could be shown that Black English was not some debased variety, this would go some way towards establishing linguistic integrity for all. There were three central strands to Labov's work. First, he justly criticized earlier studies which had elicited Black English from youngsters through interview techniques which were both unfamiliar and intimidating; these were hardly likely to produce normal, conversational samples. Second, Labov reminded us of what casual observers had known for a very long time – the Black community is verbally rich and, like other 'oral' cultures worldwide, supports and rewards those who are particularly linguistically gifted. Third, and most important of all, Labov demonstrated the regular, rule-governed nature of Black English.[11] Rules, as we have seen, are an essential feature of language, and if it were possible to show that Black English *had* grammatical regulations – not necessarily, of course, exactly the same ones as other dialects – then charges of inaccuracy and sloppiness would become groundless, and it could not be dismissed as some 'approximation' to 'proper' English.

Here, as an example, is one of the rules Labov described for Black English, a practice called 'copula deletion'. In sentences like:

She the first one started us off.
I know, but he wild, though.
We on tape.

the *is* or *are* is not present. Does this mean that the Black speakers who produced them are unaware of this verb form? Consider, next, these statements:

I was small.
She was likin' me.

Here the past tense of the verb *to be* appears. How is it that the verb appears here but not in the former sentences? Labov's studies reveal a regularity governing this linguistic behaviour: in contexts in which Standard English can *contract* (e.g., *They are going* can become *They're going*), Black English can *delete* (e.g., *They are going* can become *They going*). We have, therefore, a rule – different from the one obtaining in the standard but no less logical.

The regularity is further evidenced by the fact that where Standard English *cannot* contract, Black English *cannot* delete. Thus, a sentence like *He's as nice as he say he's* is, according to the rules of the standard variety, incorrect; contraction is not permissible in the final position. Labov notes that it is, likewise, incorrect to say in Black English, *He's as nice as he says he.*

The import of this sort of work is clear: there are no *substandard* language varieties. There are, in many languages, standard dialects and so it follows, logically, that all others are non-standard; but, this term is not a pejorative one in any technical linguistic sense. A standard dialect is, roughly, that spoken by educated people and is the form usually found in writing. Its power and place derive from history and convenience, and from the social standing of its speakers. If York instead of London had been the centre for the royal court, then BBC newsreaders would sound different and school teachers would be promoting another form of 'correct' English in England.

It has also been suggested that, although dialects may not be judged *linguistically* as better or worse than one another, perhaps they differ in *aesthetic* quality. In 1932, Standard English was defended as 'one of the most subtle and most beautiful of all expressions of the human spirit'[12] and, two years later, Henry Wyld (1870–1945), a linguist at the University of Liverpool, wrote:

> If it were possible to compare systematically every vowel sound in RS [Received Standard English – i.e., what we now more usually call RP, Received Pronunciation] with the corresponding sound in a number of provincial and other dialects, assuming that the comparison could be made, as is only fair, between speakers who possessed equal qualities of voice, and the knowledge how to use it, I believe no unbiased listener would hesitate in preferring RS as the most pleasing and sonorous form, and the best suited to be the medium of poetry and oratory.[13]

I need hardly say that such sentiments are not restricted to those speaking in and for English. The question is, can we put to the test the belief that dialect A is more 'pleasing' than dialect B?

Recent studies have, in fact, compared an 'inherent value' hypothesis with an 'imposed norm' one; the former suggests, as Wyld did, that aesthetic qualities are intrinsic, while the latter holds that they are attached or imposed by the listener who, in hearing a standard (say), considers it mellifluous because of the status of its speakers.[14] In one investigation, Welsh adults listened to European French, educated Canadian French and working-class Canadian French voice samples. Asked to rate the pleasantness and prestige of the voices on nine-point scales, the judges, who were almost entirely ignorant of French, did not single out any one of the varieties. In Quebec, however, earlier studies had shown a clear preference among French speakers for European French accents in aesthetic terms. In another experiment, British undergraduates who knew no Greek evaluated the aesthetic quality of two Greek dialects, the Athenian and the Cretan. The former is the prestige standard form, while the latter is a non-standard variant of low status. As in the first investigation, no significant differences between the two dialects were found. In fact the small, non-significant differences which did occur revealed a tendency for the British judges to rate the Cretan variety as *more* pleasant and prestigious than the Athenian.

The important element in these demonstrations is that the judges were unaware of the social connotations possessed by the different varieties in their own speech communities. The implication is that, if one removes (experimentally) the social stereotypes usually associated with given varieties, aesthetic judgements will not be made which favour the high-status standards. Anyone who watches a film or a play in which accents and dialects figure, in which (for example) a woman dressed as a duchess speaks with a Cockney accent, will appreciate the effects achieved. Equally, we can see that someone in the audience who had an understanding of English, but not of the subtle intralinguistic variations and conventions, would miss a great deal. The norms are 'imposed' by those in the know, the stereotypes which link beauty, or harshness, or comedy to a set of sounds are unavailable to others.[15] None of this, of course, rules out purely individual preferences; I may think Italian sounds the most attractive, you may believe that Gaelic is unrivalled, but we can both agree to differ on a matter of subjectivity.

There is one final, and rather neat, example I wish to provide here. In England, speakers of RP do not pronounce the postvocalic *r* – as in the words *cart* and *mar*. Thus, the absence of this feature is associated with high accent prestige. In New York, on the other hand, exactly the reverse holds. The higher the social status of the speaker, the more likely he or she is to *use* postvocalic *r*. The figures in table 4.1 represent percentages of possible postvocalic *r* pronunciations *actually* used by speakers surveyed in New York and Reading. We see that what is high class in New York is low class in Berkshire, and vice versa.

It seems clear, in summary, that having dismissed arguments for dialect superiority of either a linguistic or an aesthetic nature, we should agree that evaluations are *not* based upon intrinsic qualities but rest, rather, upon social conventions and preferences. These, in turn, are most obviously related to the prestige and power possessed by speakers of certain

Table 4.1 Percentage of postvocalic *r* pronunciation in New York and Reading[16]

	New York	Reading
Upper-middle-class speakers	32	0
Lower-middle-class speakers	20	28
Upper-working-class speakers	12	44
Lower-working-class speakers	10	49

'standard' varieties. Although I have largely restricted myself to discussions of English here, a general moral seems to be this: when social stratification is associated with linguistic variation, arguments will be made for the grammatical, lexical or phonological superiority of the variety used by those in power.

There are two exceptions to this rule, and they occur at opposite ends of the status continuum. Extremely high-status varieties may seem affected and generally 'over the top'. Opposite to this is the 'covert prestige' possessed by working-class speech, with its positive associations of masculinity.[17] Research in Britain, for example, has found that both working-class and middle-class males *claimed* to use non-standard forms even when they did not customarily do so. The actual use of such forms, by generally standard-speaking individuals, is most likely when the speaker wants to appear forceful, direct and unambiguous. A friend of mine, a middle-aged, upper-middle-class American university professor (male), was being pressed by colleagues (also male) on an academic matter. He ended an inconclusive discussion by smiling broadly and saying, 'Ain't no way I can do it!' All-male social gatherings, as at least half the readers will know, are often likely to produce such examples. Overall, though some forms of upper-crust braying may be very unpleasant to most ears, and though lower-class non-standard speech may have an attractive, rough-and-ready quality, the general moral remains potent and applicable across a wide range of social settings.

LANGUAGE ATTITUDES

If we reject linguistic and aesthetic arguments for dialect superiority we have, in a sense, only cleared away some annoying underbrush. It is very useful to know that the basis for language evaluation rests upon social convention, but we should also enquire further about the more detailed manner in which language varieties are assessed and scaled. We come then, to language attitudes.

The concept of attitude, a cornerstone of traditional social psychology, is not one about which there has been universal agreement. At a general level, however, attitude is a disposition to react favourably or unfavourably to a class of objects. This disposition is often taken to comprise three components: feelings (affective element), thoughts (cognitive element) and, following upon these, predispositions to act in a certain way (behavioural element). That is, one knows or believes something, has some emotional reaction to it and, therefore, may be assumed to act on this basis. Two points may be made here. The first is that there often exists inconsistency between assessed attitudes and actions presumably related to them. In a 'classic' study of attitude–behaviour inconsistency, a Chinese couple (accompanied by the experimenter) toured the United States in the early 1930s.[18] Visiting some 250 hotels and restaurants, they were refused service only once. When the investigator later wrote to the places visited, he found that more than 90 per cent said they would not serve Chinese. Although not without some methodological problems, this study demonstrates that what people think and feel may not always be reflected in what they do. There are, of course, a great many reasons why this should be so, ranging from immediate self-interest, to the desire to avoid embarrassment, to a difference between views of an abstraction (members of a given ethnic group, for example) and of concrete instances.

The second point is that there is sometimes confusion between belief and attitude; this is particularly so in the domain of language attitudes, and often shows up clearly on questionnaires and interviews designed to tap them. *Attitude* includes *belief* as one of its components (as just noted). Thus, a mother's response to the query, 'Is a knowledge of French important for your children, yes or no?' indicates a belief. To gauge *attitude* one would require further probing into the respondent's *feeling* about her expressed belief: for example, she might believe that French is important for her children's career success; yet, she may loathe the language. Thus, many 'attitude' questionnaires are, in fact, 'belief' questionnaires.

In his 1934 monograph (see above), Wyld hinted at a problem in comparing language varieties. If I wish to find out which of two dialects is the more pleasant, and if I therefore record a speaker of each and have the voices judged by listeners, how do I know if any differential ratings are due to features of the dialects themselves? Might they not be, at least in part, reactions to quite individual qualities of voice – tone, pitch, rhythm, pace, and so on? A way around this difficulty was devised in the 1960s by Wallace Lambert and his colleagues in Montreal. In their 'matched-guise' method, judges evaluate a tape-recorded speaker's personality after hearing him or her read the same passage in each of two or more languages, dialects or accents.[19] The fact that the speaker is, for all 'guises', the same person is not revealed to the judges (who typically do not guess this). Judges' ratings, along various dimensions, are then considered to be reflections of their stereotyped reactions to the language variety concerned, since potentially confounding individual variables are of course constant across voices.

The matched-guise technique has been criticized, most importantly for its alleged artificiality. That is, judges hear a series of disembodied voices all speaking the same words and are asked to rate the speakers on various personality scales. Do the judges, who generally comply with requests to assess speakers in this way, nevertheless feel that it is a pointless task? How would the judgements stand up in the light of more information about the speakers? The matched-guise technique *does* appear useful, however. Employed in many different contexts, it seems to provide a modest addition to, rather than a distortion of, our understanding of speaker evaluation through speech.

Finally, it is worth recalling exactly what the matched-guise methodology aims to elicit; it is not the speech *per se* which is being evaluated, but rather the speaker. The speech sample serves as a convenient identifier, facilitating the evoking of those stereotypes which, in turn, lead to language evaluation. A study by Lambert and his associates considered reactions towards French and English guises in Montreal. English-speaking judges generally reacted more favourably to English than to French guises; more interestingly, French-speaking evaluators *also* rated English guises more favourably. Thus the findings demonstrated not only favourable reactions from members of the high-status group towards their own speech but also that these reactions had been adopted by members of the lower-status group. This 'minority-group reaction' is a revealing comment on the power and breadth of social stereotypes in general, and on the way in which these may be assumed by those who are themselves the object of unfavourable evaluation.

Although the number of personality dimensions judged by listeners has varied across studies, some consistency has also been found, in the form of broad groupings of individual rating-scale assessments. Thus, some dimensions (e.g., intelligence, industriousness) are seen to reflect a speaker's *competence*, some (e.g., helpfulness, trustworthiness) reflect *personal integrity* and some (e.g., friendliness, sense of humour) underlie *social attractiveness*. The interesting thing about these broader evaluations is that speakers of high-status varieties do not fare equally well on all of them. In fact, although standard accents and dialects connote greater prestige and competence, some non-standard regional accents may evoke a greater sense of integrity or social attractiveness. Perhaps the speech patterns of non-standard speakers are seen as quaint or down-to-earth, but we have already noted the 'covert prestige' phenomenon as well. Besides, it does not take much effort to appreciate that those whose speech suggests competence, intelligence and status may not necessarily be those we can most readily identify with, trust and get on with. However, since personal competence is a factor of some importance, one might consider that the non-standard speaker, with a regional or class speech style, comes out somewhat the worse in the exchange – particularly in vital areas of life like school and employment. This matter becomes even more interesting when we recall the 'minority-group reaction' noted above, when we realize the general tendency for non-standard dialect speakers to accept the often negative stereotypes of their own variants.

Some years ago, BBC Television broadcast a series of six half-hour programmes entitled *Word of Mouth*.[20] The series considered a number of British accents and dialects (those of Glasgow, Edinburgh, London and Liverpool among them) with their historical and social associations. In the course of this, many individual speakers were presented; some of their comments were directly relevant to the issue of perceived prestige. For example, two Cockney families, resettled in a suburban area of Essex, provided personal views of their speech style. They noted that many regarded it as 'common' and that it sounded 'funny' to those who speak 'properly'. Reference was also made to a perceived link between language and occupational chances. One speaker remarked of another, 'You won't end up on the Board of Directors with a voice like that.' Overall, it was quite apparent that not only were these speakers aware of the *general* stereotypes associated with Cockney English, but also that they had personal and direct experience of such views. Again, this is only a formal example of something well understood.

Accents and dialects are not assessed in a unidimensional way. At the top of the heap, as it were, comes the standard, followed by others – rural non-standard forms usually fare better than those associated with the urban poor. But this pyramid changes if, instead of considering status and competence, we enquire about the warmth or the integrity of the speaker. As with the 'general moral' noted above, this pattern holds good in many language settings.

One further complicating factor is that among those languages having a standard form – not all do – there may be more than one standard. Common, for example, are regional standards, and perhaps a good example of this is found in the United States where an educated Texan variety of English and an old Bostonian one may each be the vernacular of educated standard-bearers and, at the same time, be viewed as non-standard from another perspective. One would expect that evaluative studies in such cases would be strongly affected by the region *within* the overall speech community.

This situation also seems to apply in Canada, where a student and I recently conducted a study in which English speakers from four places – mainland Nova Scotia, Cape Breton Island, Newfoundland and Massachusetts – were evaluated by listeners on the three dimensions of competence, integrity and attractiveness (this was not a matched-guise study, incidentally, since different speakers provided the speech samples).[21] The mainland variety was associated with the greatest competence, but no important differences were detected in evaluations made of the four varieties on the other two personality dimensions. This suggests that the mainland Nova Scotia speakers were seen to possess a *regional* standard status, inasmuch as they evoked the prestige and competence associated with standard dialects *and* – because of their local character – did not lose ground to the others on the two dimensions typically related to non-standardness.

By way of summary here, an 'organizational framework'[22] has recently been suggested in which there are two broad determinants of language perceptions: *standardization* and *vitality*. A standard (as already noted) is one whose norms have been codified and is associated with dominant social groups. Vitality (see below) refers to the number and importance of functions served, and is clearly bolstered by the status which standards possess; it can also be a feature, however, of non-standard varieties, given sufficient numbers of speakers and community support. There are also two main evaluative dimensions: *social status* and *solidarity*, the latter including the integrity and attractiveness continua already discussed here. Finally, the authors suggest three major measurement techniques: *content analysis* and *direct* and *indirect assessment*. The first of these is seen to include historical and sociological observation, as well as ethnographic studies. Direct assessment usually involves questionnaire or interview methods, while the 'matched-guise' approach is the best example of indirect measurement of language attitudes.

A similar attempt has been made to regulate the sorts of scales used in speaker assessment. The three-dimensional model first outlined by Lambert seems quite robust, however. A 'speech dialect attitudinal scale' developed in the 1970s has also revealed three dimensions underlying specific evaluation scales; they are called *socio-intellectual status*, *aesthetic quality* and *dynamism*. The first two cover the items previously accounted for under competence and attractiveness/integrity (taken together) while the third apparently taps some action–loudness–forcefulness qualities. In the 1980s another measure, the 'speech evaluation instrument' *also* found three broad dimensions, *superiority*, *attractiveness* and *dynamism*.[23] The differences among these approaches are partly due to the variations possible (and acceptable) in the mathematical exercises which 'reduce' a large number of personality-evaluation scales to a smaller set of more basic dimensions. However, it will also be apparent that, in exercises of this sort, what you get out depends very much on what you start with. If 'dynamism', for example, did not achieve prominence in the early studies, it was because scales relevant to it were not presented to listeners. Still, technicalities and 'input' problems aside, we can see that, over three decades, researchers have continued to find important language judgements made of speakers' competence, prestige and status, on the one hand, and of their warmth, integrity and attractiveness, on the other.

We have now seen something of the detailed way in which social stereotypes and views of social stratification affect reactions to language varieties. Readers will not need to be told that the attitudes here can be of considerable importance, whatever their provenance and however illogical they may be, in our dealings with individuals and groups. More illumination could be provided if further work attended to the attitude–belief distinction I alluded to earlier. Consider, for example, a case in which speaker A sounds more intelligent to judges than does speaker B. Might it not be valuable to probe further, to attempt to find out something of the reasons for the choice, to try and add the affective element to the belief component already assessed? Research along these lines would not be wholly original; it could profitably draw upon earlier work: for example, the view that non-standard varieties evoke less favourable reaction has typically been discussed in terms of speakers' differential status or prestige. It would be useful to confirm this, from the *judges'* point of view, by asking them the bases for their evaluations. This is especially interesting given that non-standard varieties do elicit positive ratings along some dimensions, and that more standard varieties sometimes are viewed positively in terms of solidarity and attractiveness. Also of interest here is the phenomenon of covert prestige. It is surely sensible to gather as much information as we can from the actual judges in language studies, as well as imposing theoretical interpretations upon their responses.

MURDER AND SUICIDE

It is one thing – and an important thing – to be able to rule out of court arguments that some language varieties are intrinsically better or more aesthetically appealing than others; it would be quite another to think that in the field, as it were, there are not bigger and smaller, more attractive and less attractive varieties. As one linguist observed: 'Only before God and the linguist are all languages equal.'[24] There are too few deities and linguists – and the two should never be confused – around these days, and consequently languages continue to be under the same pressures with which they have always had to cope. The solidarity function already discussed is, of course, a strong support for languages at risk. *All* varieties, even those associated with low speaker competence and status, have this function, and convey culture and tradition. Added to this are the perils associated with attempting to shift; years ago a French-Canadian moving to English could be labelled a *vendue*, and his or her Spanish-American counterpart a *vendido* – both terms meaning a 'sell-out', a defector to the other side. For members of groups who are visibly distinguishable from the 'other side', a shift may also be virtually useless if the intent is to acquire the status of the 'others', and for *all* the danger of 'marginalization', of falling between stools, of quitting one group yet not seamlessly fitting into the other, is a constant unwelcome possibility.

None the less people do shift, do move completely from one variety to another (i.e., without retaining the first in some bidialectal or bilingual accommodation). Many members of groups whose speakers are under pressure to shift are naturally dismayed at the process, having the understandable feeling that a large and unpleasant language is under-mining their small and attractive one. They perceive, in other words, a sort of linguistic Gresham's Law at work.[25] Where the sixteenth-century London merchant – whose 'law' was only popularized three centuries later – had argued that the concurrent circulation of two forms of exchange would lead to the disappearance of the more valuable (because, given equal nominal value, payments will naturally be made in the medium which is cheaper to produce), so the 'cheap', all-pervasive language will drive out its intrinsically superior but harder-to-maintain competitor. Thus does English threaten Irish, French loom over Breton, Spanish worry Galician, and so on. A linguistic equivalent to Gresham's economic law was provided by the Irish dialectologist O'Rahilly, who observed in 1932 that 'when a language surrenders itself to modern idiom, and when all its speakers become bilingual, the penalty is death'.[26] Well, we have seen that bilingualism *can* be a stable phenomenon, but we also have more than enough evidence of the transitional variety to be able to agree with O'Rahilly.

Yet another metaphor has been applied to languages in conflict (and it builds naturally upon the 'organic' one noted in the introductory chapter), and it is a criminal one. Languages may die: are they murdered, or do they commit suicide? Writers have discussed linguistic demise in these very emotional terms and, as one would expect, varying conclusions have been reached. Many have felt, for example, that languages do not die 'natural deaths' but are killed by those wishing to destroy the nation. Thus, Irish was murdered by English. Others have held, if not the suicide view, a perspective somewhat more complex than the linguistic murder approach. Thus, a 'persecution' theory[27] was seen by some as unable to explain the dramatic decline of Irish, and although the presence of English was clearly central, it was felt 'impossible to stamp out a language which the people are determined to keep alive'.[28] Others still expanded on this and held the Irish responsible for a linguistic suicide (as did Flann O'Brien, noted in chapter 1). The whole issue of 'murder or suicide' is muddied, of course, by ideological leanings. Those supporting the encouragement, restoration or revival of a threatened language are likely to hold the murder view; this can have the effect of simplifying things into an 'us-and-them' format in which oppressors and oppressed are easily separable and in which, furthermore, the presence of a 'victim' makes quite clear which side has the moral advantage.

The factors in the decline of languages are many and varied, and I shall be turning to them in some detail below. 'No single cause'[29] explains language loss; a 'chain of events'[30] is involved. One linguist has recently suggested that *both* murder *and* suicide occur – murder when dissimilar languages are in contact and where a high-prestige variety extends across domains, and suicide when *similar* languages come into contact but where, again, one possesses higher status; the suicide here involves the ever-increasing borrowing from the prestigious form.[31] However, it seems that both forms of decline ultimately involve suicide in the sense that, at some point, a new variety is adopted. This is the view of another linguist who notes that the *direct* cause of language death is lack of transmission to children. This occurs because a community 'sometimes "decides", for reasons of functional economy, to suppress a part of itself'.[32]

It is possible, however, that a community does not see the process as one of self-suppression, but rather of simple alteration. In this way, we might resolve the murder–suicide matter (if these terms must be used at all) by considering the social pressures under which suicide occurs. In personal suicide, stress is involved; people do not kill themselves on a whim. Usually, the pressures are varied, although there sometimes exists a 'significant other' who in some sense has caused the suicide. In linguistic suicide, on the other hand, there is *always* a significant other (language) which creates the pressures leading to language shift and decline; there is always a 'murderer'. But, just as a person may cause another's suicide without being a murderer in law, so a language can bring about another's demise without directly and actively planning to do so. Very rarely, in fact, is linguistic demise so carefully planned that one can invoke the label of murder.

LANGUAGE SPREAD AND LANGUAGE DECLINE

For languages to come into conflict, they must first come into contact, and this involves either an existing contiguity or the spreading of one or both varieties. We have already seen something of the ways in which multi-lingualism comes about, but we should consider in a little more detail some of the mechanisms at work in language spread.[33]

Ronald Wardhaugh has recently outlined a dozen or so reasons and most are interrelated within a nexus of power although, particularly in earlier times, simple geographical opportunity was also important. Even so, geographical limitations will be conquered if the power base is sufficient, and oceans and mountains have never, in themselves, stopped expansionist policies if the will and the attraction were strong enough. If the Romans built Hadrian's wall, and if they only eyed Ireland from Anglesey, we should not conclude that they could not have crossed the frontiers. Language spread was always closely allied to trade, to imperialist military ventures and to hopes for religious conversion and proselytism. Some cultures have had more explicit policies here than have others – compare, for instance, the *mission civilisatrice* of the French with the more pragmatic attitude of the English – but all imperial powers have, directly or indirectly, made their languages attractive and sometimes necessary to conquered or colonized groups. Because of power, and because of opportunities available to those who learn their languages, expansionist regimes often become associated, over time, with a cultural prestige which co-exists with the simple trappings of dominance and which often long outlives them. This is a factor in the continued adherence to European languages which exists in former colonial areas (though it is not the only factor nor, perhaps, the most central one).

Beyond these obvious matters, one or two other points should be made. First, and already implied, is the fact that the reasons for language spread in the first instance need not be those which maintain and further it. English, for example, spread initially through trade and military action. This was reinforced by political unification of an imperialist nature. But, once Britain's dominance declined, the language which it had established overseas – notably in North America – took on new and greater global significance, again animated largely by commerce and technological exigencies. Second, the degree to which a language community is open to the use of 'its' variety by others is often important. Consider, again, the differences between the English and the French. The latter have traditionally been much more possessive of their language and, while working hard to bring it to those unfortunate enough not to already speak it, have also been zealous in protecting its 'purity', even among themselves. *Québécois* speakers are often looked down on in France, but they should not feel uniquely affronted; almost any French speaker outside Paris is liable to feel patronized when visiting the capital. English, on the other hand, has not been treated in the same guarded way. We see books on the 'New Englishes'[34] and there is a journal entitled *World Englishes* – but there are no such volumes for French. English is becoming truly international in a way that French is not, at least in terms of accepted local varieties, and a language once tainted by imperialism is rapidly becoming 'ours' in many parts of the world. A power base once firmly centred in one small island has shifted to North America, and the antipodes, and on from there. India provides perhaps the best example of a developing and accepted indigenized model of the language.

A third and related point in the linguistic expansion of competing varieties is the position taken by 'third parties'. Again, English and French provide good examples. As the former became more and more international (through trade and empire), it found that French, as the established language of diplomacy, was still endorsed by others for important conferences, negotiations and treaties. Particularly after the Second World War, however, the shifting sands of global policies and alliances tended to favour English, and *it* now became increasingly favoured by others. Today, not only is English the dominant diplomatic vehicle, it also holds sway in the worlds of science and technology, finance, popular culture and so on. It has consolidated an across-the-board superiority which no language has ever achieved before.[35]

Finally, we should remember that the spread of one language is at the expense of the other (saving bilingual accommodation). Given that *all* languages are potentially capable of filling all roles, it is easy to see that those whose languages are eclipsed or threatened by others often feel understandably aggrieved. Their language, after all, has not been pushed aside because of any inherent defects, there is no fatal linguistic flaw here which might have to be grudgingly acknowledged. Rather, the power of a competing variety derives from the strength of its community and it is this which ultimately must give the most pain, especially to those who were once dominant themselves. On the other hand, the lack of intrinsic flaw and the changeability of global power structures might give a glimmer of hope. Few people could have predicted the present scope of English in 1500, when it had only 4 or 5 million speakers (well behind German, Spanish, French and Italian), and perhaps, in another half-millennium, some currently unlikely contender will predominate. It is the case, however, that so far we have not seen the re-emergence of a 'world' language once eclipsed.

One language gains, another loses; we move from spread to decline.[36] In many ways, of course, we find ourselves looking at opposite sides of the same coin, and a simple reversal will often give a factor relevant to language *maintenance*; still, the progression adopted here is dominance and spread, to decline, to revival. The first and most important point to be made (or, rather, remade) is that the fortunes of a language cannot usefully be considered in isolation from those of its speakers. To put it another way, language phenomena are social phenomena and all are intricately inter-woven. I begin the discussion here with an examination of Gaelic in Nova Scotia.[37]

Scottish emigration to Nova Scotia began in the 1770s and continued until the 1850s; it was first on a voluntary basis – if any emigration is completely voluntary – and later was a result of the Scottish Highland clearances. At the end of the nineteenth century more than 80,000 spoke Gaelic in the province, this representing the largest overseas concentration of any Celtic language. It is estimated that in *this* century Gaelic decreased by about 50 per cent every ten years and the number of people who now understand it is probably less than 1,000, of whom fewer than 100 are fluent speakers. This dramatic decline has not meant, however, the decline of 'Scottishness' *per se*, although some would see most current manifestations as commercially driven; the fact that a provincial ministry calls itself the Department of Tourism and Culture is telling. None the less, there is a strong sense of being Scottish-Canadian and a much greater sense of identity based on past and place than exists in most Canadian regions. For most people, this is now completely unrelated to the original language and, while there is a fund of passive goodwill towards Gaelic, there are few who are actively committed to it. Even the main Gaelic society, on Cape Breton Island, holds its meetings in English and, with some lingering sadness perhaps, most are reduced to praising Gaelic in the language of the *Sasannach*.

As noted above, a language is in decline if it is no longer passed on to children; it comes to be the preserve of middle-aged or elderly people who no longer see any point in transmitting it. While a minority often do still try to have the language taught – either informally or at school – a common complaint is the lack of interest among the younger generation. In fieldwork carried out in the mid-1970s only a handful of very elderly Gaelic monolinguals were found and only a few instances of active language transmission to children. Within a few years *no* monolinguals survived and among a group of Gaelic speakers surveyed the average age was 69, among Gaelic society members it was 61 and among a small group of learners of the language the average age was 57. It is of further interest that, when asked why they were studying Gaelic, no one in this last group actually mentioned speaking the language. Although classes in Gaelic are regularly held in several places in Nova Scotia and although there exist 'immersion weekends' and Gaelic playgroups, an experimental programme of Gaelic at school was recently concluded.

It is important to note that although external pressures bear heavily upon parents' decisions not to have their children learn a language, there is also a good deal of acquiescence in a shift which is – rightly or wrongly – thought to be a stepping-stone to mobility and advancement. This voluntary component takes on greater force when we realize that on other, non-linguistic matters the same population which abets language shift can resist strongly. In Scotland itself, for example, crofters were quite capable of challenging the establishment on land matters. It would be wrong, furthermore, to imagine that those taking a more docile position on language shift were without affection for their maternal variety; on the contrary, the evidence from many settings shows that a painful struggle exists between what is considered to be progressive and what is viewed as a cherished but increasingly burdensome linguistic inheritance.

Languages in decline are often confined to rural areas, and associations are made between the language and an unwanted past (and present). One observer of Nova Scotia Gaelic said that the language was one of 'toil, hardship and scarcity'[38] while English was the medium of 'refinement and culture'; another observed that, from the earliest emigrations, the settlers 'carried with them the idea that education was coincident with a knowledge of English'.[39] These sentiments were almost exactly echoed by a writer on Irish, who said that in *its* rural fastness, it became a language of 'penury, drudgery and backwardness'.[40] It becomes very difficult for a language to shake off these associations when the very rurality which gives rise to them also provides the firmest, perhaps only, foothold. It is, indeed, the case that the isolation which – sometimes for a very long time – protected and sustained a 'small' language takes on an albatross-like quality once avenues to a larger world emerge. In the same way the richness and immediacy of an oral language become an embarrassment in the face of literate forms. The language preserved in the country is forgotten in the town; and this process, which first can work within the language area itself only accelerates when even more distant attractions become available. Secondary emigration from Nova Scotia to other parts of Canada and, more importantly, to the 'Boston States' at once weakened the language and became more and more irresistible as local prospects diminished. We see, again, painful dilemmas.

The lack of concentration of speakers in heartland towns and cities is common, for while they could obviously provide a modernized and commercial base they are unlikely to do so because modernization and commercialism are part of the very threat. It is true that strong maintenance and revival movements are usually urban phenomena but their supporters, precisely because of their residence, are often atypical of the unselfconscious speakers they have in some sense left behind. The interest in Scots Gaelic in Glasgow and Edinburgh, and the networks for Irish in Dublin cannot be denied but, equally, they should not be overvalued as permanent contributors to a language maintenance which, if successful, emanates from within the core community. So, while we can applaud the urban efforts of those who are recapturing a linguistic heritage that has dimmed, we should also remember that the voluntary and conscious efforts of 'secondary bilinguals' are not of quite the same vitality as the more 'natural' ones of native speakers continuing to talk their mother tongue, in all domains, to their children. How much more significant it would be, then, if Stornoway, on the Isle of Lewis, were a Gaelic-speaking town.

There is, unfortunately for language maintenance, a rather dreary sameness in the attempt to promote a variety in an urban context, by committed individuals, and then to somehow expect this to prop up an original heartland which continues to decline. Indeed, not only is there a self-consciousness in these efforts which, while in no way reprehensible, have an artificial and temporary air, but also there is often a large element of romanticism and hazy nostalgia which is founded on urban affluence and which works best when the 'real' community is somewhere else. In the heyday of the Irish revival movement, for example, most of the leaders were Dublin-born upper-middle-class intellectuals, for whom Irish was an acquired competence rather than a maternal one, and for whom the idealized *Gaeltacht* (Irish-speaking area) was conveniently removed on the other side of the country. A place to praise and to visit, to be sure, but not a place to live in. Gellner has observed that 'genuine peasants or tribesmen ... do not generally make good nationalists'[41] and, were it not so tragic for the language, one could discern some comedy here: committed and well-meaning outsiders propping up, in their mind's eyes at least, a bucolic homeland which continues to shrink, whose inhabitants, real bearers of the linguistic torch, are forced by both circumstance and their own volition to shift, linguistically and otherwise.

It may reasonably be asked if this situation can be arrested, if linguistic support can be provided in the very place where the dwindling community still exists. The short answer is that, in the absence of dictatorial methods, the pressures which threaten the language and which rest upon historical and social evolution – not necessarily planned, especially with regard to language *per se* – are very powerful. More importantly, perhaps, they are pressures which have always existed, for all groups, and the changes they lead to, while certainly causing distress and upheaval, are not easily dismissed by most populations. We are talking, in a word, of social dynamics which swirl around language as they do all other things, and which are ultimately resisted only by those willing to tolerate self-segregation. A practical example of the difficulties here is the desire of the government to assist in the economic life of the *Gaeltacht.* It was quite clear that, if nothing were done, this Irish heartland would continue to decline for it was both rural and poor. Drawing up official *Gaeltacht* boundaries and providing extra assistance to firms and individuals within them has not, however, stemmed the loss of Irish. More than half the families, for example, now bring up their children in English. The 'paradox of the *Gaeltacht*' (and similar enclaves elsewhere) is this: a vital homeland, if left to normal social and economic forces, will shrink, being constantly encroached upon by external influence; if, on the other hand, things *are* done, then the enclave becomes artificial and those within it can take on the appearance of fish in a bowl. Also, it was found in the Irish case, that those just *outside* the *Gaeltacht* borders but equally impoverished were resentful of the special attention their Irish-speaking neighbours received. Successes in the government efforts also tended to attract outside interest, investment and even immigration and these in turn served to dilute the language base.

This, in fact, makes another interesting point. When there is strength in the heartland, or part of it, the language may suffer through in-migration of others rather than through the more traditional haemorrhage of out-migration. We see that industrialization in Brittany, for example, has attracted French speakers from the rest of the country, as well as foreign workers – Portuguese, Algerian and others – who will almost certainly learn French and not Breton. In Wales, too, anglicization followed the industrial revolution in the coalfields (though initially they actually attracted a concentration of Welsh speakers). In the Basque country, Bilbao attracts diluting elements, as does Barcelona in Catalonia. And so on, in many other contexts.

The brutal fact here seems to be that, once the numbers and concentration of speakers have fallen below a certain threshold, attempts to stem the decline of the language are extremely difficult. No one knows, of course, what this magic threshold is, but it is obviously very variable, and to a certain extent at least only has meaning within given geographical and political space. Six hundred thousand speakers of Breton no doubt feel more immediately threatened than do the 250,000 speakers of Icelandic. It would be a mistake, though, to imagine that simply creating a state to coincide with a perceived nationality would solve all the difficulties. Irish, for example, is the only Celtic language to have its own country and yet – if we consider Manx and Cornish to be effectively dead or at least moribund – it is in the weakest position of all. Other sovereign states, too, have begun to see that linguistic pressures cannot be legislated away easily, and do not vanish at the customs post. This is a process which can be expected to accelerate as the world gets smaller and English gets bigger. It is already responsible for a new galvanism in efforts to bolster smaller languages and, especially, smaller languages without a state, or state protection. In essence, though, it is simply a dramatic enlargement of age-old pressures; the avenues connecting languages have changed in form but not in influence, and what was once urban and secure has become a new type of rurality in the overall geolinguistic milieu.

It follows from points already made that some bilingual accommodation might now be the best hope of small languages. Indeed, this is recognized in many countries and by many minority groups within them. However, we have already seen that permanent bilingualism, or diglossia, depends upon a continuance of domains for each variety; this condition is less sustained, when languages come into contact, than it is eroded. One variety increasingly overtakes another across the social spectrum. I have already quoted O'Rahilly to the effect that bilingualism is often an ominous marker of things to come, and his own Irish case, that of Gaelic in Nova Scotia, and many others around the world, support the observation.

Many years ago, beginning to work on a French–English bilingual programme in Vermont, just south of the border with Quebec, I was told that elderly French-speaking people had recently started to make their religious confessions in English. At the time I did not fully understand how important this was. Here was a community which – unlike most other immigrant groups in America – had easy access to its homeland. Nevertheless, it had largely become bilingual (and many of its children knew no French at all, making their bilingual education rather poignant), and had in most outward respects embraced an American way of life. Under these circumstances one expects that private language behaviour will be a hardier survivor than more visible linguistic distinctiveness – it can be maintained, after all, with little 'cost' and does not attract the attention of others, which experience suggests is not always pleasant or beneficial. Yet here were these older men and women deciding, themselves, to engage no longer in one of the most private and important activities in their mother tongue. It was a telling indication of how far the influence of English and its associations had spread.

Once a language has surrendered, or has been forced to cede, domains of use, they are difficult to recapture. We can of course *create* settings, and we can rather self-consciously reintroduce the threatened variety but there are domains and domains. The central ones are the *domains of necessity*, which are least susceptible to the interventions of language activists. One is tempted to frame an iron law in these matters: people will not indefinitely maintain two languages when one will serve across all domains. Echoing O'Rahilly, a more contemporary linguist stated that 'to choose bilingualism is to choose the road ... to decay and extinction'. Diglossic possibilities aside, this harsh view is often correct, but I would point out, in light of all the pressures involved, that *choosing* bilingualism is often little more than Hobson's choice. This may suggest a regularity, almost a naturalness – particularly if we take the long historical view – but it also trips too easily over a transition which is painful. We may have no choice, in practical terms, but this does not necessarily mean a happy acceptance of the course embarked upon.

As implied above, *active* desire to prevent or arrest decline is usually found only in a small number of people, and they are generally not the ordinary souls whose language is at risk. There are obvious reasons for this, most of them having to do with pressing economic and pragmatic issues affecting ordinary daily life. Thus it often proves difficult or impossible to translate what may be a rather inert goodwill into something more dynamic. Revival efforts (see below) are typically characterized by a small group of activists nervously glancing over their shoulders to see how much of the population they claim to represent is following them, and how closely behind them it is. There are also less obvious reasons for the difficulties involved in arresting decline. One is that the leaders of the struggle may not, despite various protestations to the contrary, actually make much real effort to engage a broader sympathy; another is, of course, that these leaders – as we have seen in the Irish case – are usually atypical of those for whom they presume to speak. If the pure linguistic heartland is to be maintained at an almost mythological level of purity and authenticity, then it helps if one does not actually go there very often. The homeland of the 'true Gaels', the noble savages uncontaminated by modernity, was in reality a depressed area – of considerable natural beauty, certainly, as homelands always are – from which many were driven to escape. In the eternal battle between some ecological manifestation of political correctness and the grubby but life-sustaining processes of development and change, the truism that 'you can't eat the view' is a major stumbling block.

In Nova Scotia the pattern is similar, and even those learning the language show few signs of larger activity on behalf of Gaelic. One writer, discussing Gaelic in Scotland, observed that there exists a 'lightly regretful pragmatism which gives rise to general protestations about the regrettable loss of the language unaccompanied by efforts to halt that loss' and this is also applicable in Canada and other settings. Further, it has been suggested that, because of their unfortunate associations (above), languages in decline often evoke negative attitudes. We might imagine, then, that the 'regretful pragmatism' is found among those who remain sympathetic, while the negativity exists among a broader segment of the population. However, in Nova Scotia, and elsewhere, there exists, in fact. a broad *positive* attitude. Similarly, research in Ireland has shown d at symbolic support for the language, regret over the continued decline, pessimism about its future, support for some governmental maintenance efforts, desire to see a place

111

for Irish at school and a lack of personal interest in restoration activities all co-exist. This package can be interpreted as one of passivitiy, hypocrisy, lack of leadership or betrayal; it can also be seen as the reflection of an often poorly articulated accommodation of opposing pressures, a rather poignant indicator of conflicting sentiments which the speakers of unthreatened varieties, secure in some linguistic mainstream, may find difficult to appreciate or, worse, may ridicule.

There is no question that activities in support of threatened languages often produce an increase in the number of people knowing the language. This is sometimes temporary, however, and, as already noted, often rather selfconscious. Where the activities have some longer-term success, and where (for example) a place is found for the language in schools, we still must realize that 'secondary' bilinguals are less vital elements for the continued life of the language than are native speakers. The numbers game that is often played to show how an imperilled variety is making headway also often involves confusion between those who *can* speak – and the degree of fluency is clearly important here too – and those who *do*. In the 1971 Irish census about 800,000 reported themselves as Irish speakers. This was 28 per cent of the population, the greatest proportion in a century. In fact, the reported Irish speakers in 1861 formed only 24 per cent of the total. But that quarter were speakers in a sense not applicable to the later quarter. What has happened is a steady decline in native Irish speakers and, with school Irish compulsory since 1922, a great increase in more cursory competence. Outside the *Gaeltacht* today perhaps 2 or 3 per cent use Irish with any regularity; inside it, although this proportion is much higher, the language base also continues to contract. There is simply no equivalent substitute for normal, uninterrupted domestic language transmission. If this can be sustained there is always hope; if it cannot, then all other interventions remain terribly vulnerable.

A 'cultural loyalty' is often more widespread than a narrower 'language loyalty' and this is understandable in the light of what has already been mentioned. It may be seen as another perspective on the tension between old and new, tradition and change in that, while acting to support a declining language may be risky, stigmatizing and unproductive, retaining (or developing) an interest in other cultural manifestations is easier. It has been argued that 'what the son wishes to forget, the grandson wishes to remember'[42] – that is, immigrants who 'lose' their culture in the second generation regret this, and wish to recapture it in the third; the notion can be extended to all who seek this sort of 'return'. While there is a great deal of truth to this idea and while it is equally true that people – like the modern-day Scottish-Canadians with their kilts, Highland Games, bagpipes and dance – will try to ensure that the 'return' stabilizes; it is *not* generally true that a desire to learn the ancestral language is central.

Non-linguistic evidences of a continuing groupness are important, in my view, precisely because they illustrate a mechanism by which tradition and change can be reconciled and by which one's heritage can be openly acknowledged. Of course there are excesses and anomalies – the annual kilted golf tournament in Antigonish, for example – and of course commercialism, government grants and tourism blur the images of continuity. But a continuity *is* being represented none the less, and it is for those directly involved to draw the lines which separate culture from photo opportunities, and traditional music from money.

A respondent in a recent survey of Gaelic in Nova Scotia said:

> The continuance of Scottish culture should not be promoted on Gaelic language.... For the Scots many other aspects of their culture are near and dear to their hearts. Emphasis on the Gaelic language will, I feel, bring small returns. Studies in Celtic history ... are very important ... music ... all this is part of the make-up of our culture.[43]

This is not, of course, any comfort for those wishing to stem language decline, but it is not impossible to imagine that a broader and more accessible cultural base could itself provide a platform from which language activities could be renewed. A small example: the vibrant and growing Gaelic music tradition in Cape Breton has led – admittedly in a small way – to performers and others wanting to understand the words used and, if their interest extends beyond a simple page of translated lyrics, to explorations of the language itself.

What is at work here is a stronger cultural element bolstering a weaker one. A classic example is the association between religion and language. There are two related aspects to this particular linkage. The first is simply that, given a continuingly strong religion, it makes sense to exploit this strength and to suggest that it is uniquely expressible through the threatened language. The second is the belief that the language is inextricably intertwined with the religion anyway and that there is a natural and mutual reinforcement.

> The one who is taught the Gaelic acquires knowledge of wisdom and an understanding of truth and honour which will guide his steps along the paths of righteousness, and will stay with him for the rest of his life. The Gaelic is a powerful, spiritual language; and Gaels who are indifferent to it are slighting their forefathers and kinsmen.[44]

This is a general expression of the spirituality inherent in one's most intimate language. Others have been rather more pointed. In the battle with English – and the modernity it represented, which was so disliked by leaders of the movement to support Irish – the secularization and 'sordid soullessness' of that language were frequently stressed. That language was 'the casket which encloses the highest and purest religion that any country could boast of since the time of the twelve apostles';[45] Irish was 'the instrument and expression of a purely Catholic culture'.[46]

It should be noted that this sort of position could be seen as a reaction to earlier Protestant efforts at proselytism, often through the medium of Irish. In a sentiment that has echoes in other contexts, Daniel Dewar observed in 1812 that supporting Irish would hasten its decline, since suitably instructed people would obviously come to see the advantages of English; Dewar was, more pointedly, eager to see Irish used as a vehicle to convert the peasantry from the 'errors of popery'.[47] Christopher Anderson (in 1818) also bluntly stated that:

> the great object ... of teaching the reading of Irish, etc. is not to make those who are to be the subjects of that instruction a learned, or what may be called a reading people ... but almost exclusively to bring them acquainted with ... Christianity.[48]

Finally here, consider the words of Henry Mason in 1846:

> The primary object [of the Irish Society] was not proselytism from any particular sect; yet, as it was foreseen that the result of the study of divine truth would be the abandonment of human error ... it was resolved, that this Institution should be brought into close connection with the established [church] of Ireland [i.e., Protestantism] and that none but its members should be eligible to serve on the Committee.[49]

Linking language and religion is no longer done in quite the same way, of course, but the idea of the linkage itself remains strong. A related question worthy of study is that of whether and/or when secularization contributes to language decline.

Language loyalty can become a less-focused cultural loyalty when the status of the language itself changes. The distinction I have in mind here is that between language in its ordinary *communicative* sense and language as a *symbol*. For 'mainstream' speakers of strong languages these two facets co-exist; the language you do your shopping in is also that which carries your culture and history. However, the two aspects are separable, and a symbolic value – as Irish now arguably possesses for most Irish people – can be sustained indefinitely after communicative language shift has occurred. This leads to a situation of reverence without cost and one can see that, for some declining languages, the task of activists is to suggest to the wider public that what has become, or is becoming, a symbolic quantity can be revitalized into a normal medium; the thrust of the discussion indicates how difficult this will be in many circumstances.

The examples I have cited in support of the preceding generalities have been European ones but much, if not all, of the discussion is applicable in a wider context. In an earlier book I reviewed a large number of language situations around the world and, although there were, of course, many differences, I was struck by recurring themes. Those who claim that the phenomena associated with language maintenance and decline are not well understood are right at a detailed level but, in general terms, these matters are not difficult to account for. We note, for example, a powerful concern for linguistic practicality, communicative efficiency, social mobility and economic advancement. These are the greatest advantages possessed by dominant varieties and the greatest disadvantages of smaller ones. Coupled with nationalistic demands, linguistic practicality often suggests bilingualism but, in many areas, the progress of group aspirations and sociopolitical factors make this an unstable condition, particularly in the long term. Furthermore, although competence in more than one language is required in many settings, this is often restricted to highly specific situations. Formal language planning itself (below) can do little to stem the usually desired processes of urbanization, modernization and mobility – and these are the factors which *have* caused language shift and which will continue to do so. To put it simply: a decline in the existence and attractions of traditional life styles also inexorably entails a decline in languages associated with them.

Relatedly, language decline can become exacerbated when *many* languages (not just two, as in the cases I have cited above) exist within state boundaries. It is common (and sensible), therefore, to adopt a lingua franca – either a strong internal variety or a prestigious external one. The latter is usually one which has historical associations with the area, even though this can also mean a continuing reminder of colonial status. Supra-ethnic or 'neutral' varieties are often chosen to reduce possible ethnic antagonisms and it is sometimes possible for these forms to become indigenized, as it were. Kenyans are attempting to promote a particularly Kenyan Swahili, for example and in other contexts, local Englishes emerge.

Standardization and modernization efforts associated with many 'small' languages, not just with those in imminent danger, are always theoretically possible, but not always practical. When 'small' languages *are* developed to national-language status (Somali, Guaraní, etc.), the process rests upon a complex of historical variables which are not, and have not been, manipulable in any isolated fashion. There is, therefore, obvious scope for language planning here, but only in the sense of adjustments to linguistic phenomena made possible themselves by forces quite outside the boundaries of conscious planning. Furthermore, even where indigenous varieties have achieved a developed status they are still not necessarily equal in all senses to external languages. Standardized Guaraní and Somali are still much less useful, in a broad perspective, than are Spanish or English, particularly given the desired social mobility and modernization which now seem to be global phenomena.

We should recall that, historically and linguistically, change rather than stasis is the norm. Environments change, people move, and needs and demands alter – and these broad social currents have a great, almost inexorable, influence upon language. In this sense, the term 'language loss', which is often found in discussions of declining linguistic fortunes, is perhaps less accurate than language *change*. People are never, after all, at a point without any language. Language decline is often a *symptom* of social-group contact between populations of unequal political and economic status. That is, decline is an effect of a larger cause, and it follows that attempts to arrest it are very difficult. One does not cure measles by covering up the spots. The logical approach is to unpick the social fabric which has evolved, and which has caused language decline and shift, and then reweave it in a new pattern. This is difficult, given that those concerned with stopping language decline usually want only *some* reworking of social evolution, not wholesale revolution or re-evolution.

Finally here, it has become apparent that, for many ordinary people, pragmatic and economic concerns are – have to be – paramount and that it is *these* social forces, above all, which underpin language decline and bedevil attempts to halt it. Nancy Dorian, well known for her work on the declining fortunes of Scottish Gaelic, has pointed out that 'language loyalty persists as long as the economic and social circumstances are conducive to it, but if some other language proves to have greater value, a shift to that other language begins'.[50] One can appreciate that the reduction of language shift to essentially economic motives is not a popular position among linguistic nationalists or supporters of minority languages generally. While it may be that 'language allegiance is firmly rooted in the economic order rather than in any independent cultural order',[51] some have protested against 'economic reductionism' and one can easily see that talking about language in the same breath as economics is very distasteful in some quarters.

My view is that economic considerations are of central importance, although there *are* cases in which they seem irrelevant. Consider, for example, groups in which language is indissolubly tied to a central pillar of life – religion being the obvious example. The retention of religious beliefs has been so vital for some groups that they have been willing to undergo privation, suffer persecution and even make the ultimate sacrifice. This is surely 'uneconomical' of them. However, if we substitute 'pragmatic' for 'economic', then the argument still holds, since even these sorts of groups are obeying what, for them, are practical imperatives. Given sufficient strength of religious belief, what could be more practical than to obey *its* tenets when these are in conflict with purely temporary and mundane considerations? Such groups, however, are increasingly rare; and even historically, despite much glorious rhetoric, we find other-worldly considerations to be completely compelling for only a minority within the group itself. Recent reports indicate, for example, that even the self-segregating Pennsylvania 'Dutch', the Amish and the Mennonites are all under pressure.

There is a second and more common instance in which economics does not seem to apply to language matters. Groups and individuals can be found who support the retention of linguistic and cultural markers, where this does not materially advance them and where there is no link to something as central as religion. This *is* uneconomical, and there is not even some metaphysical pay-off. How can it be explained? The important feature here is that such retention may not contribute to material improvement but, equally, it does not lead to material loss. Groups in this category are secure enough to have, as it were, some psychological and economic capital to spare. Sociologists and historians have noted, generally, that cultural pluralism appeals primarily to those who are strongly positioned within society, that 'nativistic tendencies will be strongest in those classes of individuals who occupy a favored position'.[52]

Large socioeconomic factors can often influence language decline indirectly, through such things as speakers' attitudes and loyalties and this fact suggests a more subtle operation of that influence than some oversimple 'selling-out' process. Many have struggled with this subtlety within the bounds of nationalism and culture. Leaving aside Marx's well-known contributions, we find Max Weber noting in 1910, for example, that 'the fervor [of nationalism] does not, in the main, have an economic origin'[53] – but, he goes on, 'it is based upon sentiments of prestige'. This surely only pushes matters back a level, and we might reasonably want to know how 'prestige' itself originates and is assessed. Antonio Gramsci felt that economics was the major influence on culture, but he also observed that culture can itself activate emotions and sentiments which are, thus, only indirectly related to economic well-springs.[54] In a paper discussing the shaping of nationalism and its priorities, Hugh Trevor-Roper and his interviewer, George Urban, seem to agree:

> When the chips are down, national sentiment, the call of tradition, feuds and irredentism – that is to say, irrational, visceral factors – tend to determine the amount of peace we can have among nations.... Left to themselves, nations seem to have a curious order of priorities: independence first, prosperity second, internal freedom and democracy only third.[55]

To complete this circle, consider Gellner's view that: 'Men do not in general become nationalists from sentiment or sentimentality, atavistic or not, well-based or myth-founded: they become nationalists through genuine, objective, practical necessity, however obscurely recognised.'[56]

One gloss on all of this might be that nationalism is based upon practicalities (or, at least, upon perceived practicalities) but, once it exists, operates in an irrational manner. Another might be that economic and pragmatic concerns *are* central but may become buried under ever-increasing layers of culture and tradition. Given this bedrock, it follows that the mutability of language (and other markers of groupness) makes sense, given sufficiently altered social conditions. Applying, then, a 'cost–benefit' metaphor to language decline can be seen as appropriate. It does not reflect, however, any cold-blooded, formally articulated analysis, and it certainly does not indicate any eagerness to change for change's sake.

LANGUAGE REVIVAL

If language decline is complete, or nearing completion, we may see attempts made to inject new life by concerned and committed individuals and groups. It will have become clear how difficult this can be and yet there are some apparently successful cases which serve to sustain morale among revivalists. Indeed, Weinreich observed in 1953 that: 'Many "obsolescent" languages have received new leases on life through a rejuvenated language loyalty among their speakers and have made the prediction of the death of languages a hazardous business.'[57] On the other hand (with reference, perhaps, to really 'obsolescent' cases), it has sometimes been bluntly stated that dead languages stay dead; revival is impossible, once a variety has gone to that bourn from whence no traveller returns. Thus, Osborn Bergin, the Irish philologist and grammarian, noted that 'no language has ever been revived, and no language ever will be revived'.[58] Still, languages are not people – and Bergin is no Hamlet – and the 'organic metaphor' for language which I discussed in Chapter 1 is not entirely accurate.

Of course, languages are in some sense parasitic upon their human hosts, and *we* die, right enough. For the death of a language, however, it would seem that an entire group of 'hosts' must perish, either literally or by way of language shift. But, even if all its hosts die, does a language entirely succumb? Surely so long as some record of it exists, a language is not dead. A recent criticism of modern 'revived' Cornish held that it is 'self-evident that there is no way by which the pronunciation of a language that no one now living has ever heard spoken can be recovered in anything more than an approximate form, if that'.[59] Well, yes, although some modern, Holmes-like linguists have presented rather compelling cases concerning the sounds of now unspoken varieties (poetry often provides a good spoor). Pronunciation aside, however, the presence of written material suggests a continuing life of sorts, a life for which the parasite no longer needs its hosts. Besides, there is always the possibility of new hosts arriving who will, however imperfectly, take the language out of the library and back into oral society.

If determining the point of death is tricky, then *revival* itself begins on rather uncertain terrain. However, to restrict too much the use of the term through adherence to its Latin root (*vivere*) is to be unwarrantably severe.

Revival does not simply and solely mean a restoration to life after death; it can also refer to reawakening and renewal, to the restoration of vigour and activity, to a return to consciousness and to the arresting of decline or discontinuity. All of these dictionary connotations have applicability for language and, therefore, the term *revival* is entirely appropriate – if rather general – in virtually every linguistic context in which its use has been debated. For example, more than sixty years ago, Michael Tierney contributed to the arguments about Irish the observation that:

> Analogies with Flemish, Czech or the Baltic languages are all misleading, because the problem in their cases has been rather that of restoring a peasant language to cultivated use than that of reviving one which the majority had ceased to speak.[60]

While it is true that the Irish and Flemish cases are not analogous, this is not because one is a 'restoration' and the other an attempted revival. Rather, it would be more accurate to say that the *type* of revival differs in the two instances.

There is a considerable number of accounts – widely scattered both temporally and by discipline and rigour – of specific language-revival efforts, and so one might find somewhat surprising Moshe Nahir's observation that there has been little scholarly reporting.[61] He suggests on the basis of his own definition of revival (see below) that this is due to the small number of revival attempts themselves. In fact, however, there have been quite a few; Ellis and mac a'Ghobhainn, in a rather flawed survey,[62] remind us that many groups have suffered some form of language pressure and have struggled against it. They themselves discuss twenty examples, ranging from Albanian to Korean. I think, rather, that the key word in Nahir's statement is 'scholarly'; that is, there is a dearth of rigorous and dispassionate studies. It follows that there is also a lack of general or theoretical material on the dynamics of revival *per se*.

It goes without saying, of course, that the most-discussed example – which in several ways is quite atypical – is that of Hebrew in Israel; it has cast a large shadow over all revival literature. Indeed, many treatments of revival are essentially descriptions and analyses of the Hebrew case. The Irish revival, generally seen as the unsuccessful counterpart to Hebrew, is also quite widely referred to.

Nahir points out that revival presupposes the existence of a language with which a group (or nation) identifies. The *will* to renew the language is thus the first major factor. Where does this originate? One presumes a specific linguistic interest, of course, but the language itself is clearly a desired marker of groupness, and possesses symbolic value in addition to its alleged communicative function. The observation, then, that revival is a radical step[63] and an 'extralinguistic' one seems correct: a radical step inasmuch as a significant change to the *status quo* is envisaged, and a extralinguistic one in that, apart from the necessary technical processes, revival centrally involves social considerations. Relatedly, it should be clear that revivalist intervention in the social fabric is in the service of group *identity*.

The will to revive a language rests, then, upon a desire to alter or reorientate group and individual identity. It follows that the strength and scope of that will are vitally important in revival efforts, and the leaders of these typically devote considerable attention to the mobilization of public opinion. In many language and cultural matters, general public sentiment is, as we have seen, often uninformed and passive and the leadership is often atypical.

The main difficulty here was neatly captured, at the height of the Irish revival effort: 'Without scholars [the revival] cannot succeed; with scholars as leaders it is bound to fail.'[64] Eighty years later it was concluded that 'the lack of will to stop shrinking is an intrinsic characteristic of a shrinking language community'[65] – a rather gritty problem. It is a problem related, of course, to the two powerful factors already discussed: first, the contact between unequal social–political systems, and second (and relatedly), the economic and social changes produced by this contact, changes which lead to altered linguistic behaviour. I say nothing here about the *morality* of this contact which, in any event, need have little practical relevance for attempts at revival. For, on the one hand, it could be argued that *every* language revival effort presupposes an unjustified incursion of one language upon another; on the other, if it were allowed that a language had declined more because of the benign neglect of the larger system, and the relative acquiescence of the smaller (as has sometimes been claimed in the context of the British Isles) – and not because of some more blatant or outrageous suppression (Tsarist Russification policies, say) – well, this would still not necessarily mean an easier course for any planned revival.

If revival is radical, it also often involves a curious desire for stasis (once perceived inadequacies have been rectified) or, indeed, for some type of psychological 'return' to a better time. This notion of 'return' is often disputed by students of revival and nationalistic movements generally, and it is clearly not a *necessary* feature of the revival process. However, stressing such things as 'behaviorally implement[ing] ... traditions'[66] and 'remaking social reality' is surely suggestive, as is the recent observation that those active in the attempt to reverse language shift are 'change-agents on behalf of persistence'. In the Irish case at least, the conservative and romantic side of nationalism and revivalism actually veered towards a new zealotry, a 'strident authoritarianism' in fact, in which were reflected 'romantic nationalism, second-hand racialism, European radicalism, middle-class frustration and cultural awareness'.[67] This rather heady mixture is probably inevitable in any small-is-beautiful, past-is-purer, smallness-equals-morality approach (which, incidentally, probably drives further wedges between 'committed' leaders and the presumed beneficiaries of revival).

Language revivals often seem belated, and there are probably good reasons for this. For example, where populations are governed by conquering groups, attending to the linguistic practices of the natives (indeed, showing them much of an enlightened face at all) often comes as a later afterthought of the political master and is really only officially countenanced once political hegemony is felt to be secure and once interest thus develops in firmly and eternally assimilating the resident population. A second and more general reason here has to do with the antiquarian interests animating many revivalists and the relatively late realization that a dwindling group of native speakers might somehow be related to these: as I have already pointed out, the 'last' Cornish speaker, the legendary Dolly Pentreath of Mousehole, died in 1777 but the formalized concern for Cornish took another century to gear up. Sometimes, too, purely literary interests are *never* accompanied by much concern for native speakers. Recall Matthew Arnold's deep concern for Celtic literature *and* for a rapid disappearance of spoken Welsh and the full assimilation of all Celtic populations. Perhaps a more basic point needs to be underlined here, too: we cannot assume, from our own perspective, that there has always existed a great concern for minorities and their languages, nor should we ignore the fact that the upsurge in this concern in the nineteenth century was intimately connected with other large-scale social and political developments. Nor (to repeat myself again), should we be unwilling to entertain the thought that the study of languages safely dead, or on the way to extinction, or whose remaining speakers are at some remove, is altogether a neater scholastic exercise than is actually coming to grips with breathing speakers.[68] Although, for example, there were still many speakers of Irish by the time the revival effort began, the literary researches of the revivalists were not inconveniently challenged: by the 1880s, only about fifty people were literate in Irish.

It is, then, common to hear the cry, 'If only we could have started sooner.' In fact, a cynical view might hold that the very existence of a revival effort is an indication of some ultimate or penultimate chapter in a linguistic history. It is also unfortunate that, even at this critical stage, internal squabbling among revival rivals weakens an already feeble position. Thus, one observes the lack of agreement in the Irish situation, and a recent description of the Gaelic difficulties in eastern Canada in the 1930s also reveals internal strife and wrangling which held back potential government support.[69]

It all seems a tale of woe: strong external linguistic pressure, insufficient or enfeebled popular will, estranged or decontextualized leadership, the transitory nature of bilingualism. It *is*, in fact, such a tale; language revival is very problematic. However, most of the difficulties discussed here have to do with revival in the sense Nahir has described: 'An attempt to turn a language with few or no surviving native speakers back into a normal means of communication.'[70]

In line with earlier remarks about the definition and application of the term *revival*, it should be clear that the sense adopted by Nahir and others is not the only one possible. Revival efforts need not, perhaps, stand or fall on the matter of wide revernacularization alone. Before considering some successes, however, we might briefly turn to the possibility that even failures can succeed.

For a few days in September 1904, James Joyce lived in the famous Martello Tower in Sandycove, near Dublin, which is now his museum. With him were Oliver St John Gogarty and 'an Englishman named Trench'. While Gogarty is well known to be the model for Buck Mulligan in Joyce's *Ulysses*, it is not so generally perceived that Trench was the model for Haines. A few pages into the book, the following exchange occurs:

– Is it French you are talking, sir? the old woman said to Haines.
Haines spoke to her again a longer speech, confidently.
– Irish, Buck Mulligan said. Is there Gaelic on you?
– I thought it was Irish, she said, by the sound of it. Are you from west, sir?
– I am an Englishman, Haines answered.
– He's English, Buck Mulligan said, and he thinks we ought to speak Irish in Ireland.
– Sure we ought to, the old woman said, and I'm ashamed I don't speak the language myself. I'm told it's a grand language by them that knows.[71]

In any event, Trench (Haines) was a descendant of Archbishop Richard Chenevix Trench (1807–86), who published such nineteenth-century bestsellers as *On the Study of Words* and *English Past and Present*. This linguistic background reappeared, briefly, with the later Trench's only published work, a pamphlet entitled *What is the Use of Reviving Irish?* In it, he listed five reasons for reviving the language: its moral contribution to native self-respect, its intellectual value, its social concomitants, its economic benefits and, finally, its psychological significance (i.e., its status as a marker of national growth and independence). Although many others expressed similar sentiments at the time – often to a platitudinous degree – Trench concluded with the observation that even if it *failed*, the Irish revival would prove a salutary and bracing exercise.[72]

It is interesting, then, that eighty years on, Nancy Dorian proposed the 'value of language-maintenance efforts which are unlikely to succeed'. Her three major points – that such efforts can improve native-speaker attitudes, could create a healthy awareness of tradition and may have useful economic consequences – were anticipated by Trench. While none of Trench's and Dorian's points is inevitable, they are all both possible and worthy features of a revival which fails at revernacularization. Dorian makes the useful point, for example, that: 'Not all Irish, adults or children, are especially interested in their Celtic heritage. The point is, however, that if they should be, there are no obstacles whatever to learning about it.'[73] Making accessible, on a voluntary basis, aspects of a heritage which may otherwise be quite unfathomable seems a worthy objective, and any revival effort which accomplished it could hardly be judged an utter failure.

There are, as well, other aspects of success in the Irish case which are germane in other contexts. They include ensuring that everyone is given at least a thin wash of the language at school and forming an 'intellectual identification' with the culture. This is to omit entirely the associated literary revival and the important relationship between linguistic and more overtly political activism. In their rather jumbled survey of the Czech, the Icelandic, the Indonesian and (seventeen) other examples, Ellis and mac a'Ghobhainn manage to demonstrate the great variety of possibilities and 'successes' legitimately considered under the general heading of *revival*.

All of this may suggest the appropriateness of some revival typology. It would allow retention of a useful term and would help in keeping out near-synonyms, unnecessary neologisms and sundry hair-splitting exercises. (When is a revival not a revival? When it's a restoration/rebirth/renewal/renaissance / rejuvenation / revitalization / reintroduction / resurrection / reversal of shift. At least they all start with *r*.) A rough classification of revival scenarios could look like this:

1 a language with few or no speakers, where no written or taped records exist;
2 the same, except that some written material exists;
3 the same, except that written *and* taped material exists;
4 a language with some native speakers remaining, but where none are monolingual;
5 the same, but where some at least are monolingual;
6 the same, but where monolingualism and *normal family transmission* of the original language occur;
7 the same, but where substantial numbers of speakers are monolingual, where there is language transmission, and where the original variety retains important domains (especially outside the home and family).

This is a very rough outline; in fact, I am not sure that much further detail would be useful, since we would be moving into so many specificities that the exercise might dissolve. The scheme is intended only to show that, while all the situations can be subsumed under the heading of *language revival*, there are varieties. Specifically, there are degrees of difficulty, and I have arranged things such that the relative ease of revival increases as one goes from 1 to 7. Irish in Ireland, and Gaelic in Nova Scotia, for example, would both fit in category 4, while many of the European examples discussed by Ellis and mac a'Ghobhainn fall in category 7.

The term *revival* is really all that is necessary to cover a variety of situations which, while admittedly different in important ways, do not require further and apparently endlessly debatable terminology. Also, many existing formulations of revival do not come to grips sufficiently with the powerful underpinnings of *will* and *socio–political pressure*. The whole question of language revival is inextricably associated with what might be termed the *internal manifestations of external influence* and, on that basis alone, is complex and fraught with difficulty.

However, success *is* available, and the challenge is to find goals which are both desirable and reachable (for some of these, in fact, wide-ranging popular support is *not* vital). To return for the last time here to the Irish situation, we can find all manner of opinions of its success or failure, ranging from 'astounding' to the request that we 'remove our gaze from the terrible failure of Ireland'.[74] Clearly, those most closely involved must determine what action to take and what is to be aimed for. But, at the end of the day, it is ordinary people who will live with the decisions and processes, who will (or should) ultimately be the assessors and judges.

5

LANGUAGES AND
IDENTITIES

I have discussed in general terms the fortunes of languages in contact, and one of the clearest matters to emerge is the place of language within the larger social context. The symbolic attachments to language were mentioned, as was its interrelationship with other cultural aspects of life. What we observe, in a word, is the intertwining of language with group *identity* and it is to this that I wish to turn now in some greater detail; specifically, we should consider ethnic and national affiliations, and the role of language within them.

ETHNICITY

At a very simple level, ethnicity can be thought of as a 'sense of group identity deriving from real or perceived common bonds such as language, race or religion'. But, although true, this definition is very general and invites more questions than it answers. What, for example, are the most important common bonds? Are some more central than others? Are some essential? And why exactly is the phrase 'real or perceived' necessary? If we turn to the extensive literature on ethnic identity, attempting to resolve these matters, we find that we have opened Pandora's box. An examination of sixty-five studies of ethnicity found that fifty-two of them gave *no* explicit definition of ethnicity, accepting, by default as it were, the sort of general view cited above.[1] In theoretical treatments of the subject, a broad range of opinion emerges, but several themes recur and it is an examination of these that promises to lead to a comprehensive definition of identity.

First, there is the often-expressed equation of *ethnic group* with *minority* group, or with a social subgroup. Yet, even the most casual observer can see that *all* people are members of some ethnic group or other. *Ethnos* is a Greek word for 'nation', where this signifies a common-descent group, but historically it was also associated with outsiders or barbarians. Dr Johnson defined 'ethnic' as 'heathen; pagan; not Jewish; not Christian'. Perhaps a lingering sense of this has contributed to the sometimes pejorative usage of the term 'ethnic group'. Nowadays, the politics of power often means that

125

dominant groups rarely define themselves as ethnic groups. None the less, it is a logical fallacy to think of ethnicity as a minority phenomenon; while dominant groups in mixed societies may not usually consider themselves in ethnic terms, they clearly *can* be conceived of in this way.

A second factor in the discussion is the importance of emphasizing group *boundaries* or group *content*. Fredrick Barth is perhaps the most influential of contemporary scholars who have stressed that the essential focal point is the boundary between groups.[2] His reasoning is that the cultures which boundaries enclose may change, but the continuation of boundaries themselves is more long-standing. This emphasis has the attraction of illuminating group maintenance across generations; for example, third- and fourth-generation immigrants in the United States are generally quite unlike their first-generation forebears yet, to the extent to which they recognize links here (and differences from other groups), the concept and utility of group boundary has significance. Still, the cultural content within boundaries, while mutable, remains important. An examination of traits which disappear (or become less visible) versus those which show more longevity, for example, would not only clarify content change over time, but would also elucidate the ways in which boundaries are maintained in the face of changing circumstances. As a more specific instance, we might consider that the decline of an original group language may represent a change in cultural content – the loss of that language as a regular communicative instrument, and the adoption of another. But, to the extent to which language remains as a valued symbolic feature of group life, it may yet contribute to the maintenance of boundaries.

A third major feature of ethnic identity has to do with *objective* versus *subjective* definitions. On the one hand, we can consider definitions of ethnicity which include objective characteristics (linguistic, racial, geographical, religious, ancestral, etc.). From such a perspective, ethnicity is 'given', an inheritance which is an immutable historical fact. Such an 'involuntary' approach to group membership can be further understood as emphasizing common ties of socialization. It thus allows us to conceptually differentiate between ethnic groups and other forms of association, like clubs and societies, membership of which is not involuntary and does not depend upon common socialization patterns (although it might do, of course, if the organizations were to persist over generations). To this point, then, we might tentatively view ethnicity as an involuntary state in which members share common socialization practices or culture.

However, this objective approach has some serious difficulties. The main problem here is that the objective or involuntary approach – useful as it first appears as a quick means of categorization – does not adequately explain the persistence of ethnicity across generations, within rapidly changing social contexts. An obvious example is the North American immigrant experience. As noted above, continuity of group boundaries may outlive that of specific cultural content; a sense of 'groupness' may persist long after visible or tangible links with earlier generations have disappeared. On what basis is this maintained?

It is at this point that the 'subjective' perspective is useful. It has been suggested, for example, that 'an ethnic group consists of people who conceive of themselves as being of a kind ... united by emotional bonds';[3] although they may share a common heritage, 'far more important, however, is their belief that they are of common descent'. Or, consider Max Weber's observation, in 1910: 'We shall call "ethnic groups" those human groups that entertain a subjective belief in their common descent ... it does not matter whether or not an objective blood relationship exists. Ethnic membership ... differs from the kinship group precisely by being a *presumed* identity'[4] (my italics). Ethnicity, then, is seen above all as a matter of belief.

In the survey of ethnic studies noted above, common attributes cited include such things as 'sense of peoplehood' and shared values. Further, where the studies surveyed gave *no* definition of ethnicity, the implicit definition often seemed to be something as loose as 'any group of people who identify themselves or are in any way identified as Italians, Germans, Indians, Ukrainians, etc.'.[5] Yet it is very important to understand that the subjectivity here is not completely arbitrary but is, like the more material or objective perspective, based upon ancestry. There must be *some* real linkage, however much change groups and individuals have undergone.

It seems clear that some combination of objective and subjective perspectives is necessary in understanding ethnic identification. If this appears at first to require a paradoxical mingling of mutable and immutable elements, recall the distinction between group content and group boundaries. Cultural content is, of course, mutable – ethnic groups are dynamic entities, particularly when they exist as minorities within heterogeneous and developing (or highly developed) societies – but boundaries are less so. Indeed, when boundaries disappear, when even the most subjectively or symbolically sustained group markers vanish, then the ethnic group itself has ceased as a viable concept.

The final factor I want to discuss here expands the mutability of ethnic-group 'content' to symbolism. Some have seen current interest in ethnicity as representing some dying gasp, soon to be completely replaced by economic and social-class divisions (especially within 'mixed' immigrant societies like the United States, Australia and Canada). Others have reacted against the rhetoric of current ethnicity, seeing it as a chauvinistic impulse, a retrogressive longing for boundaries now very much out of place and, indeed, destructive. Thus we have portrayals of ethnicity as some anachronistic, atavistic adherence to increasingly empty symbols. But surely – in line with the subjectivity and dynamism of cultural continuity – we can see that symbolism may yet have a role to play in self-definition. Some have seen ethnic symbolism as essentially meaningless, or as reflecting empty and unworthy longings for a past that is unrecapturable. If, however, we can conceive of ethnicity as a real and continuing force, and one which is genuinely felt, then perhaps the idea of symbols is important. I have already alluded to the continuation of boundaries among some groups in which cultural content has altered dramatically over generations, and it is perhaps to these groups that we should look in order to see the power of ethnic symbols.

In 1979 Herbert Gans wrote an important article on 'symbolic ethnicity'[6] in which he commented on the apparent ethnic revival in the United States. He maintained that there had been, in fact, no real revival but, nevertheless, there *had* occurred a 'new kind of ethnic involvement ... which emphasizes concern with identity'.[7] This involvement is a minimal one, does not require traditional ethnic culture or institutions, but does give importance to symbols. One of these, of course, could be language which, having lost its communicative role, retains a sentimental and emotional grip on the group. Like many critics of the 'new ethnicity', Gans acknowledges that this symbolic version is 'an ethnicity of the last resort' but, unlike them, does not feel that this is perforce a negative quality nor one doomed to imminent demise; it is something which might persist for a long time. This reflects the fact that when ethnicity has altered to symbolic status only, it is no longer any sort of barrier to social advance and, as such, can be maintained indefinitely without cost. The ethnic 'revival' is actually symbolic ethnicity which, because of upward mobility, is a visible quantity. Some of the forms that symbolic ethnicity can take include religious *rites de passage* and holidays, 'ethnic' foods and ethnic characters in the mass media. This last manifestation is particularly interesting because, as Gans aptly points out, although 'films and television programs with ethnic characters are on the increase',[8] these characters do not engage in very 'ethnic' behaviour and 'may only have ethnic names'; thus, 'they are not very different from the ethnic audiences who watch them'.

Bearing these factors in mind, we may now attempt a definition of ethic identity:

> Ethnic identity is allegiance to a group – large or small, socially dominant or subordinate – with which one has ancestral links. There is no necessity for a continuation, over generations, of the same socialization or cultural patterns, but some sense of a group boundary must persist. This can be sustained by shared objective characteristics (language, religion, etc.), or by more subjective contributions to a sense of 'groupness', or by some combination of both. Symbolic or subjective attachments must relate, at however distant a remove, to an observably real past.

Some writers would also add the importance of the ascription of ethnic-group membership by others outside the group – and this has certainly had historical relevance, particularly for persecuted populations.

NATIONALISM

If we move on from ethnicity to nationalism we can see that they share much in common, most importantly the sense of 'groupness' or 'people-hood'.[9] They are not, however, identical, although the main difference is not one of principle but of scale. Nationalism may be thought of as an extension of ethnicity in that it adds to the belief in shared characteristics a desire for political autonomy, the feeling that the 'only legitimate type of government is national self-government'.[10] In other words, politicization changes ethnicity to nationalism (others have noted that a nation is a 'self-conscious' or 'self-aware' ethnic group, but this does not quite capture it).

It hardly needs pointing out, I suppose, that, because of historical and political dynamics, nation and state do not necessarily coincide; it has been suggested that fewer than 10 per cent of the world's countries are, in fact, true 'nation-states'.[11] Certainly the term *United Nations* is a misnomer.

Bearing in mind the link between ethnicity and nationalism, we may note that, logically, language maintenance is not a *necessary* condition for nationalism; however, it would be foolish to ignore the commonly-held assumption that it is *the* pillar of groupness.[12] Consider these sorts of slogans:

Absolutely nothing is so important for a nation's culture as its language.[13]
Language is the spiritual exhalation of the nation.[14]
Has a nation anything more precious than the language of its fathers?[15]
A people without a language of its own is only half a nation ... to lose your native tongue ... is the worst badge of conquest.[16]
A nation could lose its wealth, its government, even its territory and still survive, but should it lose its language, not a trace of it would remain.[17]
Sluagh gun chanain, sluagh gun anam. (Gaelic: 'A people without its language is a people without its soul')[18]
Hep brezhoneg, breizh ebet. ('Without Breton there is no Brittany.')
Gyn chengey, gyn cheer. (Manx: 'No language, no country.')
The care of the national language is at all times a sacred trust.[19]
Quand un peuple tombe esclave, tant qu'il tient bien sa langue, c'est comme s'il tenait la clef de sa prison.[20]
If I had to make a choice between political freedom without the language [Irish], and the language without political freedom ... I would choose the latter.[21]

Nationalism is often seen as a modern phenomenon (although this is a much-debated matter into which I cannot delve deeply here[22]), but this 'modern' view does not, *per se*, account for a necessary 'prenational' period. Consequently, it is prudent to add that nationalism – with its associated desires for sovereignty, autonomy and so on – essentially grew out of existing ethnicities. One might say that it was in the rhetoric surrounding the French revolution in 1789 that nationalism, national loyalty, the notion of the 'fatherland' and, above all, the belief in unity and autonomy first found forceful expression. It was in the German romanticism, that began at about the same time, that the notion of a *volk* and the almost mystical connection between nation and language were expounded so fervently in the modern era. Thus Conor Cruise O'Brien saw nationalism as a 'German invention under French influence'.[23] The dialects which were generally disparaged during the Enlightenment, but which had managed to survive, were idealized by the Romantics, and this fuelled the language revival movements of the nineteenth century. Thus the modern concern for minority languages also dates from the beginning of the nineteenth century, although some might say that any official recognition is either lip service only, or comes conveniently late in the day. Sapir thought it safe enough to see romantic efforts on behalf of 'small' languages as 'eddies in the more powerful stream of standardization of speech that set in at the close of the medieval period'.[24] National languages themselves, Sapir went on, 'are all huge systems of vested interests which sullenly resist critical enquiry'.[25]

Before the Romantic era, local languages and dialects may not have been well thought of, much less glorified and defended but, equally, there were often few systematic attempts to impose the language of the dominant upon subordinate or conquered populations (although, of course, language shift often occurred because of unofficial but powerful social pressures). Thus the historian Clark observed, generally, that: 'when a country was governed by a limited ruling class, it did not matter much what language the masses spoke, as long as they kept their place'.[26]

The ancient Greeks adopted such a stance. They were, however, fiercely proud of their language, and the unsurprising extension of Greek – 'a unifying language from Travancore to the hinterland of Marseille'[27] – is an example of the social pressures just mentioned. The Romans, too, often refrained from imposing Latin and considered its acquisition 'a privilege to be sought, like citizenship'.[28]

Ernest Gellner put it another way. He described a 'typical burgher in an agrarian society' who hears one morning that:

> the local Pasha had been overthrown and replaced by an altogether new one. If, at that point, his wife dared ask the burgher what language the new Pasha spoke in the intimacy of his home life – was

it Arabic, Turkish, Persian, French or English? – the hapless burgher would give her a sharp look, and wonder how he would cope with all the new difficulties when, at the same time, his wife had gone quite mad.[29]

A common practice, then, from quite remote to fairly recent times, was a benign linguistic neglect on the part of rulers, coupled with a belief that their own language was, in any event, superior and would naturally be adopted by anyone of sense. There were, of course, exceptions to this but, given linguistically diverse empires, peace and prompt payment of taxes were the major concerns linking rulers and ruled. Besides, as Einar Haugen has remarked, a *laissez-faire* policy was often quite sufficient to overcome local languages (he referred, specifically, to Celtic varieties in Britain).[30] This was the situation that changed, once a link between language and nation became strongly forged. Now, languages became a rallying-point, something to galvanize the downtrodden and to alarm the rulers.

In 1807, Johann Gottlieb Fichte (1762–1814) stressed, as absolutely crucial, the linguistic criterion of nationhood (in his famous *Addresses to the German Nation*). Indeed, Fichte not only emphasized the importance of his own language, he actively deprecated that of others, thus foreshadowing much of the negative rhetoric of nationalism. For example, he pointed out that 'the German speaks a language which has been alive ever since it first issued from the force of nature, whereas the other Teutonic races speak a language which has movement on the surface only but is dead at the root'.[31] From a linguistic standpoint this sentiment is absurd, yet it illustrates the essentially irrational (or, to be less pejorative, non-rational) power and appeal of linguistic nationalism.

Anthony Smith has observed bluntly that 'nationalism as a linguistic movement derives from Herder's influence'[32] (i.e., from the late eighteenth century). Johann Gottfried Herder (1744–1803) himself is enormously important in the literature, and the 'Herderian glorification of diversity' has been seen as inspirational by many nationalists.[33] However, this popularizer of Rousseau (as O'Brien styled him) – and, certainly, Rousseau's 'civil religion', as outlined in his *Social Contract* of 1762, does smack of nationalism – was himself quite capable of prejudice. He told Germans, for instance, to 'spew out the ugly slime of the Seine' and his followers, notably Fichte, were even more vitriolic. Perhaps this was, in fact, rather strong language for the 'meek-seeming' Herder, but surely the interesting point is this: that the high priest of cultural and linguistic nationalism was himself prone to, shall we say, lapses of taste is indicative of the dark side of the phenomenon. That is, while logic does not require that fellow-feeling be accompanied by disdain for 'out-groups', a sense of groupness has usually had just such accompaniment. The most recent notes on Herder describe a 'difficult, thin-skinned' and often rather sour individual who had a genuine enjoyment of other languages and cultures (although with a dislike of French), but who also contributed to the defeat of the Enlightenment.

It is from the beginning of the last century, then, that the term *nation* has become associated with common sympathies, sentiments, aims and will. Elie Kedourie, for example, described nationalism as a doctrine *invented* in Europe at that time. It makes three major assumptions according to Kedourie: (a) that there is a natural division of humanity into nations; (b) that these nations have identifiable characteristics; (c) that (as noted above) the only legitimate form of government is self-government. These could be summarized as follows: 'A group speaking the same language is known as a nation, and a nation ought to constitute a state.'[34] In linking language centrally to nationalism, Kedourie claimed that there are no substantive distinctions between linguistic and (say) racial nationalism, that there is simply a conception of nationalism which may embrace various features (language, race, religion, etc.). Finally, Kedourie's *own* view was that nationalism is a pernicious doctrine,[35] particularly with regard to its emphasis upon linguistic unity; possession of the same language should *not*, he felt, entitle people to governmental autonomy. More generally, political matters should *not* be based upon cultural criteria.

Kedourie's analysis of nationalism has been criticized, largely on the grounds that it emphasizes negative aspects and language. There are instances in which language may not be as important for nationalistic sentiment as are other markers; Anthony Smith claims that, in Africa, national identity is rarely associated with language *per se* since this could lead to 'balkanization' and that, in countries like Greece, Burma and Pakistan, religion has been the pre-eminent 'self-definer'. Thus, 'in general, the linguistic criterion has been of sociological importance only in Europe and the Middle East (to some extent)',[36] and is based on the German romantic version of nationalism.

We see more clearly now the conceptual link between ethnicity and nationalism. In Smith's view, for example, the 'core doctrine' of nationalism does not define the characteristics of perceived nationhood; supporting theories are required for this. Here, surely, is exactly the point at which we can insert, as it were, the previously defined concept of ethnicity. Nationalism can indeed be seen as ethnicity writ large, ethnicity with a desire for self-government (total or partial) added. Just as ethnicity does not inevitably require language (or any other specific feature) as a component, nor does nationalism.

It is important to realize that both ethnicity and nationalism rest upon a *sense of community* which can have many different tangible manifestations, none of which is indispensable for the continuation of the sense itself. The visible 'content' of both ethnicity and nationalism is eminently mutable; what is immutable is the feeling of groupness. When *this* disappears, then boundaries disappear. Any analysis of nationalism which concentrates solely upon objective characteristics misses the essential point. On the other hand, it must be remembered that the subjective fidelity which is so important is not itself arbitrary; a sense of solidarity must ultimately depend upon 'real' communalities, however diluted or altered over time. The continuing power of ethnicity and nationalism resides exactly in that intangible bond which, by definition, can survive the loss of visible markers for group distinctiveness. One of these may be language. In his famous *Qu'est-ce qu'une nation?*, Ernest Renan (1823–92) argued that *no* particular characteristic was necessary for the maintenance of nationalistic sentiment, certainly not language: 'Il y a dans l'homme quelque chose de supérieur à la langue; c'est la volonté.'[37] Above all, he felt, 'une nation est une âme, un principe spirituel'.[38]

Kedourie's view of nationalism as pernicious seems apt when we reflect upon the violent resurgences in our own time. The 'dark face' of nationalism is, of course, a disputatious matter, a fuller treatment of which would lead me too far away from my major concerns. However, it is clear that, whatever one may feel about ethnicity and nationalism and whatever criticisms may be made of them, they remain vital forces in group identity. We deal here with universal features of human life – which are, naturally, emphasized more in some contexts than in others. Minority-group members, whose identity appears at risk, are thus much more likely to stress their groupness than are majority-group members, many of whom will find nationalism and its agitations foreign and disturbing. Still, majority-group status need not be permanent, and those once secure may undergo a revitalized nationalism if they lose it.

Nationalism, for all its essential irrationality – and probably because of it – remains potent. Viewed distastefully by liberals, it has shown a continuing power to recruit intellectual support. Scorned by Marxists as outdated sentimentality, nationalism has forced from them a grudging admiration. Both liberalism and Marxism are 'rationalist creeds' which, naturally enough, have difficulty coming to terms with 'irrational attachments'. In a recent discussion,[39] Smith has suggested, further, that the 'globalization' of culture is not likely to diminish nationalist fervour and, indeed, may stimulate it. Many observers would see this as a good thing, taking nationalism here as a necessary counter-balance to faceless efficiency. Also, Smith describes nationalism as *both* progressive *and* reactionary, and this seems apt: nationalistic movements clearly want something to change but they also include a nostalgic romanticism which often manifests itself as a desire for stasis – once old wrongs have been redressed, 'melted' groups unmelted, and so on. It is interesting, but not surprising, that this duality is exactly what I described in language revival; for we can now see more precisely that this activity is part of, and is in the service of, that revitalization and reorientation of identity which is, itself, the linchpin of nationalist movement and rhetoric.

INDIVIDUALS AND COLLECTIVITIES

Ethnicity and nationalism are not to be understood as applicable only to minority groups, groups perceiving themselves at risk of cultural, linguistic or other forms of assimilation. Yet it is easy enough to see why it is within these groups that ethnicity and nationalism figure most prominently. Just as the communicative–symbolic distinction applies to all languages, but is of greater interest when, under pressure, the elements threaten to split, so larger matters of group identity have a special piquancy when that identity is being assailed. The clash here, between a threatened ethnolinguistic group and some overarching mainstream or neighbour can often become one of philosophies, too; specifically, we see a dispute between purely individual rights and those of a beleaguered collectivity. A recent apposite example is provided by the ongoing struggle to reconcile the English and French nations within the larger Canadian state.

Adherence, wherever possible, to *individual* rights is a hallmark of most democratic societies. Obvious rationales for this approach may be found when, in support of group positions, we discover ourselves supporting complete social frameworks, many of the elements of which may be reprehensible or repugnant. However, a Canadian lawyer recently observed that some accommodation with collectivities may also be required:

> The collective rights ideal operates in countries that eschew majoritarian principles. In fundamentals, the individual rights idea operating in majoritarian countries is to blunt the power of the state to interfere with individual autonomy. But in pluralist states, and in multilingual states, the individual rights thesis must be harmonized with group security.... In Canada ... fully one-third of the provisions of [the] new *Charter* [of Rights and Freedoms, passed in 1982] deals with the collective rights of semi-autonomous Canadian communities.[40]

This harmonization, of course, is often the crux of the issue.

The whole matter is clearly of central concern in the Canadian scene, where many *Québécois*, for example, see the need for legislation to protect francophone language and culture, in a collective sense. The lawyer just quoted goes on to assert that:

> Un droit d'utilisée une langue est absolument vide sauf qu'il implique un communauté linguistique qu'on peut comprendre.... Language implies a sense of community [and] in this sense language rights are not individual rights.... They are exercised by individuals only as part of a collectivity or a group. Legal protection of language rights, therefore, means protection of that linguistic community.[41]

When Quebec passed its 'sign law' (Bill 178) in December 1988, requiring all outside commercial signs to be in French only, francophone endorsement of this restriction of the use of English was not echoed widely in the anglophone community. Three anglophone Quebec cabinet ministers resigned from the provincial government – primarily because of their disagreement with the elevation of those collective rights seen to be 'at the heart of the distinct society' for most *Québécois*. The matter was of course closely entwined with that of majorities and minorities in Canada and Quebec – another minefield. A well-known columnist thus pointed out that: 'Collective rights ... represent the political weight of the French-speaking majority acting with the reflexes of a minority.'[42] But, the majority to which he referred is *only* a majority within Quebec; elsewhere it is a minority at risk.

Arguments in the press were of course both many and heated. Some contended that majorities (like francophones in Quebec) ought not to try to preserve themselves by suppressing minorities (the English), and that individual rights were absolutely fundamental to civilized society. Others took a different tack, suggesting that Quebec anglophones should understand that, although the sign law *was* a repression of individual rights (a view acknowledged by the Quebec government itself), acceptance for the greater good was called for. A former Quebec cabinet minister said: 'Let us be vigilant where language is important but generous and fair where it is only symbolic.'[43]

Another observer noted that the essence of the Quebec government's position was that 'the right of Quebec to survive ... must take precedence over the rights of individuals to advertise in the language of their choice'.[44] However, he also went on:

> If individuals have few rights ... collectivities have even fewer. There is no moral law which states that societies have a right to live on unchallenged. The British Raj ... is dead. Few would argue that it had a collective right to perpetual existence.[45]

A related view was expressed by Pierre de Bané, a federal cabinet minister during Pierre Trudeau's tenure; presuming that Canada supported individual rights, he asserted that 'if intolerance and discrimination are the price for the survival of French, it is not worth it'.[46] Indeed, history *is* the graveyard of cultures and societies, and this sort of social Darwinism is compelling.

Official Quebec reaction to these sentiments was simple and predictable: the French in Quebec *do* have *collective* rights because they are a small and threatened enclave in anglophone North America. Clearly there are no simple solutions here, and the harmonization of individual and group rights has not yet been achieved in Canada. Indeed, it is quite possible that a radical reshaping of the Canadian state will occur, or even a divorce between the 'two solitudes' of French and English Canada. If we recall the priorities set out by Urban and Trevor-Roper (above) we can understand that, for many francophones, nothing can be settled until their nationalistic aspirations are achieved – and the big question is whether these are available within the Canadian state.

LANGUAGE ECOLOGY AND LANGUAGE COMPARISON

Questions of language, of nationalism, of the protection of threatened collectivities are, as has been implied, especially significant for minority groups. Unlike powerful mainstream societies, they do not have the luxury of ignoring these matters. Indeed, given sufficient internal organization and sociopolitical opportunity, they can be expected to emphasize them. We should give minority groups some special attention here, for three main reasons: (a) because they highlight for us matters which, at one time or another, have affected all groups; (b) because it is appropriate to pay special attention to those in struggle; (c) because on purely practical grounds we see a modern swelling of minority movement. In western Europe we see increasing federalism accompanied by a concern for minorities and their cultures, and in eastern Europe we see that, as the heavy weight of totalitarianism has eased, old ethnic rivalries – never having been adequately resolved, but only stifled – again clamour for balance. In Canada, aboriginal self-government is in the air and, throughout North America traditional assimilationist policies are at least tempered here and there by concerns for pluralism. Elsewhere in the world, ethnic and national struggles continue to take on a violent aspect. In virtually all settings, violent or non-violent, language and identity are of great importance. All of this is quite visible as, indeed, is a large literature comprising case studies and descriptions of ethnolinguistic minorities. What is lacking are firm bases for comparison and, to this end, a framework of language-minority and language-contact situations could be useful – especially since, as noted above, minority concerns for language, group and identity are likely to be of broad applicability, even if secure majority populations (secure in their current positions at least) think them to be merely exotic manifestations, mere eddies in the global stream.

In an earlier book[47] I presented thumbnail sketches of forty-seven minority-language and language-contact situations around the world. The generalities concerning language maintenance and shift which I discussed in the last chapter were, in fact, drawn from these, and from a more detailed examination of the Celtic languages. However, these generalities naturally conceal rich and varied specifics which a formal typological approach could do more to highlight. In Africa, for example, the breadth of multilingualism and language contact ranges from the 400 varieties spoken in Nigeria to the relative linguistic uniformity of Somalia and Burundi. The intertwining of

French and Arabic is a feature of north African societies and, in east Africa, the power of Swahili as a lingua franca remains impressive. In the Americas, we observe the power of Spanish and English competing with the often declining fortunes of indigenous Amerindian languages; in Paraguay, though, Guaraní retains important domains and is a recognized national language. In China, standardization is promoted through Putonghua, essentially the Beijing form of Mandarin, and this has prompted the encouragement of that form in Taiwan where, however, most speak Fukienese.

India recognizes fifteen languages (Sanskrit plus fourteen 'modern' varieties) among a vast array, Singapore has made four official (Mandarin – again influenced by policy in mainland China – Malay, Tamil and English), and in Sri Lanka language forms a major cleavage between Sinhalese and Tamils. In the Soviet Union (as it was), Tsarist Russification policies, the 'cement of the empire', were altered under Lenin, although it is clear that new tolerance for minority-language rights was largely based on the hope that this would actually accelerate the moves towards Russian; later still, Russification in different guises tended to reappear.

In the Pacific, we have Papua New Guinea, with perhaps 700 native varieties and having as major lingua francas English and pidgin. Vanuatu, it is claimed, has more indigenous languages per capita (108 among 100,000 people) than anywhere else in the world. In the Philippines, more than 50 million people speak more than seventy languages. Tagalog was proclaimed a national language in 1937, and was renamed Pilipino in 1959; the 1973 constitution made English and Pilipino official – the latter is now undergoing another metamorphosis, with some elements of other Philippine varieties, to become Filipino.

In Europe, the Belgian linguistic scene continues to be animated largely by the Flemish–French contact, exacerbated by the growth of largely francophone Brussels within the Flemish half of the country. The centralist tendencies so long evident in France have perhaps relaxed slightly but regional languages like Breton, Alsatian and Occitan continue to struggle. In Luxemburg, triglossia among Standard German, French and Lëtzebuergesch exists. Spain in the post-Franco era is still working out accommodations with Basque, Catalan and Galician. German, French, Italian and Romansch co-exist in Switzerland, though separated by cantonal divisions. The linguist diversity in Yugoslavia is currently overshadowed by violent nationalistic upheavals, but language has traditionally figured in republican and provincial wrangling.

These comments are meant only to demonstrate some of the particularities of language contact around the world, and to suggest the utility of a broader framework within which they might be assessed and compared.

A typology of language situations is at once an attempt to impose theoretical/descriptive order, and a means of codifying and facilitating cross-community comparison; indeed the comparison of cases can often indicate what more we need to know about individual cases themselves. Here, I intend to outline briefly some relevant background material and some existing typological efforts, and to sketch out a new model. This, as will be seen, is at quite a rudimentary level; it is, in fact, a simple checklist of important variables. However, even a fairly thoroughgoing checklist is not without value. Some have criticized typological exercises, on the grounds (for example) that they embody prevailing assumptions, have limited analytical utility and imply permanence or stasis. These are appropriate cautions but my view is simply that since there is every reason to assume that people will continue to interest themselves in language situations, and wish to describe and account for their dynamics, since it makes no sense to assume that different contexts are unique in every element, and since we are rightly drawn to the task of theory construction or, at least, classification/description – then a comprehensive and well-specified typology may serve as a useful guide. Cross-context comparisons might well be facilitated, for example, if attention was given to the same variables in all settings; any student in the area will have experienced frustration in attempting comparisons and contrasts where this sort of attention has not been paid. Charles Ferguson, an important figure in current sociolinguistics, has just made the same point:

> It is frustrating to read a stimulating case study and find that it lacks information on what the reader regards as some crucial points ... what I have in mind is not so much a well developed theoretical frame of reference as something as simple as a checklist of points to be covered.[48]

Finally here, we can simply observe that many respected workers in the field – Haugen, Stewart, Kloss and Ferguson among them – *have* felt it meaningful to employ a typological approach. Haugen's concern, for example, was that:

> most language descriptions are prefaced by a brief and perfunctory statement concerning the number and location of its speakers and something of their history. Rarely does such a description really tell the reader what he ought to know about the social status and function of the language in question. Linguists have generally been too eager to get on with the phonology, grammar, and lexicon to pay more than superficial attention to what I would like to call the 'ecology of language'.[49]

We could expand on this by noting that, besides linguists, educationalists, sociologists, psychologists, historians and others have also often failed to give sufficient treatment to ecological variables. Also, it seems to me that useful sociolinguistic forays into minority-language matters – and many others, too – *must* be interdisciplinary; we can no longer afford the luxury of simply remaining within our own narrow boundaries, particularly since the location of these boundaries is very much open to debate.

Perhaps it is as well to begin a treatment of comparative minority-language matters by considering the question of 'minority' itself. An apposite and timely example already touched on is French in Canada. Is it a minority language? It obviously depends upon whether one takes the context to be the country or the province (Quebec). This definitional difficulty relates to many minority languages in which a concentration of population has a long- or well-established homeland within some larger political boundaries. This raises the issue of *state* and *nation*, the breadth and variability of allegiance, and the fact that state and national borders need not coincide. Even where they do, minority status may attach to the group's language, usually indicating previous historical movement (e.g., Irish in Ireland). Some might also want to point here to languages which have majority status within a state but which, not being so-called 'languages of wider communication', have in some sense a minority role on some continental or global stage (Bulgarian, for example). This leads directly to the issues of power, prestige and dominance which are often more important than mere numbers in determining majority or minority status. We could consider as an example the linguistic situation in South Africa. English and Afrikaans are official languages and have perhaps 6 million speakers. Other important languages include the Nguni group (Xhosa, Zulu, etc.) and the Sotho family (Tswana, Sotho), with a total of some 15 million speakers. Yet in what sense, other than simply numerically, could the latter be seen as of majority status? Context and power are clearly of the greatest importance. Generally, when we include the notion of dominance/subordination in the discussion, we may agree that some minorities are more minor than others: 'ils sont plus minorisés'.[50]

Furthermore, we should bear in mind that some minorities are indigenous – Celtic-language speakers in France and Britain, for example – while others are immigrant populations. Some can 'pass' more easily than others (if they wish to) into a mainstream fabric; there are differences, then, between 'white' minorities in immigrant-receiving countries and 'visible' ones, for whom no amount of assimilative effort will eradicate a stigmatized status. Some groups become minorities voluntarily, while others have little or no say in the matter. And so on.

One first element in a typology could well be geographic and, here, an adaptation of a model proposed by Paul White in 1987 seems useful.[51] This model introduces three basic distinctions. The first is among minority languages which are unique to one state, those which are non-unique but which are still minorities in all contexts in which they occur, and those which are minorities in one setting but majority varieties elsewhere. This initial distinction gives rise to the terms *unique, non-unique* and *local-only* minority. The second distinction deals with the type of connection between speakers of the same minority language in different states; are they

Table 5.1 Some examples of minority language situations[52]

Type	Indigenous minorities	Immigrant minorities
1 Unique Cohesive	Sardinian (Sardinia) Welsh (Wales) Friulian (Friuli-Venezia-Giulia)	Perhaps dialect communities (often religiously organised), where variety is now quite divergent from language in region of origin (e.g., Pennsylvania 'Dutch', Volga-German, dialects in Canada, etc.)
2 Unique Non-cohesive	Cornish (Cornwall)	As above, but where speakers are scattered
3 Non-unique Adjoining Cohesive	Occitan (Piedmont and Liguria/and in France) Basque (France/and in Spain) Catalan (Spain/and in Andorra)	Any enclaves of immigrants found in adjoining states
4 Non-unique Adjoining Non-cohesive	Saami (Finland, Norway, Sweden and Russia)	Scattered immigrants in adjoining states
5 Non-unique Non-adjoining Cohesive	Catalan (Spain/and in Sardinia)	Welsh (Patagonia) Scots Gaelic (Nova Scotia)
6 Non-unique Non-adjoining Non-cohesive	Romany (throughout Europe)	Scattered immigrants of European origin in 'new world' countries
7 Local-only Adjoining Cohesive	French (Valle d'Aosta/and in France)	French (in New England town enclaves) Spanish (South-West USA) Italian gastarbeiter (Switzerland)
8 Local-only Adjoining Non-cohesive	German (Piedmont/and in Switzerland)	French (scattered in New England)
9 Local-only Non-adjoining Cohesive	French (Apulia/and in France)	Immigrant enclaves in 'new world' countries Italian gastarbeiter (Germany)
10 Local-only Non-adjoining Non-cohesive	Albanian (throughout the Mezzogiorno/and in Albania)	Scattered immigrants in 'new world' countries

adjoining or *non-adjoining*? Finally, what degree of spatial cohesion exists among speakers within a given state? Here, the terms *cohesive* and *non-cohesive* can be used. Given that the adjoining/non-adjoining distinction does not apply to unique minorities, it follows that a ten-cell model emerges (table 5.1).

Of course, not only does this model not deal adequately with some of the issues already raised, it also suggests new difficulties. Consider, for example, the immigrant–indigenous dimension. In one sense, only Amerindian languages are indigenous to Canada yet, in another sense, French (along with English) has a 400-year claim on Canadian territory. There are also problems with the cohesiveness dimension. If a minority language is spoken sparsely over a wide area, but also possesses a concentrated centre, then it could be seen as either cohesive or non-cohesive. Yet another difficulty arises when considering a minority which is found in adjoining states; each can be classified as cohesive or non-cohesive, but the degree of cohesion of the other one may also be important. Issues also arise concerning the adjoining/non-adjoining dichotomy itself. For Basques in France and Spain, the adjoining label seems appropriate, but what of minority groups found in neighbouring states but not in their common border areas? Still, a geographical framework alone might be quite useful – for example, other things being equal or, indeed, unequal, the strength of a minority language will vary along the three dimensions of the model. The utility of a purely geographical approach is, nevertheless, severely limited; in order to apprehend more fully the complexities of minority languages and their speakers, further information from a variety of sources is clearly required.

The functions and status of competing language varieties are clearly central here, and have engaged the attention of researchers. Charles Ferguson, for example, has suggested some very basic approaches to sociolinguistic profiles.[53] For a given nation he calls for the following information: (a) number of major languages spoken (he provides some guidance here as to the 'major' designation); (b) patterns of language dominance; (c) whether a 'language of wider communication' is in use; (d) the extent of standardization; (e) the extent of written use of the language. As a scale for (e), Ferguson suggests: (i) W0 (not used for normal written purposes); (ii) W1 (used for normal written purposes); (iii) W2 (original research in physical sciences is regularly published).

William Stewart has presented classificatory information concerning language types, functions and degrees of use.[54] He thus notes seven main language types: P (pidgin), K (creole), V (vernacular: an unstandardized native language of a speech community), S (standard: a standardized vernacular), C (classical: a standard which has died out as a native language), A (artificial), D (dialect: to cover situations in which a particular dialect enjoys special status). Stewart also refers to ten important functions of language:

141

1 'g': group language, used for communication within a specific speech community;

2 'o': official language, used at the national level;

3 'p': provincial language, official only in given regions;

4 'c': capital language, communicatively dominant in the area of the national capital (other than an 'o' or 'p' variety);

5 'w': language of wider communication across language boundaries within the state (other than an 'o' or 'p' variety);

6 'i': language of wider international communication (other than an 'o' or 'p' variety);

7 'e': language used for educational purposes, at primary or secondary level (again, not to overlap with 'o' or 'p');

8 'r': language used for religious purposes;

9 'l': language used primarily for literary or scholarly purposes;

10 's': language widely taught as a school subject (other than an 'o' or 'p' variety).

Finally, Stewart specifies six degree-of-use categories, ranging from class I (where language users within the state comprise 75 per cent or more) to class VI (less than 5 per cent).

It is apparent that the use of these dimensions – or others like them – could be quite helpful in classifying minority languages. It is also apparent that, with regard to Stewart's language *functions*, there are social elements included which could easily overlap with some of the others; for example, a 'p' variety could have 'r' and 'l' status. On the other hand, a variety used primarily for 'r' purposes need have no other function. None the less, so far as it goes, Stewart's typology is very valuable. What is still needed is further refinement of *social status* factors.

In 1972, Einar Haugen popularized the term 'ecology of language', meaning the study of interactions between a language and its environment.[55] He posited ten ecological questions that should be answered for any given language: (1) how is it classified *vis-à-vis* other languages (a matter for historical and descriptive linguistics); (2) who uses it (linguistic demography); (3) what are its domains (sociolinguistics); (4) what other languages are used by its speakers (dialinguistics); (5) what are its internal varieties (dialectology); (6) what are its written traditions (philology); (7) what is its degree of standardization (prescriptive linguistics); (8) what institutional support does it have (glottopolitics); (9) what attitudes towards it are held by its speakers (ethnolinguistics); (10) where do all these factors place it in relation to other languages (ecological classification).

Haugen also refers generally to language *status* and *intimacy*. For him, status signifies the power, prestige and influence the language possesses through the social categorization of its speakers. Intimacy refers to associations with group solidarity, friendship and bonding. This has interesting overlaps with those psychological categories of language attitudes – competence, personal integrity and social attractiveness – that we have already discussed. While the first of these may be thought of as a status dimension (in Haugen's terms), the second and third clearly have intimacy and solidarity overtones.

More recently, Harald Haarmann has expanded upon the notion of language ecology, providing seven categories of 'basic ecological variables': (1) ethnodemographic variables (including size and concentration of language group, urban–rural distinctions, etc.); (2) ethnosociological variables (sex, age, social stratification, etc.); (3) ethnopolitical variables (group–state relations, institutional status of language, etc.); (4) ethnocultural variables (descent criteria, organizational promotion of group interests, etc.); (5) ethnopsychological variables (attitudes, language–identity relationship, etc.); (6) interactional variables (communicational mobility, language variety use by topic and situation, etc.); (7) ethnolinguistic variables (linguistic distance between contact languages, etc.). Haarmann provides considerable detail about these variables, including their function in language maintenance and language shift.[56]

An approach of particular psychological import is that of Howard Giles and his colleagues, in their conception of 'ethnolinguistic vitality'.[57] A three-part model has been proposed in which status, demographic and institutional-support factors are seen to contribute to the survivability of an ethnolinguistic group. Each factor comprises a number of variables: thus, status includes economic, social and linguistic attributes; demography reflects population distributions, concentrations and so on; and institutional support includes formal and informal facets like the media, education, government and religion. The particularly psychological feature here comes with the extension of the notion of ethnolinguistic vitality to perceived or 'subjective' vitality. Group members' perceptions of vitality may not always agree with objective assessment, and *perceptions* may prove more important than such assessment in determining group and individual behaviour.

There are problems with all of these models. In the case of Haugen and Haarmann, for example, there is insufficient specificity of variables – both schemes sketch out important areas, but lack of precision clearly detracts from typological utility. Some important matters are almost entirely neglected; little is said, for example, about historical, psychological, educational and geographic dimensions. The 'vitality' conception also contains elements which are too general, and neglects altogether some vital features. In presenting the original, 'objective' format, Giles does provide useful discussion of the three factors, and he acknowledges that the analysis is not exhaustive. None the less, he points out that the three-factor scheme meaningfully deals with linguistic minorities, and the subsequent expansion into 'subjective' vitality assessment might thus be seen as a premature solidification of factors. Perhaps the most important point about any typology is that it should be comprehensive. Without this quality, it may have plausibility and face validity – and it may appear to 'meaningfully group' minority populations; but, such grouping will be necessarily limited in scope.

None the less, all of these existing attempts have clearly made contributions to a language 'ecology' and, in attempting to expand upon my own geographical base (itself erected solidly on White's work) I have had to consider them closely.[58] Wanting to incorporate the earlier insights and, above all, to create a comprehensive scaffolding, I began by considering three very basic categories of variables: *speaker, language* and *setting*. These are not, of course, watertight and mutually exclusive dimensions, but they may serve as three logically important benchmarks. For example, it is possible to list all relevant variables under one or more of these headings, and they do reflect the spirit of a ecological enquiry – that is, one which emphasizes the interactions between language and environment. A second categorization takes into account different substantive and disciplinary perspectives – history, demography, education and so on. Combining these two classifications produces the framework in table 5.2. For each of the numbered cells, questions of interest can be formulated. For example, cell 3 would alert us to consider urban–rural distinctions of importance for language maintenance or decline; cell 4, the matter of within-group or without-group marriage; cell 8, the nature and degree of dialectal variation or fragmentation; cells 10/11, the matter of language attitudes and beliefs; etc.

It is obvious that these questions are not, themselves, anywhere near specific enough to comprise a completed and applicable typology; they are merely suggestions of the sort of items which could be grouped together by

Table 5.2 A typographical framework for minority-language-situation variables

	Speaker	Language	Setting
Demography	1	2	3
Sociology	4	5	6
Linguistics	7	8	9
Psychology	10	11	12
History	13	14	15
Politics/law/government	16	17	18
Geography	19	20	21
Education	22	23	24
Religion	25	26	27
Economics	28	29	30
The media	31	32	33

cell; as well, some questions could fit reasonably well in more than one cell. The reader is reminded that this is to be taken only as an approximation, in the expectation that further work will result in changes and refinements.

Clearly, much more work remains to be done. Although, to some, these typological exercises are less than appealing, although there are indeed possibilities for typological distortion, and although *no* scheme will capture every nuance of every situation, I think that the work *is* worthwhile. A comprehensive typology would be a useful tool for description and comparison, leading to a more complete conceptualization of minority-language situations, and perhaps even contributing to predictions of shift/ maintenance outcomes. We very much need to supplement individual case-studies, however rich and many-layered they are, with a comparative framework. Even if typological exercises progress no further than encouraging more rigorous and rational data gathering they will have served useful purposes.

6

THE PRESCRIPTIVE URGE

Wherever languages and dialects co-exist – wherever, that is, one sees multilingualism or multidialectalism – the elements of linguistic struggle are present. In some cases, the combatants are more equally matched than in others, and sometimes there are periods of more or less peaceful co-existence. But, as we have seen, contests do arise, and one form they often take, both between and within languages, is a prescriptive or puristic stance which, given free rein, would often lead to proscription.

I have already noted that languages and dialects cannot – linguistically or aesthetically – be seen in terms of 'better' or 'worse'. Rather, perceived qualitative differences rest upon social convention, which, in turn, derives from social inequalities and stratification, power and status relationships among speakers, and the ebb and flow of historical fortunes in a broad sense. But if these are views generally held by professional students of language, it is clear that they are not widespread. At the level of intralinguistic variation especially, people have very strong ideas about (for example) 'good' and 'bad' English, about 'incorrect' grammar and pronunciation, about allegedly deficient articulation and linguistic 'laziness', and about the failure of certain varieties to convey meaning adequately. At the same time, concern also exists for the 'contamination' of one language by another, for infiltration and borrowing, and for the bullying of small languages by larger ones; the desire to keep one's language 'pure' has always been strong. In a way, both intralinguistic and interlinguistic anxieties are expressions of a larger issue, one that is powerful precisely because it possesses emotional and symbolic qualities – the relationship between language (or dialect) and individual and group identity. We are dealing, in other words, with matters of *psychological* import, in which linguistic specifics act as markers, badges, team jerseys.

If we look at the development of psychology itself, at least in the west, we see an historical evolution from prescription to description. Before the discipline became an independent field of enquiry, and when psychological insights were produced by philosophers, theologians and ethicists, many assessments of human nature derived from positions of faith and led to prescriptions for the successful, or healthy, or purposeful conduct of life. After its divorce from philosophy – even allowing for relatively contemporary developments which have, in some areas, led to, or at least suggested, fruitful reunions – psychology became less prescriptive and more descriptive. This was due to an embrace of natural-science methods, a desire to represent psychological life as it exists, an increasing awareness of cross-cultural differences, a growing secularization and distaste for judgemental stances. While the myth of value-free science and complete objectivity has been highlighted in recent years, and while the emptiness of much of the modern psychological enterprise has prompted moves away from a narrow and anti-philosophical reductionism, no return to prescriptivism is likely within the discipline. Nowadays this exists only in the products of airport-author psychologists.

So it is with linguistics. Earlier writers – like those I have cited in the introductory chapter – were prone to prescriptive declamations, and early grammarians and lexicographers (i.e., more 'professional' linguists) produced prescriptive outlines of language in their attempts to codify, systematize and 'improve'; their works are quite understandable, given what were pioneering attempts to impose order where little or none had existed. Even in these efforts, however, one can often detect (as we shall see) feelings that, after all, usage is what ultimately counts, and that linguistic stability, variation and change are pushed from below rather than prescribed or proscribed from above. These feelings, in modern linguistics, have become very widespread and, like their psychological colleagues, linguists now see themselves as scholars whose essential remit is one of description. But if pop psychology abounds on station bookstalls and in magazines and other media, then so does an amateur linguistics in which prescriptivism still reigns. Anyone who reads newspapers, for example, knows how frequent are the cries for a return to 'standards', the laments over unwanted linguistic incursions and the complaints about slang and profanity. This, as may be imagined, is as historically constant as is disappointment with the younger generation. It is also an inevitable concomitant of multilingualism (or multidialectalism).

ANIMATING TENSIONS

Quintilian (c. 41–118) was an early language authority whose views were frequently cited in support of eighteenth- and nineteenth-century prescriptivism. Although apparently linking 'correctness' with public usage – a modern stance – Quintilian held that only 'correct' usage and 'moral' behaviour should be taken as guides to proper language; he was, after all, a prescriptivist:

> We must not accept as a rule of language words and phrases that have

become a vicious habit with a number of persons. To say nothing of the uneducated, we are all of us well aware that whole theatres and the entire crowd of spectators will often commit *barbarisms* in the cries which they utter as one man. I will therefore define usage in speech as the agreed practice of educated men.[1]

In the early seventeenth century, we find a purist railing against those abandoning *thee* and *thou*:

> Do not they speak false English, false Latine, false Greek ... and false to the other Tongues ... that doth not speak *thou* to *one*, what ever he be, Father, Mother, King, or Judge; is he not a Novice and unmannerly, and an Ideot and a Fool, that speaks *You* to *one*, which is not to be spoken to a *singular*, but to *many*? O Vulgar Professors and Teachers, that speak Plural, when they should Singular.... Come you Priests and Professors, have you not learnt your Accidence?[2]

In the seventeenth and eighteenth centuries, the concern for 'good' language (in England and elsewhere) and for standards became more widespread, and grammars, dictionaries and other linguistic manuals became increasingly common. I shall have more to say (below) about the formal efforts of language professionals, but it is worth noting here that the most sensitive among them were well aware of the tension between a prescriptivism from above and actual usage rising, as it were, from the streets. Before producing the great dictionary itself, Samuel Johnson published a *Plan* in 1747 – which he addressed to the fourth Earl of Chesterfield (having 'found that my design had been thought by your Lordship of importance sufficient to attract your favour') – in which he outlined his aim for 'a dictionary by which the pronunciation of our language may be fixed, and its attainment facilitated; by which its purity may be preserved, its use ascertained, and its duration lengthened'.[3] And, in his *Preface* to the dictionary (1755), Dr Johnson went on to observe that there were many problems with English, which had been:

> suffered to spread, under the direction of chance, into wild exuberance, resigned to the tyranny of time and fashion, and exposed to the corruption of ignorance, and caprices of innovation ... [it is] copious without order, and energetick without rules ... [its orthography] is unsettled and fortuitous ... [it has] improprieties and absurdities.[4]

Unsurprisingly, then, Johnson also thought it proper to omit many items:

> Of the laborious and mercantile part of the people, the diction is in a great measure casual and mutable.... This fugitive cant, which is always in a state of increase or decay, cannot be regarded as any part of the durable materials of a language, and therefore must be suffered to perish with other things unworthy of preservation.[5]

However, in acknowledging his work as a 'humble drudge' who was 'doomed only to remove rubbish and clear obstructions' from the paths of learning and genius, Johnson observed that some words, at least, 'must depend for their adoption on the suffrage of futurity'. More pointedly, he rejected the idea that a lexicographer 'can embalm his language, and secure it from corruption and decay, that it is in his power to change sublunary nature, or clear the world at once from folly, vanity, and affectation'.[6]

Johnson's patron, Lord Chesterfield (Philip Dormer Stanhope: 1694–1773) was, like many educated people of his day, interested in language; on the face of it, he was an excellent sponsor of Johnson's efforts. However, he was undoubtedly a less sensitive linguistic observer than was Johnson. He hoped, in fact, that the latter would prove an 'absolute dictator of standards', that a society still accustomed (or condemned) to vagaries of spelling, vocabulary and grammar would enter an age of standardization. Chesterfield himself had written to his son in 1750:

> I must tell you that orthography, in the true sense of the word, is so absolutely necessary for a man of letters, or a gentleman, that one false spelling may fix a ridicule upon him for the rest of his life. And I know a man of quality who never recovered the ridicule of having spelled *wholesome* without the *w*.[7]

Chesterfield's letters, incidentally – especially those to his son – remain well known; but he is also known, perhaps unfairly, as the uncaring patron of Johnson's efforts, a sponsor whose support was unreliable and delayed. In a famous letter (of 7 February 1775), reproduced by his biographer, Boswell, Johnson told Chesterfield:

> The notice which you have been pleased to take of my labours, had it been early, had been kind; but it has been delayed till I am indifferent, and cannot enjoy it; till I am solitary, and cannot impart it; till I am known, and do not want it.[8]

In his dictionary, Johnson defined *patron* as 'one who countenances, supports or protects. Commonly a wretch who supports with insolence, and is paid with flattery.'

Chesterfield's life just overlapped with that of William Cobbett (1763–1835), best known now for his *Rural Rides* (1830) – an anthology of pieces previously published in his newspaper, *The Political Register* (which he started in 1802, and kept until his death). A fierce social commentator often in trouble with the authorities (in America and in England) – but who nevertheless began regular Parliamentary reports, which evolved into *Hansard* – Cobbett, too, wrote letters to his son. These were published (in 1818) as:

A Grammar of the English Language: Intended for the Use of Schools and Young Persons in General; but more specifically for the Use of Soldiers, Sailors, Apprentices, and Plough-Boys. To which are added, Six Lessons, intended to prevent Statesmen from using false grammar and from writing in an awkward manner.

This is no ordinary grammar, for it mixes pedagogy and polemics. Cobbett meant both to instruct and to excoriate; he was happiest, perhaps, in assailing the famous, particularly men of letters (and university dons, 'who live by the sweat of other people's brows'). He illustrates 'collective nouns', for example, with: 'Mob, Parliament, Rabble, House of Commons, Regiment, Court of King's Bench, Den of Thieves'. At a milder level he, like Chesterfield, approved accuracy and modesty in usage. He told his son, James, that 'the only use of words is to cause our meaning to be clearly understood, and that the best words are those which are familiar to the ears of the greatest number of people'. And, further, in recounting how soldiers must know the names of parts of the musket, and sailors those of ships, Cobbett reminds his son: 'This species of preliminary knowledge is absolutely necessary in all these callings of life; but not more necessary than it is for you to learn ... how to know the sorts of words from one another.'[9]

The prescriptive–descriptive tension has hardly abated since the time of Johnson, Cobbett and Chesterfield. While, as I have implied above, formal linguistics has increasingly moved to a more disinterested description, informal linguistics – as expressed in the views of ordinary people, well-educated or not – has remained centrally concerned with questions of 'ought' and 'should', and usually employs hortatory tones: for example, George Trevelyan, the social historian, saw Johnson's 'classic age' as immensely important for English. Later linguistic developments are often seen as rather more vulgar. George Orwell, in some ways a direct descendant of Cobbett, saw the decline of English as intimately linked with politics:

> Most people who bother with the matter at all would admit that the English language is in a bad way.... It is clear that the decline of a language must ultimately have political and economic causes.... It [English] becomes ugly and inaccurate because our thoughts are foolish, but the slovenliness of our language makes it easier for us to have foolish thoughts.[10]

Orwell went on to provide six rules which he felt would arrest linguistic decline:

1 Never use a metaphor, simile or other figure of speech which you are used to seeing in print.
2 Never use a long word where a short one will do.
3 If it is possible to cut out a word, always cut it out.

4   Never use the passive where you can use the active.
5   Never use a foreign phrase, a scientific word or a jargon word if you can
     think of an everyday English equivalent.
6   Break any of these rules sooner than say anything outright barba-
     rous.[11]

This is prescriptivism, but of a relatively mild order. Furthermore, Orwell's
last rule (6) – even allowing for the reintroduction of the prescriptivism
which the ambiguous 'barbarous' suggests – makes it even milder, and
perhaps even places it, ultimately, under usage (one could, of course, see
outright anti-prescriptivism – say, the descriptive stance adopted by modern
linguists – as a type of prescriptivism itself).

The main point, I think, to be extracted from Orwell's rules is that a
tension other than the prescriptive–descriptive one exists or, more accurately perhaps, that there is a subtler *form* of the tension: it is between a
descriptive willingness to see ordinary usage as master, and the perceived
need to have some standards, some agreed-upon conventions which will
give unity to a language and its speakers. To the extent to which the need
for standard language is conceded a degree of prescriptivism and the
necessity to choose among variants become inevitable. Furthermore, even
the most broad-minded of standard-setters will likely be swayed by subjective notions of where standards might best be sought.

In 1476, William Caxton (1422–91) introduced printing to England,
having studied the process in Cologne and Bruges. He set up his press in
Westminster and published about one hundred books, 'mostly in English
and rarely in fashionable French or revered Latin'.[12] Many publications
were of his own translations and he was thus forced to attend to some
'fixing' of English, some choice among English dialects. Without dictionaries 'to cramp or to guide him' and lacking even the framework available
to Shakespeare, Caxton made a strong contribution to the dominance of
the language of London and the royal court. This is not to say that that
variety would not otherwise have triumphed, nor was Caxton free from style
and spelling variation himself; he was, however – because of the exigencies
of the new medium – one of the first in England to be formally concerned
with 'standards'. In his prologue to *Eneydos* (1490), his translation of a
French version of the *Aeneid*, Caxton reflected upon the difficulties:

> And certaynly our language now vsed varyeth ferre from that whiche
> was vsed and spoken when I was borne.... And that comyn englysshe
> that is spoken in one shyre varyeth from another. In so moche that in
> my dayes happened that certayn marchauntes were in a shippe in
> Tamyse, for to haue sayled ouer the see into Selande, and for lacke of
> wynde thei taryed atte Forlond [North Foreland in Kent], and wente
> to lande for to refreshe them; And one of theyme named Sheffelde,
> a mercer, cam in-to an hows and axed for mete; and specyally he axyed

after eggys; and the goode wyf answerde, that she coude speke no frenshe. And the marchaunt was angry, for he also coude speke no frenche, but wolde haue hadde 'egges' and she vnderstode hym not. And theene at laste another sayd that he wolde haue 'eyren' then the good wyf sayd that she vnderstod hym wel. Loo, what sholde a man in thyse dayes now wryte, 'egges' or 'eyren'?

Certainly it is harde to playse euery man by cause of dyuersite and chaunge of langage. And som honest and grete clerkes haue ben wyth me, and desired me to wryte the moste curyous termes that I coude fynde. And thus between playn, rude and curyous, I stande abasshed, but in my judgemente the comyn termes that be dayli vsed, ben lyghter to be vnderstonde than the olde and auncyent englysshe. And for as moche as this present Booke is not for a rude vplondysshman to laboure therein ne rede it, but onely for a clerke and a noble gentylman that feleth and vnderstondeth in faytes of armes, in loue, and in noble chyualrye, therefor in a meane bytwene bothe I haue reduced and translated this sayd booke in to our englysshe, not ouer rude ne curyous, but in suche termes as shall be vnderstanden, by goddys grace, accordynge to my copye.[13]

Caxton, as noted, was not invariant in his own usage, which – as we can see above – is some way removed from our own, but his standardization efforts proved very important; 'most of the spelling devices in use in current English were those chosen by Caxton'.[14] Spelling reform continued after Caxton, of course, fuelled particularly by variations in English pronunciation. Richard Mulcaster (1530–1611) was a representative reformer (or *orthoepist*: a term of the time, indicating one concerned with the relationship between pronunciation and writing): in his grammar, *The First Part of the Elementarie which Entreateth Chefelie of the Right Writing of our English Tung* (1582), he announced the need for a comprehensive dictionary and supported the borrowing of foreign words where necessary – while noting that 'I honor the Latin, but I worship the English.'[15]

The tension among outright prescriptivism, purism, descriptive linguistics and the necessity of having some standards thus brings us more or less to the eighteenth century and Johnson's dictionary. We have, however, passed over the story as it affects languages other than English, as well as formal institutionalized efforts – usually by committee – to defend and standardize languages. The latter I shall take up in a following section.

For the former, it is not difficult to appreciate that virtually all languages emerging as 'national' mediums were buffeted by the same forces I have described as affecting English. Consider, for example, the views of François de Malherbe (1555–1628). His purism, based as much on prescriptivism as on insecurity, ignorance and insensitivity, was severe: he railed against obsolete words as well as newly-coined terms, Latin forms as well as French dialect variants. He may ultimately have had the common people in mind – it is said his main concern was that even the *crocheteurs du Port au Foin* should be able to understand poetry – but his views found greatest adherence among 'court fops and light versifiers'.[16] Nicolas Boileau-Despréux (1636–1711) wrote in his *Art poétique* (1674) that: 'Enfin Malherbe vint, et, le premier en France . . . réduisit la Muse aux règles du devoir.'[17] The cost, however, was high for the language and its expression, and earlier poets like Ronsard, Villon and du Bellay were condemned as obsolete. There were some who attacked Malherbe's sterile and pedantic observations, notably Mathurin Regnier (1575–1613) and Marie de Gournay (1565–1645), but their concerns for linguistic richness and their assaults on unimaginative narrowness of vision proved to be before their time.

Another powerful figure in seventeenth-century France was Claude Favre de Vaugelas (1585–1650). At first blush he seems to adopt a descriptive stance, noting in his *Remarques sur la langue françoise* (1647) that:

> C'est une erreur . . . en matière de langues vivantes, de s'opiniastrer pour la Raison contre l'Usage. . . . On a beau invoquer Priscien, et toutes les puissances grammaticales, la Raison a succombé, et l'Usage est demeuré la maistre; *communis error facit jus*, disent les jurisconsultes.[18]

He makes, then, a grudging acknowledgement of the triumph of usage over 'reason'. When we read, further, that his standards of usage were those of 'serious' members of the royal court and the 'best' writers, we realize, however, that Vaugelas – like Quintilian – was a prescriptivist at heart. He had an aristocrat's disdain for 'la lie du peuple', and shared Malherbe's oppositions. His views were undoubtedly popular – among those who counted, and those who wished to be – and *parler Vaugelas* was to speak 'proper' and 'pure' French. (This is perhaps an opportune time to remember that prescriptivism flourishes for social reasons, that the prescriptive messages of language purists find a large and eager audience, and that linguistic regulators are group-identity guards in the eyes of many.)

I have already mentioned the views of Antoine de Rivarol (1753–1801) on the supremacy of French, and the fact that his understandable but illogical equation of French with clarity is still quoted today (often without proper ascription, of course) reinforces the general point just made. Not only did Rivarol claim *current* superiority for French, incidentally: 'Il n'y a jamais eu de langue où l'on ait écrit plus purement et plus nettement qu'en la nôtre.'[19]

At the time of the Ordonnance de Villers-Cotterêts (1539) – which decreed that French should replace Latin in all official documents – only a minority in France actually spoke the language; regional varieties still flourished. Under the *ancien régime* there was, in fact, considerable tolerance of these varieties, the official view being that political harmony and regular payment of taxes were far more important than the languages of the peasantry. By the time of the revolution, it is estimated that half the population *still* had little or no French and, in the early days, the revolutionaries remained tolerant, at least to the extent of sanctioning translation into regional languages.[20] However, when Abbé Grégoire, the head of the Education Commission, surveyed the situation in 1790, and found French still largely an élite competence and the existence of 'trente patois différents', he produced his famous *Rapport sur la nécessité et les moyens d'anéantir les patois et d'universaliser l'usage de la langue française* (1794). In the same year, Bertrand Barère – the *de facto* Minister of Cultural Propaganda, according to his biographer[21] – observed:

> Le fédéralisme et la superstition parle bas-breton; l'émigration et la haine de la République parlent allemand; la contre-revolution parle italien, et le fanatisme parle le basque. Cassons ces instruments de dommage et d'erreur.... Pour nous, nous devons, à nos concitoyens, nous devons à l'affermissement de la République, de faire parler sur tout son territoire la langue dans laquelle est écrite la Déclaration des droits de l'homme.[22]

Little wonder, then, that in July 1794 all languages other than French were proscribed: 'nul acte public ne pourra, dans quelque partie que se soit du territoire de la République, être écrit qu'en langue française'.[23]

None the less, for the rural masses, French remained weak throughout much of the nineteenth century. Laws forbidding regional varieties at school stayed on the books. Only with *la loi Deixonne* in 1951 was some provision made for Breton, Basque, Catalan and Occitan (and, later, for Alsatian, Corsican and Flemish). It would be incorrect, however, to imagine that this rather mild tolerance signalled a significant dilution of a centralist francophone tendency.

If the Ordonnance de Villers-Cotterêts[24] initiated the process of French purism (du Bellay's *Defence*, previously mentioned, appeared ten years later), then the *questione della lingua*[25] began, in Italy, at about the same time. Once it became clear, in the mid-sixteenth century, that Italian was to replace Latin, three important questions arose: one concerned the *name* of the language (Italian, Tuscan or Florentine), another involved a choice between Tuscan and other varieties as standard, and the third dealt with imitation of earlier authors as models (Petrarch and Boccaccio in particular; with Dante, they comprised 'le tre corone' of Italian literature) versus adoption of current usage. Earlier, Dante Alighieri (1265–1321) had written in his own Florentine variety which, praised by Petrarch, had given an important initial boost to Tuscan. Dante himself wrote on broader linguistic themes, most notably in his *De vulgari eloquentia* (*c.* 1300). This was not, however, a plea for a general colloquial variety, but rather expressed a desire to see some *poetic* standardization. Indeed, he was very critical of all peninsular dialects. Some he saw as 'non vulgare, sed potius tristiloquium' (not a vernacular, but a base type of speech); and he felt that the Sardinians only imitated Latin, 'as apes do men'. His solution: a 'vulgare illustre, cardinale, aulicum et curiale' (a noble, fundamental, courtly and standard-setting vernacular) – even though his own Florentine style did not meet this criterion. Again, we hear the voice of Quintilian.

In his *Diàlogo delle lingue* (*c.* 1530), Sperone Speroni (1500–88) considered all points of view, and all those who either supported or opposed them. His verdict was that the forces for Tuscan on the 'classic' model were the most compelling. Particularly important here were the puristic observations of Pietro Bembo (1470–1547), in his *Prose della volgar lingua* (1526); Cardinal Bembo noted explicitly his dislike of *contemporary* Florentine usage. However, the Italian case was not resolved until much later, largely because of a lack of political unity. In the nineteenth century, Alessandro Manzoni (1785–1873) felt that Florentine should be the model, that Tuscan teachers should flood the country. He went so far as to rewrite the famous *I promessi sposi* (1827), eliminating his native Lombardisms and replacing them with current Florentine usage. When the novel reappeared fifteen years later, it had been given a thorough *bagno nell'Arno*. By this time, Manzoni's romantic desire to reinvigorate the Tuscan standard with modern Tuscan usage had a limited appeal; the idea of a standard co-existing with accepted regional variants (as supported by Graziadio Ascoli (1829–1907), for instance) was proving more attractive. We can also note that, as elsewhere, the influence of the capital has understandably grown over the centuries; in Italy this accounts for the popular linguistic prejudice for *la lingua toscana in bocca romana*.[26]

We can easily understand that similar expressions of the prescriptivist tension were common elsewhere in Europe (and beyond). Indeed, in his excellent *External History of the Romance Languages*, Robert Hall argues that the Italian experience in particular served as a 'reservoir' for debates in other countries. The gradual emergence of a national variety, the rejection of other (earlier and contemporary) forms, the increasing need for some communicative standards, the question of whether *one* dialect should be used everywhere and in all contexts, or whether an official standard might (or should) co-exist amicably with more local forms, the requirements of political and social unity, of state-formation – all these, mixed together with linguistic judgements of widely varying levels of expertise (and ignorance), make for a heady concoction.

ACADEMIES, DICTIONARIES AND THEIR INFLUENCE

The sixteenth, seventeenth and eighteenth centuries are noteworthy, as we have seen, for a concern with language standards. Closely related to the efforts of individual philologists, both amateur and professional, were those of formal institutions. Again, the Italian experience set the scene for others, inasmuch as discussions by groups of intellectuals interested in language (and other matters) had begun in the fifteenth century. Most important towns soon had such groups, and many gave themselves rather frivolous names; there were the *ùmidi* (damp ones) of Florence, the *insensati* (foolish ones) of Perugia, and the *storditi* and *sonnacchiosi* (the 'dazed' or 'bewildered' ones and the 'drowsers') of Bologna.

The first body devoted specifically to language was the Accademia della Crusca of Florence, founded (or, at least, given royal blessing) in 1572.[27] *Crusca* means 'bran', and the motivation for the name – apart from continuing the tradition of frivolity – lay in the desire to separate linguistic grain from chaff. Its first great task was the purification and codification of the language in a grammar and dictionary. The first never appeared, but a dictionary was published in Venice in 1612 – and lexicography continues to the present. One important feature of the Crusca lexicon was its use of examples and quotations from classical texts.

In France, there were similar interest groups, one of which was the Pléiade (which included the poets Ronsard and du Bellay) in the sixteenth century, and another led by Marie de Gournay (the critic of Malherbe) in the seventeenth. As in Italy, officialdom regarded such coteries as potentially troublesome, and were moved to control them by bestowing recognition; thus, just as Còsimo 'regularized' the Florentine academy, so did Cardinal Richelieu convert the gathering of Valentin Conrart (1603–75) into the Académie Française in 1634.

In the beginning, the academy addressed quite a small number of people, many of whom saw other languages as at least equal to French for cultured discourse. Its major aim was to reinforce its conceptions of clarity, simplicity and good taste. The forty 'immortals' of the academy were given 'absolute power ... over literature and language',[28] although only two men trained in philology or lexicography have ever been members. Most academicians have been drawn from the church, nobility or military; the bodies which, historically at least, would have been considered the inheritors of the best French and the obvious arbiters of good linguistic taste. However, dictionary-making *does* require some skill, and so it comes as no surprise to learn that the academy's first effort here (1694) was 'manifestly an inferior job', as expected from 'a group of dilettantes'.

Again, however, a body of linguistic amateurs has proved very hardy, and the Académie Française continues. In modern times, it is best known for its attempts to keep French free of foreign borrowings – particularly English ones – and relatedly to create, where necessary, French terms for the products and processes of science and technology. It has thus acquired a modernizing function to supplement the original purifying objective. The special aim of keeping out English influence, the 'attacks on *anglomania* and the tendency to *anglicise*'[29] were, as might be expected, features beginning in the nineteenth century.

Similar in intent to the French academy, and much influenced by it, was the Real Academia Española, founded in 1713 by the Bourbon king Philip V. Its royal motto, *Limpia, fija y da esplendor*, emphasizes once more the desire to clarify, purify and glorify a language. The Spanish academy produced a dictionary in 1730 and a grammar in 1771; these built upon earlier work by Antonio de Nebrija, whose *Lexicon a sermone latino in ispanicum* had been presented to Queen Isabella in 1492. The work of the Spanish academy is generally considered better than that of the Crusca or the Académie Française. It was the only one to produce a 'reasonably accurate' grammar and its dictionary – again making use of many illustrative quotations – appeared first.

The Spanish body was also important in extending its influence to the new world.[30] Academies were established, in the nineteenth century, in Colombia, Mexico, Ecuador, El Salvador, Venezuela, Chile, Peru and Guatemala. In the twentieth, more were founded – in Bolivia, Costa Rica, Cuba, Honduras, Panama, Paraguay, Puerto Rico and the Dominican Republic. Indeed, there now exists an association of Hispanic academies. French influence has also extended to francophones *outre-mer*. In Quebec, for example, we find L'Office de la Langue Française. Among its activities is the production of lists of acceptable terms for trades and professions, particularly those most susceptible to English influence.

Beyond this, academies have been established in many countries worldwide: Syria, Iraq, Egypt, Jordan, Ethiopia, Sweden, Hungary, Germany, Israel, Russia – these and other states have, or had, formal institutions charged with maintaining language standards and, even where no *academy* exists, one often finds official or semi-official agencies – in Kenya and Tanzania, for example – concerned with everything from language *selection* to purification.

Conspicuous by its absence here is any English-language academy. Randolph Quirk has noted a long-standing Anglo-Saxon aversion to 'linguistic engineering' of any kind and, indeed, a 'superior scorn' in attitudes to academies and their purposes. Their goals are 'fundamentally alien' to English speakers' conceptions of language. Commenting on the work of the associated Spanish academies, Quirk feels that their intention to maintain the unity of the language would be unexceptionable in an English context (although not likely to be copied); however, the related aim of maintaining linguistic tradition 'would be totally unacceptable if not incomprehensible'.[31]

This does not mean that there was no English interest in academies. In 1605, Richard Verstegan wrote his *Restitution of Decayed Intelligence*, which called for a renewed and nationalistic pride in the antiquity of English. Indeed, it is in the seventeenth century that a language academy should, perhaps, have been established. In 1662 the Royal Society was founded and two years later it was noted that:

There were persons of the Society whose genius was very proper and inclined to improve the English tongue. Particularly for philosophic purposes, it was voted that there should be a committee for improving the English language; and that they meet at Sir Peter Wyche's lodgings in Gray's Inn once or twice a month, and give an account of their proceedings, when called upon.[32]

Many were interested, and the committee was struck; it had twenty-two members, including Dryden, Evelyn and Waller. The first of these, John Dryden (1631–1700), observed (in 1664) that:

I am sorry that (Speaking so noble a Language as we do) we have not a more certain Measure of it, as they have in France, where thay [sic] have an Academy erected for that purpose, and Indow'd with large Privileges by the present King.[33]

The poet Edmund Waller (1606–87) asked in Of English Verse, 'Who can hope his line should long last, in a daily changing tongue?'[34] The committee met several times, and Evelyn wrote a proposal, including a Lexicon or Collection of All the Pure English Words, by Themselves – but nothing came of it. A contemporary linguist has suggested that the failure of the Royal Society's committee – which might well have been the cornerstone of an academy – occurred because those members with intrinsic linguistic interests became more and more absorbed in natural-science studies, and those whose interests were based on nationalism were thus stranded without a firm scholarly base.[35]

A little later, Daniel Defoe (1659–1731) proposed, in his Essay upon Several Projects (1702), that England should follow the example of the French with a body established to:

encourage Polite Learning, to polish and refine the English Tongue, and advance the so much neglected Faculty of Correct Language, to establish Purity and Propriety of Stile, and to purge it from all the Irregular Additions that Ignorance and Affectation have introduc'd.[36]

The effort was continued into the eighteenth century, most notably with Jonathan Swift's (1667–1745) contribution entitled Proposal for Correcting, Improving and Ascertaining the English Tongue (1712). Swift felt that 'an Infusion of Enthusiastick Jargon' now characterized English, and that the 'licentiousness' of the Restoration had corrupted the language. The chaos of spelling, the 'barbarous custom of abbreviating words' (like 'rebuk'd' for rebuked, or like 'mob' for mobile vulgus), and the adoption of 'modish speech without regard to its propriety' all offended Swift. Overall, he complained that English was:

extremely imperfect; that its daily Improvements are by no Means in proportion to its daily Corruptions; that the Pretenders to polish and refine it have chiefly multiplied Abuses and Absurdities; and that in many Instances it offends against every Part of Grammar.[37]

Addressing his *Proposal* to the Earl of Oxford, Swift specifically mentioned the example of the Académie Française, and called for eminent persons to 'assemble at some appointed Time and Place, and fix on Rules by which they design to proceed ... such a Society would want your Instruction and Example, as much as your Protection'.[38] Swift's proposal was initially well received but his reactionary and prescriptivist impulses were allied – in his mind and in that of others – to his strong Tory principles. When the Tories lost power in 1714, after the death of Queen Anne, his support largely disappeared.

But, if an English academy was not to be,[39] there yet remained the need for standards – which brings us back to Samuel Johnson and his dictionary of 1755. This can be seen, essentially, as a one-man academy. Furthermore, Johnson, as noted above, rejected the linguistic 'embalming' so dear to purist hearts (although one would like to know more about Johnson's innermost predilections, as well as his practical assessments and ultimate rejection of lexical and grammatical stasis). Ultimately, he does align himself with the sentiments of John Locke (1632–1704), who, in his *Essay Concerning Human Understanding* (1689), noted: 'I am not so vain to think, that anyone can pretend to reforming the languages of the world, no not so much as that of his own country, without rendering himself ridiculous.'[40]

Influential though it was, Johnson's dictionary was hardly the last word on standards, even within his own century. For if regularization and ease of intelligibility were advanced, concerns continued about the social 'marking' implicit in dialect and accent choice. In his *Course of Lectures on Elocution* (1762), Thomas Sheridan (1719–88) said of dialects that:

one must have the preference, and become fashionable.... [This] will of course fall to the lot of that which prevails at court, the source of fashions of all kinds. All other dialects are sure marks, either of a provincial, rustic, pedantic, or mechanic education; and therefore have some degree of disgrace annexed to them.[41]

Many other influential persons held similar prescriptive views, most of which have a strong smell of Quintilian about them.[42] Among these were the writers of grammars and dictionaries (Sheridan himself produced a *General Dictionary of the English Language* in 1780, in which he largely adopted Johnson's orthographic precepts, to which he added 'correct' pronunciations).

Dictionaries before Johnson's were essentially of 'hard words' only – for example, Robert Cawdrey's *Table Alphabeticall* (1604). John Kersey compiled perhaps the first 'modern' dictionary, the first built on the assumption that all ordinary words should be included, with his *New English Dictionary* of 1702.[43] The first major effort, however, was Nathaniel Bailey's *Universal Etymological English Dictionary* (1721) which had some formative inflence on Johnson. A prescriptive grammar was that of Robert Lowth (1710–87), Bishop of London – his *Short Introduction to English Grammar* (1762). An interesting *non*-prescriptive attitude was evident in the work of Joseph Priestley (1733–1804; the discoverer of oxygen). He published his *Rudiment of English Grammar* in 1761, and *A Course of Lectures on the Theory of Language and Universal Grammar* in 1762. In the latter he stated that:

> It is absurd to pretend to set up the composition of any person or persons whatsoever as the standard of writing, or their conversation as the invariable rule of speaking.... The general prevailing custom, where ever it happens to be, can be the only standard for the time it prevails.[44]

Among the most influential of eighteenth-century productions was the *English Grammar* (1762) of Lindley Murray (1745–1826).[45] Murray, an American who moved to England after the revolution, established, or at least strongly reinforced, the 'Latinate' tradition which was to prove so powerful in schools. It was Murray's 'Rule 16', for example, which decreed that two negatives destroy one another, and are equivalent to an affirmative.

After Johnson's dictionary of 1755, the next most important work was done, in America, by Noah Webster (1758–1843). In fact, like Johnson, Webster became the one-man academy for the United States, where the institutional models of France and Spain lacked appeal because of their royalist associations. Just as in England, there were those who favoured some type of academy, the most prominent here being John Adams. Influenced by a trip to Europe, Adams recommended an academy, a body to check the 'natural tendency' language has to 'degenerate', to the Continental Congress. Adams also believed that, since England had no academy, there was an opportunity here for the United States to put *its* official stamp on English purity and preservation.[46] But Adams, often suspected of monarchist sympathies, had no success in moving Congress. There were also societies whose interests included language, among them the American Academy of Language and Belles Lettres, a body which existed only for a short time during the 1820s. Like the Académie Française, it was directly interested in standardization and purity, and had an élitist membership lacking in linguistic expertise. The founders knew well the objections to a national language academy but proceeded in spite of them. An example of their determination and sense of rightness in the face of adversity can be seen in their statement that 'happily for us, our forefathers came chiefly from that part of England where their language was most correctly spoken'.[47] The members had no more success than had Adams in getting government backing, however. The academy's publications were characterized by 'hyperbole and empty rhetoric' and demonstrated an unresolved tension between a desire to promote an American literary model and reliance upon the English of England.

Like Johnson, Webster felt that standardization was important, but he had a practical view of linguistic change and thought that no dictionary could establish final norms. Webster was, above all, concerned for the linguistic independence of the United States, and this culminated in his *American Dictionary of the English Language,* published in 1827. Earlier, in his *Dissertations on the English Language* (1789), Webster had urged spelling changes; these would underline the difference between American and British English. He also wanted Americans to stop using foreign borrowings, particularly from French. But, strangely perhaps for one concerned with a 'people's language', he also saw part of his task as the removal of 'improprieties and vulgarisms ... and ... those odious distinctions of provincial dialects'.[48] Webster further felt that Great Britain and the United States would become more and more linguistically separate, and that different languages would result in time. He was not at all opposed to this, for it reinforced his nationalistic feelings, and he was no doubt glad to be able to observe that, already, the American people spoke the purest English.

CONTEMPORARY CONSIDERATIONS

So we arrive at the nineteenth century in which, as I implied at the beginning of the chapter, descriptive linguistics became more the norm, and where prescriptivism began to wane. However, there are two important points to be made here. The first is to recall that prescriptivism has declined only within the academy; outside, it still flourishes. The second is that, *within* the academy, a 'modified' prescriptivism – albeit a necessary one – has continued in connection with standards of educated language. The dividing lines between this milder version and more strident purism have not always been easily distinguishable, however. The thesis of Tony Crowley's *Politics of Discourse* is, in fact, that the alleged shift to objective and descriptive linguistics never really occurred (in Britain, at any rate).[49] He makes the reasonable point that the 'social and rhetorical concerns' of earlier periods have not abated and, in citing supporting evidence, is able to carry this to the most recent times. For example, the phonetician Daniel Jones (1881–1967) referred, in his *Pronunciation of English* (1909), to 'Cockneyisms [and] other undesirable pronunciations'.[50] Henry Wyld, the philologist and lexicographer mentioned in chapter 4, perhaps best exemplified the subtleties of modern prescriptivism when he observed (in *Elementary Lessons in English Grammar,* 1909):

The first thing is to realise that in itself a Provincial or Regional Dialect is just as respectable, and historically quite as interesting, as Standard English. The next thing is to realise that if you want to speak good Standard English, pronunciations which belong typically to a Provincial Dialect are out of place. It is probably wise and useful to get rid of these Provincialisms since they attract attention, and often ridicule, in polite circles. The best thing to do, if you have a native Provincial Dialect, is to stick to it, and speak it in its proper place, but to learn also Standard English.[51]

Many might, indeed, read this favourably; is Wyld not advocating, at the end, an accommodation between standard and non-standard, a bidialectalism? Might he not be implying that the ridicule of non-standard forms is reprehensible? Well, perhaps, but Wyld goes on to discuss the 'obliteration' of regional varieties – a process to which he does not object. More pointed is his view (in *The Growth of English*, 1907) that standard language, since it is 'used in the conversation of the refined, the brilliant, and the learned . . . has become a better instrument for the expression of ideas than any other dialect now spoken.'[52] And so, for yet another time, we see the hovering shade of Quintilian!

The issues continue, and can be expected to remain, whenever the notion of *standard* overlaps with more restrictive sentiment – which is to say, very frequently. However, Crowley's valuable observation notwithstanding, modern linguists *do* overwhelmingly reject prescriptivism, at least in its more blatant forms. Two more or less contemporary authors whose names have become well known, and who are undoubtedly prescriptivist in at least some mild sense, are Henry Fowler (1858–1933: whose *Dictionary of Modern English Usage* first appeared in 1926) and Ernest Gowers (1880–1966), who revised Fowler's work in 1965, and who published his own *Plain Words* in 1948. Both men were amateur linguists and, more importantly, both are better described as *commentators* on usage (though not, of course, without their own opinions) than as old-style prescriptivists. Both, as well, were concerned with something that even descriptive linguists agree is important: the elimination of verbose, woolly, jargon-ridden and incomprehensible language.[53] In a world where:

a toothbrush is a 'home plaque removal instrument';
aircraft experience is 'uncontrolled contact with the ground';
an unconscious President Reagan is in a 'non-decision-making form';
a neutron bomb is an 'enhanced radiation device';
steel nuts are 'hexiform rotatable surface compression units';
paratroopers make a 'predawn vertical insertion';
(and so wearily on);

we can surely hope for some relief.

Beyond these idiocies, every reader is aware that convoluted, impenetrable or completely meaningless usage is characteristic of many professions, and is all too pervasive in modern life. Lawyers, politicians and government officials are often singled out, and rightly so; here is a note from Hackney Council in London about the refunding of overpayment of rates:

> (1) Without prejudice to ss 7(4)(b) and 18(4) of this Act, but subject to subs (2) of this section, where it is shown to the satisfaction of a rating authority that any amount paid in respect of rates, and not recoverable apart from this section, could properly be refunded on the ground that –
>
>   (a) the amount of any entry in the valuation list was excessive; or
>
>   (b) a rate was levied otherwise than in accordance with the valuation list; or
>
>   (c) any exception or relief to which a person was entitled was not allowed; or
>
>   (d) the hereditament was unoccupied during any period; or
>
>   (e) the person who made a payment in respect of rates was not liable to make that payment,
>
> the rating authority may refund that amount or part thereof.[54]

Readers can provide their own favourites here, but I cannot conclude without mentioning that social scientists are among the worst offenders:

> The examples given suggest that the multiformity of environmental apprehension and the exclusivity of abstract semantic conceptions constitute a crucial distinction. Semantic responses to qualities, environmental or other, tend to abstract each individual quality as though it were to be experienced in isolation, with nothing else impinging. But in actual environmental experience, our judgements of attributes are constantly affected by the entire milieu, and the connectivities such observations suggest reveal this multiform complexity. Semantic response is generally a consequence of reductive categorization, environmental response or synthesizing holism.[55]

Further excesses have been lovingly documented by Stanislav Andreski, who also raises (and solves) a common complaint: given that you cannot make sense of such language, how can you be sure that the fault is not your own?[56] After all, such passages often occur in books having academic seals of approval, whose authors must surely be intelligent and articulate, and altogether more elevated than oneself. Andreski's solution is to test yourself on works acknowledged to be intellectually demanding but not necessitating specialist information. He mentions Carnap's *Philosophical Foundation of*

Physics and Woodger's *Biological Principles*. If, after serious effort, you find you can understand them, but still not fathom what some politician or sociologist has said, then you can assume the failings are not yours. You will also, incidentally, find growing support from the various organizations committed to plain language and the elimination of doublespeak, gobbledygook, bafflegab and psychobabble.

But if linguists are likely to approve any efforts to reduce unintelligibility, they tend to keep a rather low profile; this is equally true when prescriptivism of the type I have been discussing appears. Appear it does, of course – and the usual linguistic response, in any public way, is to keep quiet. This is understandable from a non-interventionist standpoint, but the effect is to abandon the field to those whom Dwight Bolinger has called the language *shamans*.[57] These are the people who write books on language 'decline' and 'decay', who agonize in newspaper columns and letters over the abandonment of both standards and propriety, who berate the apathy and indolence of professional linguists in the face of attacks on the language, who anathematize any dictionary or grammar produced on descriptive principles[58] – and who obviously find a willing and worrying readership. In their rush away from prescriptivism, linguists may have abdicated a useful role as arbiters, and have left much of the field open to those less well informed.[59] While few linguists have been willing to participate in debates about the 'public life' of language, there is clearly a great need for more illumination of that persistent no-man's-land between academic linguistics and public language. If linguists refuse to acknowledge the power and appeal of prescriptivism, they will 'ensure that every enterprise of language planning will be dominated by ignorant enthusiasts and incompetent pedants'.[60]

In one sense we have come a long way from Quintilian; in another sense, we are still fighting over the same ground. This is not to be wondered at, since purism and prescriptivism – as well as the sometimes more disinterested concerns for standards and ease of intelligibility – are, as George Thomas observes, 'probably coterminous with language' itself.[61] This is especially so for societies marked by social and linguistic stratification. Thomas's recent book on purism is one of the very few works attempting an overall perspective on the phenomenon, and some of his general observations may serve to place the preceding discussion in sharper focus.

He notes, for example, that most early studies of purism were anything but disinterested, and usually involved some elevation of the writer's own variety in accordance with a nationalistic imperative. This does not, of course, mean that such studies are valueless; as objective statements they are clearly flawed, but as primary sources on prescriptivism itself they are extremely useful. In this connection Thomas provides a number of 'self-images' which have guided the work of purists. Thus, there is the purist as miller or gardener, pruning, clearing the undergrowth, promoting the growth of healthy and desirable specimens, separating the wheat from the chaff, and so on. Then there is the purist as metallurgist or grinder, involved in metal-working, refining, removal of impurities and use of the whetstone. A medical metaphor, too, can be applied: here the purist treats a diseased language – sometimes with medicine, sometimes with surgery. Genetic or genealogical work is another perspective on the purist's task, where keeping 'hybridization' at bay is often related to the discovery and promotion of linguistic 'bloodlines'. Finally, there is the picture of purist as priest, in which corruption and ritual cleansing can be seen at the highest level. All of these conceptions are related in some composite image of the purist as guardian and healer, and they all imply that prescriptivism rests upon a strong sense of knowing what is best for a language. If the gardeners and grinders, the physicians and priests, are only actors in the eyes of some, they have had very long runs, and their theatres are usually packed. And if, as Robert Hall supposed, these players are characterized by insecurity, ignorance and insensitivity, then their audiences clearly possess the same traits.[62]

Thomas also makes it clear that the puristic impulse can target any aspect of language – phonology, morphology, syntax, orthography, lexicon – but that the latter is 'archetypal'. Loanwords, calques, neologisms and dialect variations are usually seen as the main enemies. He also provides a classification of puristic orientations: reverence for the past, for some classic or golden linguistic age, attachment to the richness of folk or peasant speech, élitism, xenophobia, etc. Thomas rightly points out, here, that *anti-purism* is, itself, an orientation. One is tempted to propose an analogy between theism, atheism and agnosticism and purism, anti-purism and 'apurism'.

Thomas reminds us that the disdain many professional linguists have for prescriptivism is not merely a contemporary phenomenon. The amateurs – the *shamans*, to use Bolinger's term again – have been the most prominent. Furthermore, the writers and educators who have typically served in the prescriptivist ranks are not often the most gifted of their type. There are famous exceptions, of course, and I have mentioned some of them in this chapter, but it is also true that some of the best writers have opposed purism. Goethe, for example, mentioned: 'geistlose Menschen ... welche auf die Sprachreinigung mit zu grossem Eifer dringen: denn da sie den Wert eines Ausdrucks nicht zu schätzen wissen, so finden sie gar leicht ein Surrogat, welches Ihnen eben so bedeutend scheint.'[63] Perhaps, then, we can take heart from the fact that if prescriptivism is an enduring phenomenon then so is reaction against it. Further, it is not only the Goethes of the world who oppose purism; there are many who, in a daily, unselfconscious fashion, vote against it every time they speak. The final twist in the tale, though, is that it is from their quarter that a strong, if inarticulate, concern for 'standards' emerges. Such general concern can then be manipulated by those with more particular axes to grind, especially since general if uninformed linguistic anxieties are often intertwined with others of a nationalistic, or ethnocentric, or nativist nature.[64] We can now consider an apposite and recent example here, which demonstrates the endurance of prescriptivism, its broad appeal and its power to effect real change.

The US English movement

Many people in the United States, and elsewhere, believe that English is the official language of that country. In fact, however, the framers of the American Constitution did not enshrine it there. Still, it would be hard to deny that over the past two centuries English has become *de facto* the main language of the state, notwithstanding the many other varieties which have co-existed with it and, in some instances, challenged it. English assimilative pressures have prevailed among virtually all non-English-speaking immigrants over the course of a few generations; few would deny that acquisition of English competence is important for full social participation and that desired mobility which was often the major incentive for coming to America. It may then seem odd and unnecessary that, in 1981, Senator Samuel Hayakawa introduced a constitutional amendment to make English the official language, that others have reintroduced the proposal since and that, following lack of action on his original measure, Hayakawa (together with Dr John Tanton) founded the organization called *US English* in 1983 to support and actively promote the cause.[65]

Hayakawa had said, in 1981, that 'a common language can unify; separate languages can fracture and fragment a society',[66] and that learning English was the main task of immigrants. In 1983, Senator Huddleston observed that 'for the past fifteen years [i.e., since the advent of federally-sponsored bilingual education], we have experienced a growing resistance to the acceptance of our historic language, an antagonistic questioning of the melting-pot philosophy'.[67] Such views were held by many within and without government, including President Reagan himself, who was in any event merely echoing earlier national leaders. Teddy Roosevelt, for example, was a great believer in the American crucible, and Israel Zangwill (1864–1926) dedicated his play, *The Melting Pot* (1909), to him. In 1915, Roosevelt said that 'there is no room in this country for hyphenated Americanism ... [the foreign-born] must talk the language of its native-born fellow-citizens'. He also observed, in a famous passage, that 'we have room for but one language here, and that is the English language, for we intend to see that the crucible turns our people out as Americans, of American nationality, and not as dwellers in a polyglot boarding house'.

Now, US English – self-described as a national, non-profit, non-partisan organization established to defend the public interest in the debate on bilingualism and biculturalism – has some 400,000 members, a large annual budget, and a board of advisors with such luminaries as Jacques Barzun, Saul Bellow, Alistair Cooke, Sidney Hook, Gore Vidal and Arnold Schwarzenegger. It speaks generally of English as a common bond and a 'blessing' integrating America's diverse population. It sees a dangerous and growing rejection of the melting-pot ideal, distressing trends towards institutionalization of government-funded programmes of bilingual education and a spread of foreign-language use in officialdom. US English often refers to Canadian bilingualism as a source of disharmony; Hayakawa has said that, of all people, Canadians know best the 'pitfalls' of a bilingual society.

Apart from its overriding concern that English be made official, US English advocates integration (assimilation) over separatism (pluralism) and holds that every effort should be made, particularly via education, to assist newcomers in the acquisition of English. At the same time, it rejects linguistic chauvinism, nativism and xenophobia, encourages foreign-language study, supports individual and private rights to use and maintain languages other than English, and would not prohibit forms of bilingual education intended to ease children into English ability. Both Tanton and Linda Chavez (former president of US English) have, furthermore, explained why the organization was founded when it was; why there is now a rejection of traditional assimilation which must be combatted. In the past, many other languages came to the United States but none were strong enough to withstand English; this has changed, they argue, with the current large Spanish-speaking population existing in concentrated areas.

It might be appropriate here to say something about the history of language legislation in the United States since opponents and proponents of official English differ over whether or not the framers of the US Constitution were supporters of a multilingual society. We know that Benjamin Franklin and others expressed anti-German sentiment, but we also know that the Constitution did not enshrine English. Why? It is important to recall that the English tradition was not, and has not been, one of language legislation (see above), and the United States has inherited the English reluctance to regulate language politically. This tolerance, and the allowance for social forces to settle language questions, was no doubt sustained by the thought that English dominance was obvious and unendangered. The antagonism to German demonstrates, perhaps, that if this assumption had not been generally met, legislation supporting English might well have occurred.[68] The story of laws restricting languages other than English is best described by Heinz Kloss in *The American Bilingual Tradition*, but it is clear that there has been a general tolerance for 'foreign' languages, and that these and English have been more subject to socioeconomic pressures than to legal ones. Repressive language legislation early this century (often connected with war emotion) was relatively quickly dismissed as unconstitutional.

There would certainly seem to be considerable popular and political support for official English in the United States. A so-called 'sense of the Senate' measure declaring English official has been passed three times as an attachment to immigration legislation, although these declarations do not have the force of law. At another level, seventeen states have made English official, with legislation pending or planned in others; with few exceptions, all made the move since the mid-1980s. As well, public-opinion polls in a variety of locations have shown considerable support for English. Most of these have been markedly unscientific, often conducted by newspapers, radio and television, but others have been taken by survey organizations (although even here the questions asked vary widely and are often poorly phrased or 'loaded'; this also applies, incidentally, to polls cited as showing support for languages other than English, such as the *Newsweek* survey of 1984, conducted by Gallup).

US English has, since its inception, been subject to a barrage of opposition, and many ethnic-group spokesmen and academics, particularly, have seen it as a nativist, ethnocentric organization. Chavez reports being called a fascist, a traitor to her own Hispanic heritage, and has been picketed at speaking engagements. The president of *La Raza* (an Hispanic political movement) likened US English to the Ku Klux Klan, and a journalist has linked the group – through a larger body, *US Inc.*, and another association, the *Federation for American Immigration Reform* (also founded by John Tanton) – to allegedly racist funding agencies, including the Pioneer Fund, created in 1937 to promote 'racial betterment' through eugenics. This same journalist, James Crawford, has discussed in some detail a leaked memorandum written by Tanton, a statement which led to the resignation of Linda Chavez. In it, Tanton demonstrates a fear of Hispanic control in America, asks if 'homo contraceptivus' can compete with 'homo progenitiva', and lists cultural 'threats' associated with Hispanic Americans – the tradition of bribery, Roman Catholicism and so on. Tanton replied to Crawford, whom he called a practitioner of the 'big lie', admitting the memorandum included mis-statements and stupidities.

Other American organizations have either explicitly or indirectly attacked US English and the official-English philosophy. These include the powerful teachers' union, the National Education Association, TESOL (Teachers of English to Speakers of Other Languages), the National Council of Teachers of English, the Linguistic Society of America, the Modern Language Association and the Center for Applied Linguistics. Many see US English as promoting an English-only policy rather than simply an English-official one (this is denied by the group), and one reaction has been the *English Plus* movement, whose purposes are obvious. It had its genesis in statements by the Spanish–American League Against Discrimination (SALAD – so now we have a salad-bowl to counter the melting-pot) and it has established an information clearing-house. Adherents to the English Plus idea have also proposed a constitutional amendment of their own; it is the Cultural Rights Amendment, which would formalize the preservation and promotion of ethnic diversity.

The preceding discussion shows something of the scope and vehemence of the debate surrounding the official-English issue and US English. Is the latter a racist, nativist organization, and does the proposed English Language Amendment mask an Anglo-conformist, anti-Hispanic hysteria? Are the opponents of US English overreacting, are they out of touch with mass opinion? Do they represent a constituency committed, for self-interested reasons, to linguistic diversity and a dual- or multilanguage America, who try to claim in the face of contrary evidence that multi-lingualism is not a divisive force in the world? These are some of the weighty questions involved.

In one sense, the whole matter is a non-issue, only the current symbol perhaps of a jockeying for place among groups and interests, and part of the evolving story of a diverse 'receiving' society. After all, the dominance of English is hardly in doubt, and Hispanic immigration and concentration show the familiar signs of surrender to pressures for language shift and assimilation. But objective data on ethnic-group dynamics do not neces-sarily spring to the minds of English speakers in Miami or southern California who are confronted with many marks of Hispanic vitality. Equally, disclaimers on the part of US English notwithstanding, a nativist sentiment is being projected which arouses and reinforces old anxieties among non-English speakers. If an English Language Amendment is objectively unnecessary – it would, incidentally, be quite difficult to pass such a measure because of the voting patterns required; the American Constitution has been amended only sixteen times – it is *seen* as needed by some and as an unsubtle attack on diversity by others. It is not, then, a benign matter, nor is US English a non-partisan body. While it is clear that not all the members of the group, nor all those in favour of making English official, are racist, there is yet a strong nativist element, a desire to maintain a social *status quo*. This reflects, at the least, insecurity, apprehension and regret that an old order is perceived as changing – hardly an uncommon phenomenon. Hispanic Americans with their linguistic distinctiveness are symbols, then, of unwanted change. Given their origins, social status, skin colour and historical position *vis-à-vis* the American mainstream they are, unfortunately, targets.

The question of whether or not US English is really an English-only organization is interesting. The group itself claims not, pointing to its support for linguistic diversity and bilingual education. Yet it has argued against bilingual education on the grounds of 'identity confusion' and 'resegregation'. It also clearly advocates programmes other than bilingual education to expedite linguistic assimilation, and its own 'Golden Door' project – the words come from Emma Lazarus's famous poem on the Statue of Liberty, 'The New Colossus' – aims to teach English to adult immigrants through direct instruction. It seems reasonable to assume that US English, while giving this grudging and ambivalent nod in the direction of bilingual education, would prefer a return to only English-as-a-second-language interventions or, indeed, to old 'submersion' methods.

Norman Podhoretz, the editor of *Commentary* and a US English board member, has noted his gratitude for being humiliated at school for his lack of English, for being forced with many immigrants to learn the language in a sink-or-swim manner, since this proved a spur towards social mobility and success. It is, by the way, a striking fact, one pointed to by US English itself, that so many board members and officers are themselves of non-English-speaking background. This is surely meant to be taken as a sign that the organization could hardly be xenophobic, and that it is securely aligned with the masses of American 'ethnics'. But as safe and successful individuals themselves, may not the immigrant officers be falling prey to the idea that there is some innate virtue in rising up the old way, the hard way? Could there be resentment here that newer immigrants are having an easier time adjusting, at government expense, and that their own achievements are somehow diluted, their own positions less exclusive? The feminist who finally cracks the prestigious all-male law firm may just as easily pull the ladder up after her as lean back to help others up the rungs.

It is not original to suggest that, where at all possible, matters of language may be best left unlegislated. Most countries, for example, do not have explicit constitutional provisions declaring an official language; while in many cases a particular language has an obvious pre-eminence, there is at least here a legal flexibility which could accommodate shifting social tides. Some may see lack of government legislation as ignorant or discriminatory, but a lack of legislative response to appeals like the English Language Amendment (or, indeed, the Cultural Rights Amendment) can itself be a considered government action. One would hope, of course, that refusal or unwillingness to rule on matters of language and ethnicity goes hand in hand with tolerance for groups to define themselves as they see fit – this tolerance could well be supported in law, through anti-discrimination measures and so on. It might also be thought, however, that such an approach fails to protect group languages and cultures at risk of assimilation in a society like the United States. But, where such risk exists largely because of unlegislated social pressures, it cannot be removed without legislation so draconian as to be intolerant and perhaps counter-productive.

The best prediction is that US English will continue to flourish for some time and will engage the sympathies of many people for many different reasons. Certainly, its existence and success are not surprising. However benign its aims and procedures are in the eyes of its supporters, it will also continue to be a focus of nativist–pluralist controversy. This is likely to exist largely at an unintellectual and highly emotional level, to heighten rather than assist to resolve social tensions.

Loose canons

Related to, and often predating, the emergence of a standard dialect is a collection of literary works which achieve high status on the assumption that they represent the finest writings of the finest authors. This collection is the written culture's showcase, and a work allowed entry has attained a permanent position in the pantheon. This enshrinement, then, results from a sort of mega-prescriptivism: the highest and purest achieve immortality while, on the other side of the boundary, lesser works jostle for attention, with some proving very ephemeral, others managing an existence of considerable longevity. But longevity alone is an insufficient criterion for membership in *the* collection; accompanying it, and contributing to it, there must also exist the accolades of the academy.

Thus arises a literary *canon*. Its presence is formidable and unmistakable, and although quarrels may arise over the qualifications of junior members, the old guard are secure forever in their leather chairs. The canon of English literature includes Shakespeare, Milton, Byron, Yeats, Joyce and Eliot – to list only a few of the authors represented in one of the major canonical collections, *The Norton Anthology of English Literature* (similar lists can, of course, be easily assembled for all national literatures).[69]

At the moment some canons, having traditionally been quite capable of repelling boarders, are under fierce attack, and the çanon-foundries and canon-makers are deeply suspect. The problem is not so much that Shakespeare and Yeats are likely to be ejected from the canon, but rather that others are seen to have been unfairly excluded from canonical consideration. It is not only from the wilder regions of political correctness that the matter emerges; there is a more general and more sustainable conviction that members of minority groups and, especially perhaps, women have never had a fair kick at the canon. The club has always been exclusive and, as elsewhere, power, dominance and old-boy interconnections have triumphed.

It is not only history that is written by the winners. It is not difficult to see that current unease in the literary world is but one manifestation of a more general desire to redress perceived social imbalances and inequities. Fuelling this further is the apprehension that we have missed a great deal historically, that many writers and many works have been irretrievably lost through ignorance, neglect and prejudice. On the other hand, some dismiss the modern agitations on the ground that the literary canon *does* represent the best, the classic, the standard, that it *is* the embodiment of great literature and that the possibility of dethroning Shakespeare – or any other Dead White European Male member of the establishment – on ideological grounds is repugnant and barbaric.

Although Shakespeare is not in imminent danger, the idea of making the club less exclusive, of an expanded and more inclusive canon, may be useful. There is certainly a mustiness in some quarters, and the self-righteousness of the canon's entourage has on occasion been excessive. In America, the *Norton Anthology*, which has come to symbolize all that is wrong with the literary canon, is printed on the same thin paper, and has the same heft and substance, as the sacred canon itself! However, influential collections (like *Norton*) are really scapegoats, for the essential difficulty is this: *any* collection, *any* selection, *any* reading list for students implies value judgement and choice. Some canons are of lesser calibre than others, but the necessity of choosing what is to be read is an insoluble practical problem. Furthermore, innovations like canon expansion (to include hitherto neglected writers), canon multiplication (canonical collections of women writers, of Black writers, of homosexual writers, and so on), or canon elimination (give students of literature a free choice of what to read) are not likely to stop questions of *standards* being raised – and answered. All collections might be equal, but we can be assured that some would be more equal than others. One observes, as well, that (as in linguistics) anti-prescriptive injunctions here are, themselves, prescriptive. Are we to welcome replacement of a tyranny of the centre by a tyranny of the previously 'marginalized'?

One useful outcome, perhaps, of the current *Angst* is a new attention paid to 'canonicity' itself – that is, to the processes by which canons are created and maintained. While canons may always be with us, we might begin to admit that unswerving and dogmatic allegiances may have stifling effects. It might be salutary to consider, now and again, what exactly would be lost if we were to replace Charles Dickens by Stephen King. A recent straightforward suggestion was that we would simply lose interesting things to talk about – but, I suppose, this assumption is, itself, a product of a particular training and tradition. Luckily, the issue of cultural and literary yardsticks need not be taken up here. Standards and canons are likely to remain (and remain useful) and literature will sort itself out, as it has always done. However, it is heartening to think that, in future, the application forms for entry to the club might be more widely distributed.

LANGUAGE PLANNING

As we have seen throughout this chapter, prescriptivist interventions have usually been built on unscientific bases. We have also noted, however, the gradual emergence of standard forms of language, a process which is clearly prescriptive but which is also usually seen as a necessary form of regulation. It can also be seen that such standardization is not the only type of regulatory activity that might be required. In some societies, choices among different *languages* may be necessary – for example, to select forms which will receive some official imprimatur in education and officialdom. Orthographies may have to be developed (or invented), lexicons may need to be modernized and so on. Given that these matters demand attention, it seems reasonable that linguists – despite their traditional reluctance to prescribe, despite their sense that language change is a constant and natural process, despite their view that broad usage is the ultimate criterion of 'correctness' – might bring their skills to bear and might, by their contributions, forestall other, less disinterested action.

Over the last twenty-five years, *language planning* has become a formal topic within applied sociolinguistics – in the sense of a research-based approach to some of the requirements noted above.[70] As a field having its own journals, books and conferences, it is of course constantly evolving. Various language-planning 'paradigms' and theories have been proposed, and the area has its own internal rivalries and controversies. Indeed, it has matured sufficiently to have attracted critical scrutiny and summary.[71]

The major features of language planing were presented in a model by Einar Haugen in 1966.[72] There are four aspects to the model: norm selection, norm codification, functional implementation and functional elaboration. Here, selection and implementation (often called 'status planning') are extralinguistic features, societal in nature; codification and elaboration ('corpus planning'), on the other hand, deal directly with language itself. The operation of language planning along these lines is, theoretically at least, quite straightforward. A linguistic problem arises, such that a choice has to be made between or among varieties. Following this, standardization is often needed to codify the chosen variety – to give it a written form and to regularize its grammar, orthography and lexicon. Implementation involves spreading the variety through official pronouncements, education, the media, etc. Various evaluation procedures are often employed at this stage to monitor the degree of acceptance of the chosen norm. Finally, elaboration means keeping the norm viable in a changing world; obvious necessities here include lexical modernization and expansion. Haugen's classification overlaps to some degree with Moshe Nahir's 'aspects' of language planning – purification, revival, reform, standardization and modernization. One can see that Haugen's model deals with the planning process, while Nahir emphasizes applications.

However, language planning is far from straightforward: for example, the purely linguistic aspects (codification and elaboration) of planning are very much less important than the social ones (selection and implementation). In this sense, language planners essentially engage in technical activities, *after* important decisions have been taken by others. It is, of course, an important task requiring a great deal of skill to attempt linguistic codification and elaboration, but language planners should not delude themselves into thinking that they are prime movers here. In fact, to some ears at least, language planning has an altogether too grandiose ring about it. Those involved *do* usually realize that their work does not occur in isolation, but it is not always so clear that they appreciate the radical difference of magnitude between their contribution and that of the *real* planners – politicians, administrators and rulers.

Also, it is clear that language planning, especially selection and implementation, is a heavily value-laden exercise. Certainly, any disinterested theorizing becomes compromised in practice, and language planning is usually concerned with applications in highly controversial settings – involving 'small' languages at risk, the establishment of a lingua franca, large degrees of linguistic diversity and so on. Planning here is inevitably coloured by ideological imperatives and what may appear as progress to some will be persecution to others. Language planning is, after all, prescriptivism.

If not from the beginning, then certainly at the point of application, language planning is subservient to the demands of non-academic interests, with social and political agendas. Planners are usually called in 'after the fact' to work out the technical details for the implementation of policies desired by those in power. It is not language planners themselves, nor the results of academic argument, which sway the real policy-makers. As in other areas of public life, 'experts' are called as needed, and their recommendations are either implemented or gather dust according to how well they support or justify desired positions. The language planner has been likened to the 'management scientist' who rarely makes real decisions, but is rather employed to organize and analyse data; the 'decision-maker' – manager or politician – may then balance this work with other information which is considered important. In the world of language planning, such 'other information' usually encompasses far more than language alone.

None of this means that professional linguistic assistance is trivial. On the contrary, as implied above, one would hope that relevant expertise *would* be solicited. But language planning is a species of social engineering and, as such, is commissioned and implemented by those in power. Of course, to be *successful*, language planning does not only depend upon the blessing of the powerful; it also requires acceptance from those whose linguistic habits are to be affected. Even the most dictatorial policies may result in social upheavals if they are repressive and/or unpopular enough, and many tensions in the world today can be seen as manifestations, often violent, of concern with language policy and practice (among other things, of course). More benign policies, on the other hand, may languish due to misreading of the social context. There is in some sense, then, a natural check on the implementation of 'top–down' planning that fails to engage the sympathies of its intended recipients – but, unfortunately, this may come too late to avoid distress or social disturbance (or, the response of policy-makers may be unfeeling, inadequate or otherwise deficient).

7

LANGUAGES, CULTURES AND EDUCATION

All of the preceding discussion has emphasized the social aspects of multilingualism and has interwoven the story of languages with the sociology and psychology of their speakers. Here I want to turn to a closer examination of the relationship between multilingualism and multiculturalism; this, in a sense, picks up a thread first exposed in the chapter on bilingualism, where an *integrative* motivation for second-language acquisition was seen to grow from the desire to know more about and perhaps to eventually take on the characteristics of another culture. Beyond an individual level at which multilingualism and multiculturalism might overlap, it is also clear that social recognition – perhaps at a policy level – of one involves the other, too. Here we must consider issues of pluralism and assimilation. Related to this is the linkage between language and groupness (ethnicity or nationalism) which is centrally the relationship between language maintenance and cultural continuity.

The school is an arena in which these matters have often been treated and discussed, so we must consider education here. But, in doing so, it will also be necessary to expand the horizon from multilingualism and multiculturalism to multidialectalism and multi-subculturalism (if such an ugly word is permitted). The school which deals with different languages and cultures is *also* a point of contact for dialects within one given language, and subgroups within one given culture. Of particular interest, perhaps, is the more or less conscious use of schools as agents of linguistic and cultural policy – sometimes, some would say, of repression.

Also in this chapter I must say something about the great internal division found in all cultures, that between men and women. Without necessarily going so far as to suggest that the sexes comprise two subcultures – although in some societies this seems a reasonable description – it *is* apparent that language use and language choice can vary according to the sex and situation of speakers.

This chapter, then, will touch briefly on some very broad groupings indeed: social class, ethnic/national and sexual. I may as well say at the outset that the treatment is likely to be flawed, part of the reason being that

175

brevity often reflects oversimplification. The groupings to be discussed here are not unitary or monolithic in themselves, nor do they exist in isolation from one another. That is why I discuss language, education and culture at this point in the book, trusting that readers will make the appropriate connections with what has gone before.

MULTICULTURALISM

The existence of many languages in the world implies the existence of many cultures. Beyond lists and typologies, we have seen that it is the *interrelation-ships* among languages and their speakers which create interest and tension. So it is with cultures: how do they connect, interpenetrate and conflict with one another? In fact, given that closeness between language and culture already discussed, one can appreciate that to talk about language contact and cultural contact is, very often, to discuss the same thing. A common example is found where – as is clear in at least some facets of the US English movement – debates about language reflect larger cultural anxieties, where language is, in fact, a convenient and visible peg upon which to hang broader social concerns. Official or *de facto* policies which recognize more than one language are sometimes driven by political necessity and do not always indicate deep philosophical convictions about the value of multi-lingualism *per se*. Equally, multicultural adaptations may arise through circumstance rather than from a wholehearted desire to celebrate diversity.

On the other hand, there *do* exist strong, disinterested sentiments supportive of cultural and linguistic pluralism; sometimes these are strengthened because of modern perceptions that some global 'mono-culture' threatens. And, of course, we could recall here the 'parochialism' discussed by de Saussure (and many others, in different ways) and the larger group-identity functions of specific languages and the specific cultures which surround them. Add to all this contemporary, liberal concerns for the importance of 'roots', and the philosophical marriage between such concerns and 'green' environmental and ecological stances, and the current interest in multiculturalism becomes clearer still. It is not the case, of course, that multicultural matters – either grudgingly acknowl-edged or wholeheartedly embraced – are purely modern. It *is* the case, however, that they are more conspicuous today. In the summer of 1992, for example, the Council of Europe endorsed a charter for regional/minority languages which clearly stresses 'interculturalism'. Considering that, at other levels, Europe is continuing towards continental federalism, one sees diversity valued within unity.

Large issues remain, of course. It cannot be assumed that legislating about cultural diversity means anything more than lip service, for example. Even if it does, there may still be strong unofficial pressures militating against cultural continuity. Furthermore (and relatedly), if there is a broader base nowadays for the protection and maintenance of cultures, particularly those seen to be at risk of assimilation, there are also continuing fears – not always of nativist or racist provenance – of social fragmentation, of the dilution of a common civic polity, of an undesirable strength afforded to ethnic or national groups, and so on.

Many of these matters can be seen most transparently in immigrant-receiving countries, particularly perhaps in those new-world states whose very origins are multi-ethnic and multicultural. Before continuing here I should remind the reader that we have *already* covered some multicultural ground in the previous discussion of official or state-recognized multi-lingualism. Recall the policy and practice in Switzerland, for example, or Belgium, or Singapore, or in those African and Asian countries where provision is made for some pluralistic accommodation, within state borders, of different groups and languages. Recall also the reference made to the almost fifty capsule portraits of language-contact dynamics worldwide, presented in my earlier *Language, Society and Identity*.[1] In all cases information can be deduced about *cultural* as well as linguistic recognition. My discussion here can be seen, therefore, as an amplification, particularly in North American contexts, of the tensions which obviously exist very widely. I would go further, however, and claim that, in the arguments surrounding cultural pluralism (and assimilation) in the 'new world', we see matters in very clear focus, for very obvious reasons.

The American scene[2]

The very terms *pluralism* and *assimilation* seem not, after all, to be such polar opposites as might first be thought. Pluralism is certainly concerned with the persistence of social diversity, and assimilation signifies some blending, some amalgamation of elements into a unified, perhaps emergent, culture. But in practice, as we shall see, the two interpenetrate in interesting ways; indeed, their relationship is not unlike that between *individualism* and *collectivities* in stratified societies (as discussed in chapter 5) – these two 'opposites', as well, are rarely seen in pure form at policy levels.

We have already noted that, in the United States around the turn of the century, important forces (from Teddy Roosevelt down) supported the assimilation of immigrants in that melting-pot popularized by Israel Zangwill. But this idea was often tempered with racist notions that some should be refused immersion into the pot altogether. In addition, not all members of all immigrant cultures were interested in such thoroughgoing reworking. Beyond this, it was evident that an *overall* amalgamation was not widely envisaged; only *some* identities were to be melted down and recast. That is, some thought that assimilative forces should be brought to bear upon various categories of newcomers, whose task it was to accommodate themselves to an existing, and largely unchanged, mainstream. That is why the term *anglo-conformity* seems more apt, in America, Canada and Australia, than some metaphor of a crucible in which *all* would be mixed, and from which would emerge, phoenix-like, a new culture.

An early architect of cultural pluralism in the United States was Horace Kallen, who, in 1915, wrote an article called 'Democracy versus the melting pot'. He argued that there was no overarching American nationality but, rather, a collection of distinct groups who would perpetuate themselves indefinitely. His ideal was a harmonious diversity, a stable cultural pluralism. Of course he made provision in his model for some assimilation through consensus, allowing for a *unum* in the national motto while emphasizing the *pluribus*. Part of the *unum*, incidentally, was English as the common language.[3]

Kallen's work notwithstanding, most academics both believed and hoped that the assimilation of immigrants would proceed in what was called 'straight-line' fashion. However, a roaring and insensitive melting-pot was rarely what they had in mind. Robert Park, for example – one of the foremost members of the 'Chicago School' of sociology and an important participant in the 'Americanization Studies' sponsored by the Carnegie Foundation – felt that assimilation was not something to be forced upon immigrants. They should, rather, be helped towards full participation in national life. Indeed, a natural progression was perceived, from competition and conflict to accommodation and incorporation (assimilation) – the famous 'race-relations cycle'. Recent interpretations strongly suggest that Park (and other academics) were liberals (some were romantics) caught in a dilemma.[4] He felt that civilization subverts attractive and egalitarian 'small' cultures with their 'redemptive' solidarity; and he was, in many ways, a champion of what he termed 'parochial culture' (one wonders if he had read de Saussure). At the same time, he did not wish to repudiate larger society, whose attractions and advantages were clear. Park and his colleagues were both progressive and pragmatic, but they also wished to incorporate earlier and 'smaller' group values in a broader society which was, itself, still developing. They struggled, as liberals often do, with the competing attractions of past and present, rural and urban, diversity and unity. These sorts of struggles continued up to and beyond the Second World War; during this time the problems of racial integration and democracy became more prominent, too, and were the subject of Gunnar Myrdal's classic *An American Dilemma* (1944).[5] Arguing that assimilation was the norm for ethnic groups, Myrdal essentially rejected the idea of preserving an Afro-American heritage, saw Blacks as an American 'issue' only, and thus aligned their integration (*mutatis mutandis*) with that of other minorities.

It was in the 1960s that the great wave of interest, academic and otherwise, arose in ethnic 'revival' or 'resurgence'.[6] Many commentators suggested that this was surprising, that the recrudescence of 'ethnic mobilization' was an assault on 'straight-line' assimilation which had somehow crept up unseen. One prominent apologist for diversity observed in 1970: 'One of the most extraordinary events of our time has been the resurgence of tribalism in a supposedly secularized and technocratic world ... ties of race, nationality and religion seem to have taken on new importance.'[7] In fact, however, it is debatable whether there was any ethnic resurgence; it might be more apt to describe an ethnic *persistence* which became more visible in times which were at once more 'monocultural' (or, at least, in which some global tendencies were seen to be increasingly threatening) and more sympathetic to the plight to small-group identities. One might recall here the earlier discussion of the ability of ethnicity to persist and to maintain itself in the force of radically changing conditions (both within and without the group).

It is certainly true that the 'resurgence' of pluralist demands was not solely an American phenomenon, nor one restricted to 'receiving' societies. Nor has it disappeared since the 1960s; on the contrary, it has grown stronger. We see opportunities for reasserting smothered nationalisms and ethnicities being grasped in eastern Europe and the former Soviet Union; we observe unprecedented moves on behalf of western European linguistic minorities at the same time as continental federalism is on the march; we note the constitutional crises in Canada, most pointedly between the French- and English-speaking communities, but also involving demands for increased autonomy among aboriginal groups.

Twenty years after the comment cited above was made, we thus see it reiterated; the 'extraordinary' events in America are now global. Benjamin Barber notes: 'a retribalization of large swaths of humankind ... a threatened Lebanonization of national states ... a Jihad in the name of a hundred narrowly conceived faiths'.[8] Yet, at the same time, he observes: 'economic and ecological forces that demand integration and uniformity and that mesmerize the world with fast music, fast computers, and fast food – with MTV, Macintosh and McDonalds's – one McWorld'.[9] And, looking at the former Yugoslavia and the former Soviet republics, Barber sees an irony: the nationalism that once unified now divides. 'The planet is falling precipitantly apart *and* coming reluctantly together at the very same moment. These two tendencies are sometimes visible in the same countries at the same instant.' In fact, neither the 'powerful irony' of nationalism nor the joint operation of separation and cohesion are very surprising. They reflect tensions already discussed (think, again, of Saussure's *parochialism* and *intercourse*, or Ferdinand Tönnies's classic distinction between *Gemeinschaft* and *Gesellschaft*).

Returning to the American scene, one observes that the ethnic 'revival' was, predictably, welcomed by many. Some, indeed, celebrated pluralism and gleefully trampled on the image of the melting-pot:

> [The new ethnicity] stands for a true, real, multicultural cosmopol-
> itanism.... Struggling to be born is a creature of multicultural beauty,
> dazzling, free, a higher and richer form of life. It was fashioned in the
> painful darkness of the melting pot and now, at the appointed time,
> it awakens.[10]

Indeed, in the well-known *Beyond the Melting Pot* (1963) of Nathan Glazer
and Daniel Moynihan, it was alleged that, awful as it was, the melting-pot
had not worked – an opinion much cited by pluralists.[11] In fact, they did *not*
mean that assimilation had not occurred in America; they *did* mean that,
although some ethnic markers had succumbed (communicative language
being the most obvious), other group manifestations had remained. The
way was theoretically open, then, to a discussion of marker retention and
loss, which culminated in some sense with Herbert Gans's work on *symbolic*
ethnicity (see chapter 5).[12] Gans has recently returned to his theme,
reminding us that, while theorists of the 'new ethnicity' were right to
criticize the older 'straight-line' approach, and to suggest that people in
America essentially 'construct their own ethnicity'[13] – others had earlier
pointed out, too, that the 'distinctive' cultures of American ethnic groups
were *not* those of the original homeland, but were largely 'creations
growing out of their experiences on American soil'[14] – they neglected the
other pole of the argument: 'people also construct their own acculturation
and assimilation'.[15] All of this occurs in an American society which
obviously had (and has) many attractions, which drew people from all over
the world, which seemed to offer rewards unavailable at home, which would
obviously exact some accommodations. In a word, people felt that the
material and psychological cost of dislocating themselves would be repaid
(with interest).

Grappling with the difficulties and attractions of cultural pluralism has
led many contemporary writers to come up with theories and models
which, in one way or another, reflect an accommodation between unity and
diversity. Terms like *pluralistic integration, participationist pluralism, modified
pluralism, liberal pluralism, multivariate assimilation* and *social accommodation*
(among others) are indicative here. Some are critical that any 'modified'
sort of pluralism is simply a stage on the road to complete assimilation, but
three points can be made here: first, any term which attempts to capture
some intermediate position between total assimilation and group segrega-
tion is probably an accurate reflection of what ordinary immigrants aim for;
second, private and symbolic manifestations of ethnicity, which can
contribute importantly to a sustained pluralism, can remain in place for a
long time – as long, in fact, as groups and individuals want them to; third,
even *if* seamless assimilation *is* the ultimate destiny, it is difficult to see how,
short of draconian measures unlikely to be acceptable in democratic
societies, it might be avoided for significant segments of the population.

Beyond this, cultural and ethnic change is probably not best seen as some blind or insensitive repudiation of the past, of one's social roots. Stasis is hardly the historical norm, and alterations in ethnic practices and markers – particularly for immigrants, but also for indigenous minorities and, indeed, for everyone – are likely. Force in these matters is, of course, unconscionable, but the record in the more tolerant societies where pressures are largely of an unofficial nature shows that it is not, in any event, required; many writers have commented that the process of change caused by social contact is often welcomed and sometimes sponsored by ethnic groups themselves.

In the process of finding some intermediate position, immigrant and other minorities make adaptations in non-random ways. Thus, private markers of groupness are likely to outlast public, visible manifestations and, as noted, groups may reach a position where only ethnicity of a 'symbolic' kind is evident. However, precisely *because* of its nature, this 'marking', this intangible sense of groupness, can endure. I do not believe it is sensible to dismiss this symbolic quantity on the grounds that it is merely some ethnic 'residue', although I agree, of course, that many most directly concerned are unhappy with what they often see as a cultural retreat to psychological distinctiveness only. However – given that loss of more public, visible markers (including language, in its ordinary communicative sense) seems inevitable for many groups – perhaps this form of identity continuity should be more thoughtfully considered. As a psychologist myself, I think it is better to ask questions like 'What is it that sustains a continuing sense of groupness, once objective markers – dress, customs, religion, language and so on – have disappeared?' than to accept the view that once these boundary-stones have gone, everything has gone.

Canada

Multiculturalism in other contexts – Britain, Australia, Canada and elsewhere – is affected by the same issues and pressures just noted for the American case. However, some further discussion is warranted, particularly of the Canadian context, where, in addition to multicultural accommodation for a wide range of ethnic groups, there exist *two* 'mainstream' populations.

Whatever its earliest origins, with its two 'charter' groups, its two 'founding peoples', Canada is now seen as a multicultural society in which the presence of the 'others', the 'allophones' (as, collectively, those of non-francophone, non-anglophone provenance are called), is just as central as that of the two official-language groups. Simple population profiles support this. At the turn of the century, the British constituted 57 per cent of the population, the French were 31 per cent and the others 12 per cent. Over the years the proportion of both British and French has decreased (the former dramatically and the latter slightly), while that of the 'others' has grown. Thus, the figures in 1940 were 50 per cent British, 30 per cent French and 20 per cent 'other' and, by the 1981 census, these had become 40 per cent, 27 per cent and 27 per cent, respectively (the remaining 6 per cent report themselves to be of more than one ethnic origin; of these, almost three-quarters had non-British, non-French origins). The 'non-charter' population has thus reached the same level as that of the French and, outside the province of Quebec, greatly outnumbers them.

The demographic situation was one of French–'other' equality, therefore, when the Canadian policy of multiculturalism was announced by the government in October 1971. Coming as a response to the report of the Royal Commission on Bilingualism and Biculturalism, the new policy had four main aims: (i) to assist all cultural groups in their efforts to develop and to contribute to society as a whole; (ii) to help these groups overcome any cultural barriers to mainstream participation; (iii) to promote 'creative encounters' among groups; (iv) to assist immigrants to learn at least one of the two official languages of Canada. It is important to note (with special regard to the fourth provision) that the multiculturalism initiative was to be embedded within a bilingual framework; while all cultures might now expect some increased government support, only the two 'charter' languages were to be emphasized – meaning that the others would not be. Thus, one view from the very outset was that an enduring difference between the status of 'other' ethnic groups and that of the French and British was to be enshrined.

Jean Burnet commented on the multiculturalism policy, seeing it:

> as encouraging those members of ethnic groups who want to do so to maintain a proud sense of the contribution of their groups to Canadian society. Interpreted in this way, it becomes something very North American: voluntary marginal differentiation among peoples who are equal participants in the society.[16]

She went on to note that if the policy was construed as some wholesale maintenance of 'foreign' cultures in Canada, then it would not endure – thus touching upon a theme, a disparity of perspective, which has caused confusion and difficulty in this country and in other immigrant-receiving states.

The multiculturalism policy has attracted criticism from its inception. At a theoretical level, the late John Porter observed that such a policy might prove a regressive force, might promote and sustain an ethnic stratification which is historically naive and which, by emphasizing *group* interests, could act against the advancement of *individuals*; to use his own phrase, multiculturalism could support a continuing 'vertical mosaic' of social status and power.[17]

A further criticism has been that the whole multicultural thrust has been politically opportunistic, both in a larger sense of attempting some national reconciliation between the two 'founding' groups and the 'others', and in the more specific desire to co-opt 'ethnic' voters. Indeed, some have seen a possibility that the government, with the assistance of well-ensconced and secure 'spokemen' might do a real disservice to cultural groups by visibly and vociferously promoting various cultural manifestations while side-stepping (or giving only lip-service to) real problems of an economic, social and political nature.

Another problem stems from the intention to support multiculturalism within a continuing official French–English bilingualism. A Ukrainian-Canadian academic, Manoly Lupul, noted in this regard the great difficulty in the reconciliation of charter dualism with ethnocultural pluralism. He described the federal policy as one of 'political pragmatism' which:

> pleased no one.... The failure to provide multiculturalism with a linguistic base especially displeased the Ukrainians; the loosening of the ties between language and culture angered the francophones who disliked any suggestion that the status of their culture was on a par with that of other ethnic groups.[18]

Much criticism of multiculturalism has indeed come from the francophone community. Guy Rocher, for example, pointed out that multiculturalism might undermine official bilingualism, might be incompatible with national unity, and could generally prove a regressive step for the French who have their own long-standing concerns with dominance and equality. The fear, above all, is that the francophones might be reduced to the status of the 'others'. It could logically be argued that a multiculturalism policy has a similar effect on the anglophone community, but this latter group is not in the same precarious position as the French; indeed, a cynical view is that the greater support for multiculturalism from the English sector (see below) exists because it has been seen as a defusing of the French 'problem' in Canada. There is a dilemma here for francophones: a rejection of multiculturalism on the grounds just noted may have some substance but, equally, a non-interventionist policy on the part of the government would be a tacit acknowledgement of ethnic 'melting' which would ultimately enlarge the anglophone proportions of the country; linguistic 'melting' proceeds apace, in any event.[19]

Concerns about assimilation bring us back to larger political and social matters. Many, both within and without 'ethnic' communities, have questioned a policy which might be seen – especially given what is sometimes a regrettable emphasis on folk-dance, costume, cuisine, music, 'brotherhood rhetoric' and other such manifestations, many of them trivial or trivializing – as supporting some unnatural and non-developing maintenance of cultures. Also, there is a general public unwillingness to see government funds used for cultural maintenance, the risk of favouring (or appearing to favour) some groups over others, and the general difficulties attendant upon the involvement of officialdom in internal ethnic politics. Canadian multiculturalism is, in considerable measure, a product of political ideology and it might be argued that, because of this, and because of its intrinsic difficulties, it is unlikely to succeed. Raymond Breton, a prominent researcher on ethnic and cultural matters, has summarized:

> Those who saw the policy as an attempt to maintain ethnic cultures argued that this was a futile exercise, since the structural conditions for the preservation of ethnocultures – such as parallel institutional systems – did not exist in Canada. They could perhaps exist in relatively isolated rural settings, but it was unrealistic to expect to establish them in cities.[20]

It is, finally, instructive to note here that, despite all the rhetoric about the Canadian 'mosaic' (as opposed to the American 'melting-pot'), most commentators have agreed that, in both contexts, anglo-conformity has been the prevailing force. Indeed, making the obvious exception of Quebec (and, even there, the force of English has had a great deal of historical strength in institutional life), even casual observation supports this.

With all this as brief background to multiculturalism in Canada, we can turn now to more recent developments which demonstrate the ongoing tensions associated with the policy. Official pronouncements, for example, continue to be noteworthy. James Fleming, then the Minister of State for Multiculturalism, said in 1982 that 'multiculturalism in Canada isn't a weakness, it's a strength. It forces people to be tolerant of differences and eccentricity.'[21] *Forcing* people to be tolerant has an odd ring to it, and the minister may not have found the *mot juste* in 'eccentricity'. At the first federal–provincial conference on multiculturalism, the new minister, Jack Murta, made three points of interest: (i) most Canadians oppose the 'melting-pot' notion; (ii) multiculturalism is not in opposition to official bilingualism; (iii) the Progressive Conservative party (his own) had done more for multiculturalism than had the Liberals.[22] In fact, many *do* consider multiculturalism and bilingualism to be uneasy companions, the whole issue *is* very politicized (and, we can now note, party politicized as well), and popular opposition to a more blatantly assimilationist stance is not proven.

Murta's remarks became the subject of a 1985 editorial in the *Globe and Mail* (Toronto). It suggested that many 'ethnics' born in Canada were not very interested in their cultures of origin: 'They do not derive their identity from their immigrant forebears, but from their own experience in the northern half of North America' (a view I have already noted).[23] Murta had said that while the Liberal policy had been one of 'celebrating difference', the Conservatives held that all were Canadians first; he also felt, however, that Canada would never be a melting-pot. The *Globe and Mail* piece found some possible contradiction here, and went on to ask if the multi-culturalism policy helped new arrivals or kept them 'in their place'. Although the overall tenor of the editorial was favourable to what might be termed the *ideals* of multiculturalism, it also stated that:

> multiculturalism is a highly ambiguous concept. At one level, it affirms the legitimacy of all the world's cultures.... At another, it encourages immigrants and their descendants to perpetuate original values and customs [not all of which, the implication is, are positive]. It is often said that only by nourishing their differences can immigrants hope for equality within Canada, a thesis hardly confirmed by experience.[24]

It is always important to know about grassroots support (or the lack of it) for particular policies. In the area of multiculturalism, the optimism expressed by Murta and others is not strongly underpinned: for example, a well-conducted poll of about 1,400 Canadians in 1989 found that 58 per cent thought immigrants should integrate with 'Canadian culture' and only 38 per cent supported government efforts to promote particular heritages.[25] The greatest degree of support for multiculturalism came, unsurprisingly, from visible-minority individuals (still only 53 per cent, however). Among the general population, attitudes were most favourable in Ontario (43 per cent); in the west they averaged about 39 per cent and in Quebec favourable views of multiculturalism comprised some 32 per cent.

Despite the obvious importance of ethnic issues in Canada, there has been little academic investigation of direct relevance, and no major attitude studies pertaining to multiculturalism were undertaken before the mid-1970s. In a 1976 survey of non-official languages in Canada, most respondents were found to be in favour of multiculturalism, but only about 20 per cent actually *knew* much about the policy (ten minority groups in five cities were sampled).[26] Support for multiculturalism, in this and other surveys, tends to be of a passive nature and would not necessarily extend to endorsement of *active* governmental involvement in cultural promotion. There is, then, a general tolerance but little more: 'The majority of Canadians tend to support multiculturalism as an ideal, so long as it does not affect their own lives, the sociocultural institutions in which they participate, or their pocketbooks.'[27] In other words, the multicultural *symbol* is what appeals, not a reality which might actually alter things. Even this symbolic quality has less force in francophone quarters than in anglophone ones.

A study that a student and I conducted in 1987 assessed the views of language, multicultural and identity matters of 400 respondents (university staff and students, and townspeople) in Nova Scotia.[28] A slight majority, overall, were supportive of the notion of multiculturalism, but further probing revealed that few had any idea of the policy's actual substance or intentions. It is surely noteworthy that a policy so widely endorsed by government should have been broadcast so ineffectively. The study also found that when respondents were asked to explain their stance on multiculturalism, those in favour tended to support their position with generalities – multiculturalism was endorsed as 'enriching' and as promoting equality, diversity was viewed as a good thing *per se*, and so on; those opposed, however, formulated more specific answers. Most of these touched upon criticisms already noted: crass political motivations, divisiveness, idealism without reality, difficulties inherent in government involvement with culture, etc.

Across a range of recent studies:

> the research results on popular attitudes do not indicate a strong and widespread demand for state intervention in the ethnocultural field, except for the symbolic affirmation of Canada as a multicultural rather than bicultural society. The demand for a federal policy of multiculturalism seems to have come primarily from ethnic organizational elites and their supporters, from government agencies and their officers, and from political authorities.[29]

A broader observation is that the Canadian population has a certain (unspecified, perhaps unspecifiable) level of tolerance for diversity, a certain fund of passive goodwill, a certain willingness to see the 'others' shape their lives as desired. It does not appear to have any great sympathy for real changes in social institutions, for direct (especially financial) official involvement in ethnocultural affairs, for any substantial alteration to an anglo-conformity pattern. In these respects it is not unlike other socially heterogeneous societies. One could, of course, dismiss public opinion here as uninformed and narrowly self-concerned. The question of whether it would be wise or expedient to do so, and the even more interesting question of the degree of acuity revealed in public surveys might suggest, however, that such a blanket dismissal would be inappropriate.

A Canadian Multiculturalism Act was passed in July 1988 and it appears as if a greater awareness of linguistic matters distinguishes it from previous post-1971 policy; there is now a call for the maintenance of the 'other' languages. However, it immediately goes on to advocate 'strengthening the status and use of the official languages' and promoting multiculturalism 'in harmony with the national commitment to the official languages'. It remains to be seen, then, what precisely the Act may signify for the so-called 'heritage' languages of Canada.[30]

Of course, both multiculturalism and bilingualism, as official policies, have come under renewed scrutiny in the last few years, as Canada wrestles with constitutional problems which have, at their heart, an attempted reconciliation of the francophones of Quebec with what the press has now taken to referring as the ROC (Rest of Canada). The most recent failure came at the end of October 1992, when a national referendum on unity was held. Overall, voters rejected a package of constitutional proposals, which included recognition of Quebec as a 'distinct' society (see chapter 5). While Quebec nationalists and separatists had become increasingly concerned to point out to the rest of Canada that their province was a nation, and that constitutional arrangements must acknowledge this, the message was obviously unacceptable to many outside the province. Given this tension, it is clear that federal policies of multiculturalism are now more tenuous than before. As for official bilingualism, it remains a peripheral phenomenon for most Canadians, and seen as irrelevant, intrusive and irritating for many. The *Québécois* themselves have increasingly rejected it in favour of a desired French unilingualism. At the broadest level, then, federal bilingualism has failed to bring together the 'two solitudes' of the classic Canadian partnership. In general, recent events in Canada have demonstrated – once again – the centrality of issues of language and culture in political life. They remind us of what John Stuart Mill said in 1861 about the obstacles to internal cohesion and effective government which are created when a state contains more than one nationality. Many in Quebec would no doubt endorse his view that it is 'a necessary condition of free institutions that the boundaries of governments should coincide in the main with those of nationalities'.[31]

Mill also noted, however, that if arrangements cannot be found, then there might be a need to break existing connections, to separate the parties. Afterwards, 'there may be cases in which the provinces, after separation, might usefully remain united by a federal tie'.[32] Such post-separation federation may yet prove applicable in some reworked Canada; it certainly seems to accord with the idea of 'sovereignty-association', which was first suggested by Quebec nationalists more than a decade ago. Any reworking, however – as the preceding discussion has indicated – must now embrace a broader 'multiculturalism' than that envisaged in previous constitutional arrangements. That is, it will have to go beyond the French and English 'founding groups' and embrace the native peoples and the allophones. It is the nature of this embrace, the way in which diversity can be accommodated within a federal system, that is crucial. And, finally, it is in the inevitable tensions here that we can see links between the Canadian experience and situations elsewhere – in the emerging Europe, for example (as mentioned above), but also in *all* pluralistic societies.

MULTICULTURALISM IN EDUCATION

The impulse behind multicultural education is very largely a positive one. In a postmodern and politically correct environment it has, in many eyes, a motherhood quality; also, however, one need not be a modern ideologue (of any stripe) to see in such education a progressive and liberalizing force.

Indeed, one would be hard pressed to deny (in theory, at least) the utility and justice of an educational thrust which aims to alert children to the varied world around them – which may exist, in microcosm, in their own classroom – to inculcate cross-cultural respect, and to form a bulwark against racism and intolerance. The problems arise from definition and interpretation, on the one hand, and from implementation, on the other. As I have already discussed some theoretical issues attaching to multi-culturalism and, perforce, to its educational arm, I can turn now to more practical matters.

What should a multicultural programme look like at school? There are many possibilities, of course, and probably no two programmes could be identical, if only for the reason that local ethnic realities (which should, at least to some extent, be reflected in such programmes) alter with context. However, there are two broad approaches. One, now almost entirely rejected at an intellectual level but still much in evidence, is a sort of ethnic show-and-tell in which cultural manifestations are paraded in a self-conscious and often trivial fashion. While such elements do have a place in a more thoughtful programme, little can be expected if they are presented essentially as varieties of the exotic. Children (and teachers) may look forward to these experiences, but largely as light relief from the *real* work of the school, taking their place with unexpected but welcome school assemblies and old-style lessons in religion and citizenship.

The second approach involves a broader and less superficial stance on multiculturalism. Programmes here are often heavy with objectives and curricula and, while well-meaning, may be either leaden and insensitive or woolly and arbitrary. One recent writer discusses a multicultural curriculum focusing upon the 'subjective content of the teachers' and students' own consciousness'.[33] He continues: 'As an action system, the classroom of teacher and students would examine the historical process which creates each individual. The shared solidarity, when related to common experi-ence, would plant the seeds of collective change.'[34]

These insubstantial vapourings surprisingly manage to suggest two important points. The first is the implication that schools possess power for social change which history shows to be rare. Schools acting in relative isolation from other social currents – and the imparting of multicultural awareness and its ramifications *are*, unfortunately, often largely seen as educational matters which can proceed independently – have a very limited potency. The realization of this is important for all those who wish schools to act as agents of change. Recent calls for schools to 'empower' minority students are thus likely to prove naive. Schools can, through their example and practice, legitimize cultural varieties and markers (including language) – at least in the eyes of their possessors – but educational legitimation is not empowerment. It may lead to it, or contribute to it but, again, not when schools are asked to shoulder the load almost unassisted.[35]

The other point to be extracted from the quotation is that the vagueness of the language may well reflect the disembodied nature of the multicultural programme under consideration. There may be few who would deny the psychological and social benefits potentially associated with a heightened cultural awareness, but in order for this latter quality to be realized a minimum requirement, a necessary condition, is that the multicultural thrust be firmly embedded within an appropriate, valued and systematic context.

This context already exists in the subject-based curriculum, although there are, of course, many difficulties with it; for example, the breaking down of artificial barriers erected among topics, for convenience, would surely magnify the impact of any multicultural programme. Thoroughgoing social studies, history, geography and so on should be strongly interconnected and a strong multicultural strand might then run through them. Can we conceive, in fact, of a meaningful history (for example) which is not multicultural? I cannot go into further detail here, but this is clearly the foundation for a solid and insightful programme. I have suggested elsewhere, simply, that '*all education worthy of the name is multicultural*'.[36] A fully integrated multicultural thrust of this kind would go some way towards alleviating the concerns of minority-group members themselves, incidentally. Many are rightly suspicious of the agendas here, both overt and hidden. The West Indian writer, Maureen Stone, for example, wants schools to stress 'core' knowledge and rejects what are seen as the vague, 'affective' goals of much modern multicultural education: 'I want to suggest that MRE [multiracial education – the term in favour in Britain] is conceptually unsound ... while at the same time creating for teachers, both radical and liberal, the illusion that they are doing something special for a particularly disadvantaged group.'[37] Another Black parent and educator made a related comment: 'Black parents don't want black studies or multicultural education for their children – that is for white children; black pupils need to be good at science, history, geography – at what society thinks of as things of worth.'[38]

It will be apparent that I believe that Black children – all children – can have *both* the strengths of a multicultural curriculum *and* those of a necessary 'core-knowledge' one. The not ignoble aim (apologies to George Orwell: see chapter 4) of promoting multicultural awareness and tolerance must, however, become an inextricable part of the whole educational enterprise. If it does not, it will fall between stools. It will be viewed as a quaint, diverting but largely insubstantial adjunct to the real business of schools by mainstream pupils and the 'others', plus evidence of a lack of meaningful concern in the eyes of that latter group, whose presence reminds us of what a fully-formed education should be.

We see, then, that the *general* tendencies associated with dealing with diversity in unity are found in more particular form in the classroom. I want to conclude here by mentioning one important specific: the relationship between cultural respect – which should, presumably, be a central feature and product of multicultural education – and value judgement. While a thoroughgoing relativist might claim that all cultures and all value systems have validity (perhaps equal validity), this stance is often difficult to maintain in practice (see chapter 4). Multicultural education may thus find itself in dangerous waters.

LANGUAGE AT SCHOOL

School is traditionally a strong arm of culture, and central to its aims has always been a strong emphasis upon language. On the one hand, school has attempted to refine and develop communicative skills with the language or languages of its constituency; on the other, it has been the centre for foreign-language acquisition. In both (but especially in the first) there has often existed a strong prescriptivist tendency which, given that schools reflect the larger society, is hardly surprising. In 1800, Thomas Morton (1764–1838) wrote a play entitled *Speed the Plough*, in which appeared the famous Mrs Grundy, whose name is now synonymous with narrow linguistic purism and 'morality'. 'What will Mrs Grundy Say? What will Mrs Grundy think?' are apprehensions with which those readers who remember their grammar classes will no doubt be familiar. They may be less familiar with Miss Fidditch, one of those schoolteachers who would rather 'parse than eat'.[39] In Martin Joos's book on style (discussed in chapter 3), Miss Fidditch plays a central role, and sees herself as the prophet of the great god, Webster. Both Mrs Grundy and Miss Fidditch endorse the sort of rigid grammatical principles of a Lindley Murray (for example), whose Rule 16 – 'two negatives destroy one another, or are equivalent to an affirmative' – we came across in the last chapter. Grundy and Fidditch, perhaps mother and daughter, have had many relatives in the schools and, although those still there are fewer now, and longer in the tooth, their influence continues.

In chapter 4, I presented some evidence of the linguistic validity of all languages and dialects. While we may retain the non-pejorative term, *non-standard language*, we must entirely reject *substandard*. Further, we know that the distinction between standard and non-standard varieties rests upon social pillars alone. We also know, however, that the continuing power of social stereotypes, preferences and prejudices effectively translates *different* language into *deficient* language. Given the relationship between school and the society in which it exists, it is clear that this translation is made in the classroom as well as in the street.

Thus, certain groups of children whose language is not of the standard variety typically taught and encouraged at school – lower-class children and ethnic minority-group members in particular – have been seen as linguistically disadvantaged and in need of remedial or compensatory attention.[40] The aim here has often been to *replace* their allegedly flawed maternal variety with a 'correct' form, although there is perhaps an increasing tendency to opt for a policy of repertoire *expansion* – that is, to *add* standard fluency to the mother tongue. This is, from a linguistic point of view, a more enlightened approach, but putting it into effect is a delicate exercise which is rarely handled well, even when teachers are informed and sympathetic. Replacement is still the policy in many parts of the world, however, and even where more 'progressive' views obtain, it regularly reappears whenever 'declining standards' are an issue.[41]

At one time, the problems of so-called 'linguistically disadvantaged' children were seen to derive from inherent or genetic deficiency. A slightly more enlightened view was, subsequently, that deficits derived from poor or inadequate social environments (particularly within the family) and – as we have seen – a third perspective is that *different* environments produce *different* attitudes and behaviour. It would seem that this third perspective, which is the correct one on the basis of the best available evidence, has not percolated down to the educational community to the extent one would wish.

A recent study of teachers in Nova Scotia provides a good example here.[42] Among a group of about one hundred primary and secondary teachers, whose pupils included Black and French Acadian children, virtually no endorsement of the inherent-deficiency argument was found. Rather, teachers stressed the home-background aspects of linguistic disadvantage; unfortunately a language-deficit perspective was common, rather than one which accepted, simply, that families and speech communities in which non-standard language is the norm will naturally produce children whose speech reflects this. Here are some typical teacher comments:

> [Disadvantaged children have] lack of experiences, poor language development . . . usually disorganized.

> [Children often cannot] articulate their thoughts and feelings in such a way that they satisfy both themselves and their audience. Both receptive and expressive skills seem to have low levels of value and priority when it comes to developing accuracy and fluency. Blacks have a slang language all their own. They will not use proper English when opportunity arises.

In general about half in this group of teachers felt that certain groups of children had more speech and language problems than did others – singled out here were, unsurprisingly, Black and Acadian youngsters. The problems mentioned included poor vocabulary and grammar, lack of articulation of ideas, mispronunciation, regional dialects and accents, slang and foul language. Evidence from other studies suggests that the views of these Canadian teachers are not unique to them: minority-group children whose language is non-standard are generally seen to be suffering from deprived social environments which hamstring their linguistic and cognitive capabilities. In the context of this book, this can be seen as a rejection of normally-occurring multilingual, or multidialectal, competence. In a well-meaning but ill-informed way, teachers continue to categorize children unfairly, exacerbating sociolinguistic difficulties which, unfortunately, may dog these children throughout their life. I have already implied that repertoire *expansion* may be necessary for non-standard speakers, and that this is a delicate business. Having treated the matter in detail elsewhere, I note here only that it *can* be accomplished. The process is not likely to be assisted, however, where attitudes of the sort just discussed remain prevalent.

Foreign languages at school

Schools have always implicitly recognized that competence in other languages is a mark of education. Beyond this, it is apparent that it is *necessary* to expand one's language capabilities in many contexts, and the classroom is an obvious setting in which this can take place. In situations of necessity it is also clear that the efforts of the school are driven and reinforced by extra-educational forces. Conversely, where necessity is not perceived, schools must act more in isolation. These simple facts account for the great disparities observed in the success of language teaching and learning; one need not be a Solomon to see that there are more difficulties with school German in Iowa than in Nijmegen. In the Iowas of the world – and there are many of them, especially in English-language communities – the difficulty of creating an instrumental need for foreign languages means that language attitudes may become more important. To put it another way, if there is no pressing *need* for German, and if school learning thus risks becoming an artificial exercise – a perception reinforced, curiously enough, by schools' continuing attempts to present language classes as somehow different from others, as means to ends – then motivation and interest cannot be taken for granted; they need to be stimulated.

Here, of course, schools have often done a poor job (see Chapter 3). Traditional classes, with their emphasis upon grammar and writing skills, have made the learning of languages a passive, receptive matter for students; the activity lies in the teaching. This is hardly likely to induce in pupils any sense that learning German is a different sort of exercise from learning trigonometry or ancient history. It does nothing to reduce the artificiality of a classroom in which teachers and pupils routinely but rather unnaturally use a language which is neither their maternal variety, nor one which can be put to more or less immediate use. It is, additionally, neither an extension of the way first languages are acquired – where communication is stressed, and where grammatical refinements come afterwards – nor a representation of normal, interactive conversation. Modern methods have, of course, attempted to remedy this. The chief development is to encourage a more 'natural' conversational interplay and there have been real strides made here. But, without going into the large literature on methods, which is peripheral to my purpose here anyway, it can be appreciated that school language learning will always either benefit from externally imposed necessity or suffer for the lack of it.

Bilingual education

In bilingual education, teaching *through* two languages is a permanent feature in the classroom.[43] Again, this can arise for non-instrumental reasons, as part of an educational philosophy; more commonly, though, bilingual education is driven by need. If, for example, the maternal language of pupils is a minority variety of limited national or international scope, then the desire to sustain and encourage that language while, at the same time, providing access to a 'bigger' form may suggest bilingual education. On purely pedagogical terms it may be considered vital to have, at least, early schooling through the medium of children's first language – especially where this is a minority variety, and relatively lacking in social status; not only may the primary educational foundations be more securely fixed, but also the pupil's linguistic identity and general sense of self-esteem may be supported.

Bilingual education has, of course, a long history.[44] I have already discussed the regard in which Greek was held by the Romans, and it is not surprising that this would be reflected in formal educational arrangements. Indeed, Greek was often introduced to Roman children – of the aristocratic class, of course – before formal Latin instruction. Cicero and Quintilian preferred Greek to Latin as the medium of schooling and children were often bilingual *before* arriving at school, since they were generally cared for by Greek servants and tutors. Formal instruction in both languages was largely modelled on the Greek curriculum. It was recognized, however, that an overemphasis on Greek might create problems. Both Quintilian and Cicero, for example, were concerned about children speaking Latin with Greek intonation. And the possibility of somehow overburdening a child's time and 'limited' cognitive capacity – a worry that has persisted (see Chapter 3) – was also recognized. Haaroff, in a study of classical education, cited the complaint of Paulinus:

> Quae doctrine duplex sicut est potioribus apta
> Ingeniis, gemenoque ornat splendore peritos,
> Sic sterilis nimium nostri, ut modo sentio, cordis

Exilem facile exhausit venam.[45]

'It's all very well for the clever ones
to be asked to learn two languages –
they get double glory. For the average
schoolboy like me, the need to maintain
both languages is trying and exhausting.'

Haaroff also reports the view (of Augustine and others) that Greek imposed for its own sake was 'barren' and 'unnatural', condemning the young to boredom and drudgery. As these concerns increased, as Latin expanded its literary scope and as competent Greek teachers became harder to find, Latin–Greek bilingual education declined; by the end of the fifth century it was virtually gone. Once the need for Greek vanished, so a knowledge of it became (and remained) important only for a scholarly élite. We see again, then, that necessity drives learning *through* foreign languages as much as it does the more basic acquisition and teaching *of* them.

However, the need for bilingual education has been repeatedly demonstrated throughout history. A contemporary survey showed that bilingual schooling in various formats and at various educational levels is a very widespread global phenomenon.[46] French and Arabic in the Maghreb, English/French and indigenous languages in sub-Saharan Africa, Welsh or Gaelic and English in Wales and Scotland, Greenlandic and Danish in Greenland, English and Maltese in Malta, English and Chinese/Tamil/ Malay in Singapore, Swahili and English in Tanzania – these are just a few examples.

In all examples of bilingual education, there are recurring questions. When should it be introduced, and for how long? What instructional weight should be given to each language? How best can it be integrated with a pre-existing and non-bilingual curriculum? Should it be available to all students or only to those of 'normal' intelligence or more? Should it be extended to a broad range of pupils, or restricted to those whose mother tongue is a 'minority' one? And so on.

One of the most interesting aspects of bilingual education – and most pertinent for present purposes – is its role as an agent of social change, as a bulwark of ethnolinguistic pluralism, as a force for sustained group identity seen to be at risk. That is, if we move beyond the immediate pedagogical utility of a bilingual education which at some point fades into a monolingual scholastic mainstream (and the timing of this is quite a contentious point in the literature), and if we consider a more permanent arrangement, then social and political factors may come to outweigh the more purely linguistic and educational ones. If we maintain bilingual education for minority-group children beyond the point at which fluency in the mainstream language has been reached, or if we see bilingual education also as an appropriate format for adding a second-language capacity to the maternal competence of majority-group pupils, what assumptions, desires and problems are involved?

A main assumption would seem to be that society at large will profit by having more bilingual members and that, therefore, the educational programmes for bringing this about will be welcomed. It remains, however, difficult in many settings to convince people that such a change to the *status quo* is either necessary or desirable, especially when one strong language holds undisputed sway in the society; if that language *also* has international clout, the difficulty increases. Allied to the general sense that bilingual competence is unnecessary are the more specific fears of social fragmentation and divisiveness. Sometimes these fears derive from the desire to protect the mainstream group; sometimes they are expressed out of sympathy for a minority population which, it is thought, might be better served by being brought into the main linguistic channel as soon as possible (even though, on the latter point, some academic evidence suggests that bilingual education could actually *expedite* social integration). It need hardly be said, I suppose, that sometimes expressions of sympathy for minorities are cloaks for more nativist sentiments.

We find the American president observing, in 1981, that:

> It's absolutely wrong and against the American concept to have a bilingual program that is now openly, admittedly dedicated to preserving their native language and never getting them adequate in English so that they can go out into the job market and participate.[47]

We can also find such sentiments among (originally) non-mainstream members, too. Norman Podhoretz, as noted in the last chapter, found his 'humiliating' lack of English a spur towards social mobility and success.[48] We know, from millions of cases, that the old-style 'submersion' which Podhoretz endorses works. We also strongly suspect, however, that the psychological costs may have been high and, more to the point, unnecessary; perhaps even a limited bilingual provision at school would have helped all those early immigrants to America, both in their linguistic progress and in their psychological identity. But this, of course, is not the point. President Reagan, Norman Podhoretz and the many others like them, have a vision (of America, in this case) of a linguistically efficient and socially united country where one language is seen to integrate, and where more than one is both largely unnecessary and potentially balkanizing. We return, then, to necessity (or, at least, to *perceived* necessity among those in power). The brutal fact is that most 'big' language speakers in most societies remain unconvinced of either the immediate need or the philosophical desirability of officially-supported cultural and linguistic programmes for their small-language neighbours.

Some among the minority also share this doubt and it is, in many instances, a minority within a minority who actively endorse the use of schools as instruments of social engineering. Given that *all* education can be seen as an arm of policy – as Kedourie put it bluntly, 'to bend the will of the young to the will of the nation'[49] – then the desires of activists here are unsurprising. At the same time, having an eye to social practicalities and power, they should ensure that school children are not made to suffer for their own wishes and principles (see the comments cited in chapter 1). I certainly do not mean to imply that only minority-group members must face these concerns, that majorities can remain educationally smug in their secure social positions. It would also be contrary to the spirit of this book to suggest that supporting linguistic diversity is unwarranted in itself. However, it should be pointed out that, though reliance upon school – often in virtual isolation – to effect change in these contexts is to be expected, it is rarely successful.

Many groups who see school programmes as saviours are those in which strong linguistic and cultural pressures are seen as threats to continued identity. These pressures are, if anything, more powerful now than before, as the global village becomes increasingly anglicized and westernized. A 'parochial' reaction (to use de Saussure's term) is thus predictable. Whether one looks at the capitalist world or the erstwhile communist one, at contemporary times or historical ones, at small societies or empires, at immigrant minorities or indigenous groups, one sees, increasingly, an inexorability and similarity of pressures which force change and throw populations into transitional states; these, naturally enough, have unpleasant consequences as well as perceived benefits. To deny this is to deny an historical sweep which, at one time or another, has affected *all* groups – even those now securely placed (but whose security is of course not likely to endure forever).

Immersion education

A final format of language at school which I should briefly mention here is that in which pupils with mother tongue A receive all their education – at least in the early years – through language B. This so-called 'immersion' method was developed in Quebec in the 1960s, where anglophone parents were dissatisfied with their children's accomplishments in French as taught by traditional methods at school. In a rare example of harmony among parents, educators and researchers, the immersion programme was initiated. It was designed to capitalize on young children's language-learning abilities, relative unselfconsciousness and attitudinal openness, to attempt to emphasize from the first the communicative purpose of language (and thus capture, as far as possible, something of the atmosphere of first-language acquisition), and to ensure that children's development in other areas was not retarded.[50]

Readers may ask how immersion differs from the historical practice of throwing foreign-language-speaking immigrants into the deep end of a mainstream-language classroom in their new country. This practice, usually referred to as *submersion*, is unlike immersion education in that no special provisions are usually made for the newcomers. More importantly, since the language of the school is the dominant community variety, the maternal language of these minority-group children is not reinforced; thus, submersion expedites linguistic assimilation. In immersion schooling, on the other hand, majority-group children (anglophones in Canada), whose language is dominant and under no threat, learn through French. The co-operative beginnings of immersion education are also relevant here, in that it has always been a voluntary programme in which the participants (or, at least, their parents) are usually highly motivated. These positive attitudes are typically found among the teachers, too. It is most important, then, to distinguish submersion in a mainstream language for minority-group pupils from immersion in a 'secondary' language for majority-group children. Many in the United States, for example, have looked at the Canadian immersion experience and, through ignorance or by design, have claimed that its success indicates that non-English-speaking children in America ought to be 'immersed' in English without delay, without benefit of any bilingual provision. It should be clear that this sort of linguistic baptism is a submergence and that its 'success' will probably mean a new monolingualism, not the bilingualism of immersion education.

Immersion certainly has been successful in Canada, where, it is estimated, some 300,000 children are or have been involved. Evaluations of the programmes suggest that it is an effective way to acquire a second language, that transfer of skills occurs from one language to the other, and that any lag in English-language development is only temporary (English language arts are usually not introduced for two or three years after first school entry). Refinements have included immersion for the middle or later school years, and immersion for children whose backgrounds are not the comfortable middle-class ones often associated with enthusiasm for immersion. None of this, I think, should come as a surprise, given the very positive social context in which immersion programmes operate.

While it has been claimed that early-immersion pupils have acquired, by the end of primary school, a comprehension of spoken and written French equal to that of their native French-speaking counterparts, their French–English bilingualism is *not* equivalent to that more 'naturally' acquired. One researcher observed that their competence should be viewed in terms of rather more 'specific measures of understanding, speaking, reading and writing'.[51] The French produced by immersion students has been variously described as 'somewhat artificial'[52] or 'Frenglish'[53] or 'fossilized interlanguage'.[54] In fact, arguments over whether or not immersion 'works', and over the quality of the French produced, have been very vigorous at times.[55] As with discussions of other educational innovations which are linked to broader social agendas, debate here has usually provided more heat than light.

At a broader social level, immersion education has not proved to be the catalyst uniting the two Canadian linguistic solitudes; its beneficiaries

> as they become more and more adult tend to shy away from the play-acting language of childhood in favour of the everyday language of the adult world. Such 'bilingual' uni-ethnic schools do not in themselves tend to promote societal bilingualism.[56]

A recent study suggested that some expected (or hoped for) behavioural differences between immersion students and those studying French in more traditional ways may be slight.[57] The former do little French reading and, like the latter, report instrumental rather than integrative reasons for learning French. Although more likely (unsurprisingly) to use more French in personal encounters, immersion pupils did no more than the others to seek out or initiate such encounters (even where opportunities exist, as in Montreal). Thus, the admitted superiority in basic competence which the immersion children possess may not be carried through to actual *use*; this, presumably, is a large part of what the whole exercise was thought to be about.

None the less, despite some of the grandiose claims often made for immersion education, despite the real difficulties with the French produced and the use made of it, the concept remains vital for two obvious reasons: first, it is a superior alternative, for language learning and cultural sensitivity, to anything else on a similar scale; second, its existence as a voluntary exercise grows out of a valuable commitment to the ethos of multilingualism. This is particularly noteworthy given recent political and social developments in Canada which have illustrated real difficulties with officially-promoted bilingualism (and multiculturalism). In some ways, perhaps, those parents who lobby for immersion programmes are the contemporary counterparts of that historical élite which always valued foreign-language learning. If so, this modern movement is much more broadly-based and open to new membership.

LANGUAGE AND SEX

We have seen how intimately language is associated with broad social groupings of nation, ethnicity and class; indeed, the whole thrust of this book is to illustrate languages in context. It would be remiss, therefore, not to include some brief mention of language variations with speaker sex.

The greatest variation, of course, would be found in a speech community in which men and women spoke different languages. This may seem unlikely, to say the least, but a famous instance was reported 300 years ago by Europeans in contact with the Carib Indians of the new world. How could this come about? The Indians themselves provided this explanation:

> When the Caribs came to occupy the islands these were inhabited by an Arawak tribe which they exterminated completely, with the exception of the women, whom they married in order to populate the country.... [Thus] there is some similarity between the speech of the continental Arawaks and that of the Carib women.[58]

A more considered analysis, however, indicated that:

> The men have a great many expressions peculiar to them, which the women understand but never pronounce themselves. On the other hand the women have words and phrases which the men never use, or they would be laughed to scorn. Thus it happens that in their conversations it often *seems* as if the women had another language than the men.[59] (my italics)

It would indeed be odd to find men and women unable to understand each other's language, but there are examples in which women customarily speak language A, and men language B, and where the two sexes are bilingual. One such is found among Amazonian Indians living along the Vaupés river.[60] The language of the longhouse is Tuyuka, which is used by all the men and between women and children. However, since men must marry outside their tribe, the first language of the wives is not Tuyuka; thus, a woman might be a native speaker of Desano and continue to use it with her husband – who answers her in Tuyuka.

More common is the Carib scenario, in which certain features of men's and women's speech differ. Typical here are variations in pronunciation or morphology. Among the Gros Ventre of Montana, for example, the women say *kyatsa* for 'bread', while the men's form is *jatsa*. In Yana, another North American variety, the words of men and women differ because the former typically add a suffix. The word for 'deer' is *ba* (for women) and *ba-na* (for men), and 'person' is *yaa* or *yaa-na*.[61]

Beyond this, there are many examples of vocabulary differences between the sexes, although these are never extensive. In the 1930s a classic study was undertaken of Koasati, a language of Louisiana, which revealed sex differences with verb forms.[62] To say 'you are building a fire', men used the term *osch* while women said *ost*; for 'I am saying,' the male variant was *kahal*, the female *kahas*; and so on. Vocabulary differences are seen even more clearly in Japanese, where women say *ohiya*, *onaka* and *taberu* for 'water', 'stomach' and 'eat' and men say *mizu*, *hara* and *kuu*.[63] Or consider Chiquito, a Bolivian language: here a woman says *ichibausi* to mean 'my brother' where a man would say *tsaruki*; 'my father' is *ishupu* for females, but *ijai* for males.[64] These variations say more, of course, about an elaborate system of kinship designation than about sex differences *per se*. After all, the relationship of a sister to her brother is not the same as that of brother to brother.

There are languages in which the sex of the *listener* determines the variant used, not that of the *speaker*. There are, further, languages in which the sex of *both* speaker and listener is influential. In Kūrux, a Dravidian language of India, a man speaking to either a man or a woman, and a woman speaking to a man, would say *bardan* (I come); a woman speaking to another woman, however, says *bar?en* (the symbol *?* indicates a glottal stop – as *better* becomes Cockney 'be'er'). Speaking to a man, either sex says *barday* (you come) but speaking to a woman, a man would say *bardi* and another woman would use the form *bardin*.[65]

Why do such differences exist?[66] In some cases, social and religious taboos can have linguistic consequences. In other cases, women's forms appear to be older than the men's; changes have occurred in men's speech which the women have yet to adopt (it is a common observation that women's linguistic patterns are more conservative than men's). Related to this and supporting the maintenance of distinctions is the view that these older, women's forms are *better*.

The sorts of variation we have looked at so far are of what one linguist has called the 'sex-exclusive' variety.[67] More recognizable to most readers of this book are 'sex-preferential' features – linguistic practices and markers which are more *common* to one sex than to the other. The most general observation is the one just noted: women's speech tends to be more conservative, more standard, more 'polite' than men's. In a much-quoted study, John Fischer found, among New England children aged between three and ten years, that girls were much more likely than boys to use *-ing* rather than *-in* for the ending of the present participle.[68] Although the degree of differentiation varies, this has proved a robust finding in other contexts. Research in Detroit demonstrated, unsurprisingly, that the use of multiple negation (as in phrases like *I don't want none*) is much more common among lower-class speakers than among upper-class ones. In addition, however, women use it much less frequently than men. In lower-middle-class men, for example, the study revealed that 32 per cent employed multiple negation;[69] for women in this group, the percentage was 1.4. Lower-working-class men used it a great deal (90 per cent), their female counterparts 59 per cent. Similar work has demonstrated that more men than women drop the *h*.[70]

Why should women's speech be more standard than men's? Most explanations centre upon women's allegedly greater status-consciousness.[71] Perhaps they are less socially secure than men and wish to gain status through the use of standard forms. Relatedly, they may be traditionally more likely – lacking obvious occupational and income markers – to use speech as a status indicator, to present a more favourable appearance.[72] They may, in their maternal role, be more conscious of the importance of their children's acquisition of prestigious speech variants and thus see part of this role as linguistic model. Beyond this, there is also the association between working-class speech and masculinity which, for males of *all* classes, can constitute so-called 'covert prestige' (see chapter 4). Research has shown that males often *claim* to use more non-standard forms than they actually do while females are more likely to over-report *standard* usage.

If women's and men's speech differs because the status (and hence, status-consciousness) of the two sexes differs, then it is clear that large social issues of power and subordination are involved. If women are expected to use 'better' forms than men, if they are supposed to be more 'polite', if their use of profanity and obscenity is more severely sanctioned, then we might conclude that they are a subordinate group whose linguistic (and other) behaviour has limits placed upon it. It is an irony, of course, that the forms this limiting takes are often velvet-lined – is it not good to be polite and to avoid swearing? The fact remains that if women are on some sort of linguistic pedestal in these regards, they have been *placed* there – and pedestals offer little room for movement.

A subordinate social role implies less freedom of movement, greater insecurity, uncertainty and lack of confidence. It is exactly these features which were elucidated by Robin Lakoff in her studies of women's language during the 1970s.[73] These include:

1 lexical 'hedges' or 'fillers' (*you know, sort of, you see*);
2 tag questions (*She's very nice, isn't she?*);
3 'empty' adjectives (*divine, charming*);
4 precise colour terms (*magenta, taupe, mauve*);
5 intensifiers (*I like him so much*);
6 excessive politeness, indirect requests, euphemisms, avoidance of swearing;
7 emphatic stress (*It was a BRILLIANT performance*).

While Lakoff's methodology was questionable, while her analysis lacked linguistic precision, while her lists were hardly comprehensive and while she implicitly adopted a 'male-as-norm' perspective (see below), her insights and observations have obvious value. Whether the linguistic feature acts as a 'hedge', weakening the strength of a statement, or as a 'booster' – which implies that the speaker feels the listener will require reinforcement of an otherwise unconvincing message – we observe nervousness and insecurity. These features of women's language are related to sex differences in conversational interaction: men dominate conversations, men interrupt women more than women do men, women provide more conversational feedback than men – that is, they make more encouraging and facilitating remarks during exchanges – and so on.

It would be easy, though incorrect, to see all of this as evidence of clearcut dominance of one sex by the other. Two points should be made: first, 'women's' features are not exclusively theirs, and do not always signify the same thing; second, a dominance–subordination dichotomy simply does not fully account for all the observed differences.

Consider tag questions, one of the most widely discussed features of women's speech.[74] Do they always imply uncertainty?: do they always invite the listener to make a correction or at least expand upon a dubious utterance? Some do – *It's a wonderful picture, isn't it?* – but others may be *facilitative*, giving the listener a comfortable conversational entry (*You've just changed jobs, haven't you?*), or may soften a criticism (*That was a bit silly, wasn't it?*). Tags can also be *confrontational* (*You understand what I'm telling you, don't you?*). A study by Janet Holmes which analysed these varieties also plotted their distribution, by sex, in a large corpus of speech. She found that 59 per cent of women's tag-question use was facilitative, 6 per cent had a 'softening' function and 35 per cent expressed uncertainty. Men's use was less facilitative (26 per cent) but *more* softening (13 per cent) and expressive of uncertainty (61 per cent).

More fine-grained analyses of sex differences in speech reveal that 'women's' features, greater female politeness and increased use of the standard may indicate more about women's facilitative and supportive desires than they do about insecurity and lack of confidence. That is, men and women may use language for different social purposes, having been socialized in different ways from earliest childhood. Differences in men's and women's 'gossip' are instructive here. One sex focuses on personal relationships, experiences and problems, in a generally supportive atmosphere; the other is more concerned with factual information, in an often competitive or combative format. One writer has suggested that, in conversation, men typically ask themselves 'Have I won?' while women ask 'Have I been sufficiently helpful?'[75]

Of course, each sex may, in its way, be contributing to group solidarity. One must also remember that these are very general descriptions – women are also interested in fact, and much of their 'networking' is driven by practical necessity; men's gossip, equally, can be intensely personal. There are also class divisions which intersect with these sexual ones. Still, the point that men and women use language, at least some of the time, for different purposes is surely reasonable. It also seems quite generalizable across a wide range of cultures.[76] Finally, it should alert us to the danger of seeing the speech of one sex (need I say which?) as the norm from which that of the other differs or deviates. Why say women are more polite than men, or swear less, or are more conversationally facilitative, or hedge their linguistic bets? Why not ask, rather, why men are ruder, more confrontational and more unreasonably assertive? An answer is provided in the following:

> If it were shown that men speak more surely than women, hesitating less, this would certainly be greeted as another sign of masculine

superiority. The halting speech of women would be seen as evidence of their tentative, feminine nature. Yet, when Jespersen found just the opposite phenomenon, that men hesitate more than women when speaking, he naturally attributed this fact to a greater desire for accuracy and clarity among male speakers, which leads them to search for just the right word.[77]

This is the same Jespersen who, in heading a long list of subsequent authors – both male and female – felt obliged to include in his *Language* a chapter on women but none on men.[78]

8

CONCLUSIONS

Recently, a school superintendent in Arkansas refused a request to have foreign languages taught at secondary level; he said, 'If English was good enough for Jesus, it's good enough for you.'[1] This is a rather unusual way to deny the value of other languages and – who knows? – the story may be apocryphal or, at least, heavily embroidered. The idea, however, that expansion of the linguistic repertoire is unnecessary remains common among speakers of 'large' languages. Equally common is ignorance of the scope of multilingualism, past and present, and of the powerful relationships between languages and all aspects of social and psychological life. One of my most basic aims in this book has been, simply, to provide information which might counteract such ignorance. From the initial presentation, in Chapter 2, there is a logical progression to the ramifications and implications of multilingualism: what problems and challenges for communication it creates, how and why languages compete, why the defence of languages is such a vital and enduring part of the story and so on.

There are some key concepts which, directly or implicitly, have recurred in the discussion. One of the most central is surely *necessity*: given the existence, from earliest times, of different language communities, there has always been a need for multilingual facility. Sometimes this is seen at a personal level, sometimes translators act as agents of communication and sometimes official policies exist which recognize these communities and – theoretically, at least – unite them under some acceptable state umbrella. We have also seen that the bridging of language barriers can be accomplished through shared second languages, through agreement on a lingua franca. I was concerned to point out early in the book, however, that communicative necessity often sits uneasily with the powerful sentiments attached to maternal varieties: there is a strong tension, then, between the pull of parochialism – and the special perspective on the world which is often seen to be uniquely associated with a first language – and the very obvious attractions and rewards of moving out of the shadow of *le clocher*. It seems to me that this tension is an extremely important one, and that to ignore or dismiss it is to severely hamper our understanding of the social

204

life of language. Consider, for example, the limiting influence that parochialism, the appeal of home and hearth, has upon the *scope* of multilingualism; it helps to ensure that linguistic competence extends only as far as necessity dictates. Of course, one could say that where necessity is absent, repertoire expansion will not occur. This is true, but I am suggesting, further, that the centripetal forces of parochialism keep an especially close watch on the borders of necessity, and may in fact influence our very perceptions of where those frontiers lie.

We have moved here to another key concept, personal and group *identity*, and though the most immediate focal point here is the discussion of 'groupness' in Chapter 5, it, too, is a recurring theme. Indeed, to return to de Saussure's terms yet again, the requirements of identity maintenance and cultural continuity, on the one hand, and the pressures of material advancement and 'progress', on the other, form the background to the linguistic struggle between parochialism and intercourse. We can understand better the drama inherent in most situations of language shift, decline and revival if we keep this background in mind. We can also appreciate the use of such highly charged terms as 'murder' and 'suicide' (and, indeed, 'revival' itself), terms which would probably not arise if change, or threatened change, was of a purely instrumental nature. And, to give another example here, we can realize in a deeper sense the problems associated with the introduction of constructed languages like Esperanto.

Matters of identity are important when we consider prescriptivism, too. In Chapter 6, I suggested that the urge to prescribe and 'purify' might best be seen along a continuum. At one extreme, there exists a *laissez-faire* attitude towards language which has never been widespread; it is found largely among contemporary linguists whose views, for better or worse, have generally failed to percolate to either the educated public or the masses. The perceptions of the latter two groups are distinguished mainly by the *degree* to which they are able to articulate their sense of outrage at linguistic 'contamination'. Somewhere along the continuum we find what seems to be a reasonable form of prescriptivism – the desire to standardize, for purposes of communicative efficiency, and the abhorrence of inflated, or jargon-ridden, or downright incomprehensible language. Finally, at the other end of the scale, we arrive at the Priscian-like narrowness, that disdain for all varieties but one, that constitutes purism writ large.[2]

If we admit *prescriptivism* as another central theme here, we must also remember the importance of *power, prestige* and *status*. In all linguistic struggles, both within and between languages, in all situations of language maintenance and decline, in all language-planning efforts, we observe a competition which is not between languages themselves but, rather, between language communities or linguistic 'interest groups'. It is perhaps a good idea here to remake the point that neither languages nor dialects can be compared in terms of 'better' or 'worse' and that the strong preferences for given varieties, which have always existed, are based upon sociopolitical considerations; central here are the dominance and prestige of speakers. Matters of power, then, interlock with *perceptions* rather than with any intrinsic qualities of language. The basic dynamics here are historically very stable, although, of course, specifics vary enormously and contemporary contact and conflict are often more visible – and more global – than once they were.

All of these 'key' concepts are to be understood within social situations in which language intertwines with other cultural matters. I hope that readers will thus realize that the study of languages and their interrelationships, while a fascinating topic in itself, remains incomplete – indeed, seriously flawed – without reference to issues central to fields other than sociolinguistics or the sociology of language. The reverse could be said with equal accuracy: language is an important window into society. If we charted, for example, the fortunes and functions of Black English in America, we would have a useful perspective on the vicissitudes of Black life itself. From earlier assessments of substandardness we have moved, in more enlightened circles at least, to an appreciation of a dialect which is *non*-standard, but which is as 'valid' as any other. Among speakers of Black English, we have seen a progression from that 'minority group reaction' in which the recipients of negative evaluations accept, themselves, their unfavourable linguistic status, to a realization of their dialect's legitimacy – sometimes to the extent that what was previously stigmatized is now consciously exaggerated as an expression of group pride and solidarity. Much the same could be said of speakers of working-class Canadian French, and of many other minority populations.

The coverage in this book is, of course, incomplete, and readers may have found that some areas have been omitted and others given shorter shrift than they would have liked. I can only say that the breadth of the subject has made selection and brevity necessary for present purposes. I have tried to provide useful references for further reading without, as noted in the preface, making them intrude into the text; this, I hope, is coherent without them. Beyond this, I should make two points: first, the treatment here has a generally western bias and, in some places, a more particularly anglophone one. While I believe that many of the generalities have a broad applicability I have, in making the selection just referred to, naturally emphasized those settings, those examples with which I am most familiar. I will no doubt hear about my limitations in this regard.

The second point is that I have frequently presented, where possible, information, examples and, especially, quotations of an historical nature. Without wishing to dredge up clichés about ignorance of history condemning us to repeat it, I do want to note that the disembodied nature of much work in social science places great limits on our understanding. 'Presentism' – to use an ugly contemporary word – is rightly rejected in many quarters: only a foolish historian would attempt to explain Elizabethan conduct solely within a modern framework; only a foolish reader rejects out of hand literary styles and themes which do not conform to current ones. Yet in sociology, psychology and sociolinguistics we are still regularly presented with snapshots in which the necessary background is either ignored or given very brief, and sometimes blurred, attention. I cannot understand, for example, what enduring usefulness attaches to studies of ethnolinguistic groups in contact, or restrictive language policies, or the relationship between language and group identity, which do not embed themselves, at least minimally, in what has gone before. Finally here, I must confess my own preference for that vivacity and bluntness which character-izes many historical accounts – even those which now seem, and perhaps always were, inaccurate or insensitive, dyspeptic or partial – and which are now so rare in the scholarly literature, where the endless qualification and bet-hedging often leads only to emptiness. Modern academic writing is often, indeed, 'writing that never leaves the school ... always seeking the approval of a higher authority'.[3] Perhaps, too, historical treatments are more appealing because they originate before the understandable but, none the less, regrettable specialization which has elevated technically detailed narrowness above broadly-educated discussion. I do not want to condemn all social-scientific writing, I realize *why* academic literature has become what it is, I know that there are good scientific reasons for qualification and conservatism of expression and, finally, I am hardly free of excesses myself – but readers, I think, know what my complaint is here. Perhaps readers will also agree that the difficulties and frustrations referred to are particularly heightened when we think of the themes of this book, and their broad interest and relevance to ordinary people in ordinary life.

One implication – and I touched upon this in chapter 6 – is that linguists and other 'professionals' interested in language and society have a greater responsibility than others to attempt, at least occasionally, to speak to non-professionals. We do not expect that experts from the starriest echelons of nuclear physics will (or should) very often descend to our level – although some of the best *have* managed to do so quite successfully. In part, this is because their researches and their results need never touch our lives in any direct manner. *We* do not need to know *their* field. But language is not nuclear physics and one could make a case – perhaps I have made one in some sections of this book – that it touches more lives more immediately. Even those linguists working in the most mysterious recesses of grammar and morphology have a potentially closer connection to the public than do latter-day Einsteins. Those experts in the *social* life of language are closer still. Alas, communication with ordinary people is still largely left to the shamans; we still have too few Bolingers among us.[4]

The loss here is not only to the non-professional public, for debate about important language matters becomes unnecessarily restricted. One result of professionals attempting to reach the 'others' is a more substantial grounding of the professionals' own discipline. That is, leaving aside entirely any insights flowing back *to* these professionals, the very exercise of communicating with the public is salutary for the subject, in just the same way that teaching a topic one knows very well to essentially uninformed students can be. For sociology-of-language matters specifically, however, unlettered opinion can *also* have the wider utility just hinted at, can temper more academic study in useful ways.

Many applied linguists – often members of minority ethnolinguistic groups themselves – take a keen interest in the survival of threatened languages. That is, they blend their academic training with a position of advocacy; the usual rationale is that the loss of any language diminishes us all, and that any 'small' group at risk deserves special attention and action. The views of Michael Krauss, cited in the notes to chapter 2, are representative here: linguists have a special responsibility to intervene where they can to support endangered varieties. We protect animals, we agitate to save old buildings from the wrecker's ball, we try and preserve physical environments – why should we not be equally zealous, then, in aiming to sustain languages?

Other applied linguists have not seen things in quite the same way. In a direct response to Krauss's plea, Peter Ladefoged has recently pointed out that not all speakers of threatened languages see their preservation as possible or even, perhaps, desirable.[5] He mentions the Toda, speakers of a Dravidian language in India, who now number fewer than 1,000. They have apparently accepted that the continued daily use of their mother tongue is incompatible with their social aspirations. Ladefoged himself claims that the task of the linguist is to 'lay out the facts' and he describes how he and his colleagues did just that in a study of langauge in Uganda. They assessed linguistic similarities among the major Ugandan varieties – some thirty languages – and determined patterns of proficiency, language use in the media and at school, and so on. They then presented their findings to the government. Throughout his short article, Ladefoged states that this 'detached' stance is the appropriate one, that linguists should not assume that they know best and, more particularly, should not attempt to persuade people that language shift is a bad thing, *per se*. Perhaps linguists who are, themselves, strongly committed to the maintenance of linguistic diversity, might consider that one of the 'facts' that could be presented to groups or governments is that very commitment (and the reasons for it). The latter could then weigh this along with more objective language data and percentages. Ultimately, though, Ladefoged is surely right: it is those who are most directly concerned who must make final decisions and it is possible to imagine that periods of transition and distress might be aggravated by well-meaning professionals afflicted by linguistic tunnel vision.

The intent of this book has been to present a wide range of information about multilingualism to a non-specialist audience. Beyond that, it may also prove useful as a primer for students; here, I hope the notes and references provide a suitable entry to the more technical literature. Throughout the work I have tried to communicate something of my own enthusiasm for a rich and varied facet of human life.

Multilingualism arises and is maintained through necessity, real or perceived. In order to explore it further, we need more information from 'ordinary' people about language and the way in which it is woven into the larger social fabric. Data-gathering should become more substantive, should aim for fuller accounts, should go from the study of *beliefs* about language (usually assessed on 'attitude' questionnaires, interviews and surveys) towards a broader understanding of *attitude*. Ethnographic approaches should also be encouraged because, despite the phenomenological excesses to which they are sometimes prone, they *do* aim at the elucidation of particularities *within* contexts, they reject narrow reductionism, and they adopt the *Gestalt* view that the whole, especially the subjectively assessed whole, is greater than the sum of all its elements.

If we collect more, and more sensitive, information *from* 'ordinary' people we ought, equally, to make more sustained attempts to give findings back *to* this same constituency (as I have already implied). I have never met anyone who is not interested in language at some level, and there is thus an ever-present receptivity which demands attention. When, further, we recall the many varieties of linguistic misinformation, prejudice and myopia, we realize how important it is not to abandon this educational role to the shamans.

It is clear that we also need better information about the linkages between languages and identities; both historical and contemporary studies have much to tell us and, indeed, we cannot be fully informed without an integrated knowledge of both. We have ample evidence of the relevance of ethnicity and nationalism and it is not an unreasonable prediction that these phenomena will grow, not shrink, in global importance. The collapse of the Soviet empire and the ending of the Cold War do not mean world harmony; on the contrary, they permit and facilitate the rise or resurgence of many 'smaller' conflicts in which ethnolinguistic matters figure prominently. There is historical precedent for this: to go back no further than the nineteenth century, we note that the *pax Britannica* hardly diminished smaller actions; in fact, Britain was virtually never free of foreign engagements, most of which involved struggles whose linguistic components I discussed in Chapter 4.

One perspective on the language-identity relationship, to which I have frequently referred, is the tension between parochialism and 'intercourse', between continuity and change. I have implied throughout the book that this stress is a common one, underlying many specific social manifestations.

Under what circumstances can desired change co-exist with cultural coherence? What are the chief items to be entered in any ledger of costs and benefits pertaining to language shift? What does the historical record teach us, and what innovations are possible, likely or wanted? I hope that partial answers can be gleaned from the material I have presented, but more remains to be discovered. Indeed, this is a never-ending task, if only because generalities here must always be tempered with localized particulars. The kaleidoscopic picture constantly alters, even though it is always constructed from the same brightly-coloured elements.

NOTES AND REFERENCES

PREFACE

1 A useful outline of the early centrality of language issues in social psychology, their virtual disappearance and their very recent reappearance is provided by Rolf Kroger and Linda Wood, 'Whatever happened to language in social psychology?' (*Canadian Psychology*, 1992, 33, 584–94); see also John Edwards, *Language, Society and Identity* (Oxford: Blackwell, 1985).

2 Joyce Hertzler, 'Toward a sociology of language' (*Social Forces*, 1953, 32, 109–19) and *The Sociology of Language* (New York: Random House, 1965). The proceedings of the California sociolinguistics conference were edited by William Bright as *Sociolinguistics* (The Hague: Mouton, 1966).

3 The preface to Joshua Fishman (ed.), *Advances in the Sociology of Language*, Vol. 1 (The Hague: Mouton, 1971).

4 Anthony Edwards, *Language in Culture and Class* (London: Heinemann, 1976, p. 9).

5 S. Herman, 'Explorations in the social psychology of language choice' (*Human Relations*, 1961, 14, 149–64).

6 Noam Chomsky, *Dialogues avec Mitsou Ronat* (Paris: Flammarion, 1977). Published in English as *Language and Responsibility* (New York: Pantheon, 1979). The quotations are from pages 55 and 56. See also Chomsky's *Language and Politics* (Montreal: Black Rose, 1988).

7 Ronald Wardhaugh, *An Introduction to Sociolinguistics* (Oxford: Blackwell, 1986, p. 10). See also Roger Andersen's criticism of Chomsky's 'armchair' philosophy in his *The Power and the Word* (London: Paladin, 1988). Further useful discussion of Chomsky and his critics may be found in F. Newmeyer (ed.), *Linguistics: The Cambridge Survey* (Cambridge: Cambridge University Press, 1988) – particularly in Volume 4 (*Language: The Sociocultural Context*).

8 Chomsky, 1979, p. 57.

1 AN INTRODUCTORY OVERVIEW

1 Indian examples: P. Pandit, 'Perspectives on sociolinguistics in India' (in W. McCormack and S. Wurm (eds), *Language and Society*, The Hague: Mouton, 1979); D. Pattanayak, 'On being and becoming bilingual in India' (in Joshua Fishman *et al.*, *The Fergusonian Impact*, The Hague: de Gruyter, 1986).

2 From a study by John Gumperz, cited by David Crystal, *Cambridge Encyclopedia of Language* (Cambridge: Cambridge University Press, 1987, p. 363).

3 George Steiner, *After Babel* (London: Oxford University Press, 1975).

4 Pattanayak, 1986.

5 Steiner, 1975, p. 122.

6 J. Waterman, *A History of the German Language* (Seattle: University of Washington Press, 1966, p. 138).

7 John Milton, *Prose Writings* (London: Dent, 1958, pp. 319–20).

8 The lines by Butler appear in an essay of Hazlitt's called 'On the ignorance of the learned' in *Table-Talk* (London: Richards, 1901). See also R. Lamar, *Samuel Butler: Satires and Miscellaneous Poetry and Prose* (Cambridge: Cambridge University Press, 1928).

9 H. de Quehen, *Samuel Butler: Prose Observations* (Oxford: Clarendon, 1979).

10 Steiner (1975) comments, naturally, on the myth of Babel, suggesting that humanity was not destroyed by the scattering of tongues but was, rather, kept vital and creative by it. See also Einar Haugen, 'The curse of Babel' (in M. Bloomfield and E. Haugen (eds), *Language as a Human Problem*, Guildford: Lutterworth, 1975) and his *Blessings of Babel* (The Hague: Mouton, 1987).

11 Translations may be *belles infidèles* but we need them. Nietzsche said that to translate meant one had conquered 'but only with the anticipation that conquest would become a most pleasant assimilation by the enemy in the end'. This seems less than crystal-clear, however; if Englishmen translate from Sanskrit, who is conquering who? This, perhaps (for the French, at any rate), is what adds the *belles* to the *infidèles*. An interesting article on these matters, specifically in the modern European context, is Wolf Lepenies' 'Translation's role in national identity' (*Times Higher Education Supplement*, 2 October 1992). He claims that the 'burden' of translation has been historically vital; the Schlegel brothers' translations of Indian culture added much, then, to *German* classicism. A modern difficulty is found between the two Germanies where, Lepenies says, speaking the same language has 'nurtured the illusion that we understand each other.' This brings to mind, I suppose, Wilde's idea of England and America being separated by a common language (or was it Shaw's idea? see Nigel Rees, *Why do we Quote?*, London: Blandford, 1989).

12 Richard Carew, *Epistle on the Excellency of the English Tongue* (London, 1605).

13 G.W. Lemon, *English Etymology* (London, 1783, pp. 6–7).

14 Cited by H. Sharp, *Selections from Educational Records, Part I* (Calcutta: Government Printing Office, 1920, p. 110).

15 Edwin Guest, *A History of English Rhythms* (London, 1838, p. 703).

16 George Marsh, *Lectures on the English Language* (New York, 1860, p. 23).

17 E. Higginson, *An English Grammar Specially Intended for Classical Schools and Private Students* (London, 1864, p. 207). The citations from Lemon, Guest, Marsh and Higginson are all given in Tony Crowley's excellent *The Politics of Discourse* (London: Macmillan, 1989).

18 The Irish references can be found in John Edwards, *The Irish Language* (New York: Garland, 1983).

19 Bertrand Russell, *Unpopular Essays* (London: Allen & Unwin, 1950). This is related perhaps to what Madsen Pirie has described in *The Book of the Fallacy* (London: Routledge & Kegan Paul, 1985, p. 109): 'The poor may indeed be blessed; but they are not necessarily right. It is a fallacy to suppose that because someone is poor they must be sounder or more virtuous than one who is rich. The *argumentum ad Lazarum*, after the poor man, Lazarus, takes it that the poverty of the arguer enhances the case he or she is making.' One also thinks of the famous Monty Python sketch in which a curious status is achieved by the one who can demonstrate the most deprived background: '*You* weren't poor; at least you had a hovel. *We* lived in a paper bag', etc.

20 Thomas Jones's book was published in London in 1688; only ten copies survive,

but Scolar Press (Menston, Yorkshire) issued a facsimile edition in 1972 from a copy in the Bodleian Library. It is interesting that Jones uses the word 'infancy' – it signifies one without speech.

21 Cited by Otto Jespersen in *Language* (London: Allen & Unwin, 1922, p. 65).

22 Joachim du Bellay, *The Defence and Illustration of the French Language* (1549) – only translated into English in 1939, by Gladys Turquet (London: Dent). The citation is from page 21 of this translation.

23 Jean Aitchison, *Language Change* (London: Fontana, 1981, p. 208).

24 See John Edwards, *Language, Society and Identity* (Oxford: Blackwell, 1985) and 'Did English murder Irish?' (*English Today,* 1986, 6, 7–10).

25 Cited by Breandán Ó Conaire, on p. 125 of 'Flann O'Brien, *An Béal Bocht* and other Irish matters' (*Irish University Review,* 1973, 3, 121–40).

26 Details on language situations and classification may be consulted in John Edwards, 'Notes for a minority-language typology' (*Journal of Multilingual and Multicultural Development,* 1990, 11, 137–51), 'Socio-educational issues concerning indigenous minority languages' (in J. Sikma and D. Gorter (eds), *European Lesser-Used Languages in Primary Education,* Leeuwarden: Fryske Akademy/Mercator, 1991) and 'Sociopolitical aspects of language maintenance and loss' (in W. Fase, K. Jaspaert and S. Kroon (eds), *Maintenance and Loss of Minority Languages,* Amsterdam: John Benjamins, 1992).

27 A related matter is the question of whether linguistic uniformity correlates with economic well-being. A casual observation might suggest that countries with many languages tend also to be poor; indeed, Jonathan Pool noted that 'a country that is linguistically highly heterogeneous is always undeveloped, and a country that is developed always has considerable language uniformity' ('National development and language diversity', in Joshua Fishman (ed.), *Advances in the Sociology of Language,* The Hague: Mouton, 1972, p. 213). However, dealing with a large number of countries, and with a very large number of possibly important variables, is a daunting exercise; recent studies which have employed sophisticated statistical techniques have suggested that linguistic homogeneity or heterogeneity is 'only indirectly and insignificantly related' to measures of economic strength (Joshua Fishman and Frank Solano, 'Cross-polity linguistic homogeneity/heterogeneity and per capita gross national product: an empirical exploration', *Language Problems and Language Planning,* 1989, 13, 103–18). Equally, however, much more work remains to be done, especially concerning any possible *positive* consequences of linguistic heterogeneity; see Joshua Fishman, 'An inter-polity perspective on the relationships between linguistic heterogeneity, civil strife and per capita gross national product' (*International Journal of Applied Linguistics,* 1991, 1, 5–18). See also Kenneth McRae, *Conflict and Compromise in Multilingual Societies: Switzerland* (Waterloo, Ontario: Wilfrid Laurier University Press, 1983) and Ralph Fasold, *The Sociolinguistics of Society* (Oxford: Blackwell, 1984).

28 Information about education is in Edwards, 1985.

29 Brian Bullivant, *The Pluralist Dilemma in Education* (Sydney: Allen & Unwin, 1981).

30 Elie Kedourie, *Nationalism* (London: Hutchinson, 1961, pp. 83–4).

31 p. 268 in E. O'Doherty, 'Bilingual school policy' (*Studies,* 1958, 47, 259–68).

32 Donald Akenson, *A Mirror to Kathleen's Face* (Montreal: McGill-Queen's University Press, 1970, p. 60).

33 Language academies and dictionaries are discussed in Edwards, 1985.

34 On French and English academies, see Robert Hall, *External History of the Romance Languages* (New York: Elsevier, 1974) and John Ayto, 'English: failures

of language reforms' (in I. Fodor and C. Hagège (eds), *Language Reform: History and Future* (Vol. 1), Hamburg: Helmut Buske, 1983).

35 The authors of *The Plight of English* (Newton Abbot: David & Charles, 1975) and *Strictly Speaking* (Indianapolis: Bobbs-Merrill, 1974) are Basil Cottle and Edwin Newman respectively.

2 LANGUAGES IN THE WORLD

1 The 'extended' Tower of Babel story was related to me by Bernard Spolsky.

2 The details about Psamtik, Frederic II, James IV and Akbar are from David Crystal, *Cambridge Encyclopedia of Language* (Cambridge: Cambridge University Press, 1987).

3 Roger Shattuck, *The Forbidden Experiment* (New York: Washington Square Press, 1980, pp. 54–5). Montaigne himself had a rather unusual linguistic upbringing. Hardly had he 'learned to lisp' when he was handed over to a 'German savant' named Horstanus who spoke only Latin with him. As well, all others in the household spoke to Montaigne only with 'such few words of Latin as each had learnt'. Thus, he acquired colloquial Latin before he could speak 'the *patois* of Perigord or the language of France' (from Thomas Seccombe's introduction to the three-volume facsimile edition of *The Essays of Michael Lord of Montaigne* (London: Grant Richards, 1908) – the John Florio translation, originally 1603).

4 Shattuck, 1980.

5 The Société de Linguistique de Paris had only formed the previous year (1865). It was quite happy to endorse the study of 'legends, traditions [and] customs' but firmly rejected any communication on language origin (and, incidentally, on the creation of a 'universal' language). See James Stam, *Inquiries into the Origin of Language* (New York: Harper & Row, 1976). This book is excellent, documenting all the eighteenth- and nineteenth-century philosophers who wrote about language origins.

6 Otto Jespersen, *Language* (London: Allen & Unwin, 1922).

7 Henry Alexander, *The Story of Our Language* (New York: Dolphin, 1962, p. 42).

8 Charles Hockett, 'The origin of speech' (in William Wang, *Human Communication*, San Francisco: W.H. Freeman, 1982). Originally published in *Scientific American*, September 1960). Ved Mehta, *John is Eager to Please* (New York: Farrar, Straus & Giroux, 1971) has an interesting chapter on Chomsky, Hockett, Jakobson and other contemporary linguists.

9 From Robin Dunbar, a British anthropologist; reported by Carl Honoré, 'Say what?' (*Globe and Mail* (Toronto), 26 September 1992).

10 Hockett, 1982, p. 12.

11 Edward Sapir, *Language* (New York: Harcourt Brace, 1921, pp. 19, 222).

12 Definitions of language are many. The essence of the one given here comes from C. Morris, *Signs, Language and Behavior* (Englewood Cliffs, NJ: Prentice-Hall, 1946).

13 William Mackey, 'Bilingual education and its social implications' (in John Edwards (ed.), *Linguistic Minorities, Policies and Pluralism*, London and New York: Academic Press, 1984).

14 John Firth, *The Tongues of Men and Speech* (London: Oxford University Press, 1970).

15 See Crystal, 1987; Ronald Wardhaugh, *Languages in Competition* (Oxford: Blackwell, 1987); Bernard Comrie, 'Languages of the world: who speaks what'

(in N. Collinge (ed.), *An Encyclopedia of Language*, London: Routledge, 1990).

16 John Edwards, 'Gaelic in Nova Scotia' (in C. Williams, (ed.), *Linguistic Minorities, Society and Territory*, Clevedon, Avon: Multilingual Matters, 1991).

17 Peter Ellis, *The Cornish Language and its Literature* (London: Routledge & Kegan Paul, 1974). In 1984 I visited Mousehole and was interested to read on the Paul memorial that Pentreath was *said* to have been the last Cornish speaker and, on her house plaque, that she was *one* of the last speakers.

18 Matthew Arnold, *On the Study of Celtic Literature and on Translating Homer* (New York: Macmillan, 1883).

19 See Nancy Dorian, *Language Death* (Philadelphia: University of Pennsylvania Press, 1981) and *Investigating Obsolescence* (Cambridge: Cambridge University Press, 1989). W. Elmendorf's 'Last speakers and language change' (*Anthropological Linguistics*, 1981, 23, 36–49) discusses two Californian languages, each having only one remaining speaker; the notes and references are particularly useful. A recent article by Michael Krauss, 'The world's languages in crisis' (*Language*, 1992, 68, 4–10) points out that as many as *half* of the world's languages may be moribund. In fact, Krauss, considering worst-case scenarios, says that it is 'a plausible calculation that – at the rate things are going – the coming century will see either the death or the doom of 90 per cent of mankind's languages' (p. 7). He urges, at the least, grammatical and lexical documentation 'lest linguistics go down in history as the only science that presided obliviously over the disappearance of 90 per cent of the very field to which it is dedicated' (p. 10). On Celtic language, see the informative but flawed work by D.B. Gregor, *Celtic: A Comparative Study* (New York: Oleander, 1980).

20 Noted in *Language Problems and Language Planning*, 1985, 9, 82.

21 Michael Foster, 'Indigenous languages in Canada' (*Language and Society*, 1982, 7, 20–4).

22 Ronald Wright, 'Beyond words' (*Saturday Night*, 1988, 103, 38–46).

23 Dr. Johnson's observation was, 'I am always sorry when any language is lost, because languages are the pedigrees of nations', made while travelling with Boswell in Scotland, in September 1773. Apart from the sentiment itself, the word *pedigree* is an interesting one. In his own dictionary of 1755, Johnson said that it comes from *père* and *degré* (on the authority of Skinner who, in the dictionary's preface, Johnson described as 'often ignorant, but never ridiculous'). Skinner *was* wrong here, for *pedigree* derives from *pié (pied) de grue* – crane's foot – because the triple-lined mark genealogists drew to signify lineage resembled the bird's claws. Later, the term was mistakenly seen as *pied degrue*, and the latter word was thought to mean degree, or rank – not a ridiculous error (nor is Skinner's assumption of *père*, in this context). The surname *Pettigrew* is related.

24 Bernd Heine, *Status and Use of African Lingua Francas* (Munich: Weltforum, 1970); and Barbara Grimes, *Ethnologue* (Dallas: Wycliffe Bible Translators, 1984).

25 K. Petyt, *The Study of Dialect* (London: André Deutsch, 1980); Peter Trudgill, *Sociolinguistics* (Harmondsworth: Penguin, 1974).

26 O. Maurud, 'Reciprocal comprehension of neighbour languages in Scandinavia' (*Scandinavian Journal of Educational Research*, 1976, 20, 49–72). Mackey (1984) cites a study showing that while 40 per cent of Danes said they understood Swedish, almost 90 per cent of Swedes thought Danes could understand them. Three-quarters of the Danes said they were understood by Norwegians, but only half the latter admitted understanding Danish.

27 H. Wolff, 'Intelligibility and inter-ethnic attitudes' (*Anthropological Linguistics*, 1959, 1, 34–41).

28 Crystal, 1987. The total represents, in effect, a reduction of more than 20,000 language and dialect *names*, a reduction made on the basis of factors I have discussed up to this point. See C. and F. Voegelin, *Classification and Index of the World's Languages* (New York: Elsevier, 1977); M. Ruhlen, *A Guide to the World's Languages* (Stanford: Stanford University Press, 1987); and B. Comrie, *The World's Major Languages* (London: Croom Helm, 1987).

29 See W.B. Lockwood, *Indo-European Philology* (London: Hutchinson, 1969).

30 See Frederick Bodmer, *The Loom of Language* (London: Allen & Unwin, 1943); N. Collinge, 'Language as it evolves: tracing its forms and families' and Vivien Law, 'Language and its students: the history of linguistics' (both in Collinge, 1990).

31 Gesner and Adelung named their works for Mithridates, a king of Pontus who – according to Herodotus – could speak all the languages of his kingdom (about two dozen). It was also Mithridates who protected himself against poisoning by taking repeated small doses.

32 Other encyclopaedic efforts of limited utility included those of Pallas, whose 1787 work was entitled *Linguarum Totius Orbis Vocabularia Comparativa* (it dealt with 200 Asian and European languages) and Hervas – his *Catálogo de las Lenguas de las Naciones Conocidas y Numeracion, Division y Clases de estas segun la Diversidad de sus Idiomas y Dialectos* (1805) covered 300 varieties (see Bodmer, 1943).

33 A new book edited by Agnès Bresson, *Lettres à Claude Saumaise et à son entourage, 1620–1637* (Florence: Olschki, 1992), presents 66 previously unpublished letters to Saumaise from Nicolas-Claude Fabri de Peiresc (1580–1637). These throw more light on Saumaise's activities and, of course, on those of Peiresc who was a collector, patron, organizer and researcher across an incredibly broad spectrum. He was interested in comparative linguistics, and particularly in Coptic.

34 Cited by Crystal, 1987, p. 296 and Bodmer, 1943, p. 180. Further information about 'Oriental Jones' can be found in R. Robins, 'The life and work of Sir William Jones' (*Transactions of the Philological Society*, 1987, 1–23) and in a new biography by Garland Cannon, *The Life and Mind of Oriental Jones* (Cambridge: Cambridge University Press, 1991).

35 Law, 1990, p. 819.

36 Rask's 1818 work was *Undersøgelse om det Gamle Nordiske eller Islandske Sprogs Oprindelse.*

37 Bopp's 1816 grammar was entitled *Über das Conjugationssystem der Sanskritsprache in Vergleichung mit jenem der Griechischen, Lateinischen, Persischen und Germanischen Sprache.*

38 Bopp's monumental 1833 work was *Vergleichende Grammatik des Sanskrit, Zend, Griechischen, Lateininschen, Litthauischen, Gothischen und Deutschen.* Zend (or Avestan) is an old Iranian language of Zoroastrianism.

39 Law, 1990, p. 819.

40 Brugmann's work was entitled *Grundriss der Vergleichenden Grammatik der Indogermanischen Sprachen.*

41 See Crystal, 1987; J. Payne, 'Language universals and language types' (in Collinge, 1990).

42 See Ralph Fasold, *The Sociolinguistics of Society* (Oxford: Blackwell, 1984).

43 K. Murray, *Caught in the Web of Words* (New Haven: Yale University Press, 1977, p. 70). Sir Richard Burton, the Victorian scholar–explorer, spoke more than

two dozen languages according to his biographer, Edward Rice (*Captain Sir Richard Francis Burton*, New York: Scribners, 1990). His case is also illustrative of a tendency: the more languages you know the easier it is to add a new one. Other notable linguists in history are mentioned by John Firth, 1970. Nowadays, a linguist need not know more than one language to merit the title. Roman Jakobson, a founder of the 'Prague School' of linguistics (based on the insights of de Saussure), noted, for example, that 'Chomsky's epigones' often know only English. Jakobson himself, although obviously a linguist in the 'new' sense, was also one in the traditional sense of one who knows many languages. He claimed he could lecture in six languages, and could read virtually all western European and Slavic varieties (see Mehta, 1971).

44 John de Vries, 'Some methodological aspects of self-report questions on language and ethnicity' (*Journal of Multilingual and Multicultural Development*, 1985, 6, 347–68).

45 Crystal, 1987.

46 De Vries, 1985; see also his 'On coming to our census' (*Journal of Multilingual and Multicultural Development*, 11, 57–76).

47 John Edwards, *Language, Society and Identity* (Oxford: Blackwell, 1985).

48 Edwards, 1991.

49 Brian Weinstein, *The Civic Tongue* (New York: Longman, 1983) and Dorothy Waggoner, 'Statistics on language use' (in Charles Ferguson and Shirley Heath (eds), *Language in the USA*. Cambridge: Cambridge University Press, 1981).

50 Weinstein, 1983. In the United States, in the last two decennial censuses, 40 per cent of *all* Hispanics said they were neither white nor black, but racially 'other'. Among Puerto Ricans in New York in 1980, 44 per cent said they were white, 4 per cent said black, 48 per cent said 'other' – and then wrote in some Spanish description – and 4 per cent simply said 'other'. See Clara Rodriguez and Hector Cordero-Guzman, 'Placing race in context' (*Ethnic and Racial Studies*, 1992, 15, 523–42).

51 Edwards, 1985; Sumiko Tan, 'Strangers in their own country' (*Straits Times*, 14 December 1991).

52 Roland Breton, *Géographie des Langues* (Paris: Presses Universitaires de France, 1983).

53 K. O'Bryan, J. Reitz and O. Kuplowska, *Non-Official Languages: A Study in Canadian Multiculturalism* (Ottawa: Supply & Services Canada, 1976).

54 See Linguistic Minorities Project, *The Other Languages of England* (London: Routledge & Kegan Paul, 1985).

55 The 'Original' (but clearly not the first) lingua franca ('language of the Franks') was probably a pidgin composed of Provençal, which was common along the Riviera from Marseille to Genoa, and Italian, with the latter dominant. It dates from the time of the Crusaders' struggles in the eastern Mediterranean. Early uses of the term *lingua franca* in English typically allude to a 'mixed language' or 'jargon' used in the Levant (from *lever*, referring to the eastern sunrise); from this the term became generalized to any 'contact' language. In the seventeenth century, Dryden observed that a lingua franca was a composition of 'all tongues'. By the end of the nineteenth century the term had expanded to include instances where a single language provided the necessary bridging (e.g., Urdu, for much of India) but the earlier idea of some fairly haphazard mixture of varieties was also retained. See also William Samarin, 'Lingua francas of the world' (in Joshua Fishman (ed.), *Readings in the Sociology of Language*. The Hague: Mouton, 1968).

56 Bodmer, 1943.

57 George MacDonald Fraser, *Flashman and the Mountain of Light* (London: Fontana, 1991, p. 378). See also Henry Beard's amusing books, *Lingua Latina Occasionibus Omnibus* and *Lingua Latina Multo Pluribus Occasionibus* (New York: Villard, 1991). Some of Beard's stock-phrases are: 'Quanta mora volatui fiet?' ('How long will the flight be delayed?'); 'Salve, socie. Pone mihi, sodes, alteram locustam marinam in caminello' ('G'day mate. Will you please put another shrimp on the barbie for me?'); 'Interdum ascende ut me visas' ('Come up and see me sometime.'). Since 1989, Radio Finland has broadcast a Latin news bulletin a dozen times each weekend. What began as a publicity effort for its international programming became a serious venture. Foregoing some of the Vatican circumlocutions, Professor Tuomo Pekkanen adopts a 'lean and economical' vocabulary where *television*, for example, is *not* 'machina ad vim electricam trasmittendam ita instructa ut sine intervallo imagines ac voces e longinquo indicet', but rather *televistrum* (actually a Greek-Latin hybrid). Since the programme is listened to worldwide on shortwave, perhaps one should not see in modern Latin simply some religious anachronism (Carl Honoré, 'Calling all Latin lovers', *Globe and Mail* (Toronto), 28 March 1992).

58 See Robert McCrum, William Cran and Robert MacNeil, *The Story of English* (New York: Viking, 1986) – the book accompanying the outstanding BBC/PBS television series of the same name.

59 See the Oxford English Dictionary.

60 On Berncastle, see Loreto Todd, *Pidgins and Creoles* (London: Routledge & Kegan Paul, 1974) and, on pidgins and creoles generally, see also Suzanne Romaine, *Pidgin and Creole Languages* (London: Longman, 1988) and Dell Hymes, *Pidginization and Creolization of Languages* (Cambridge: Cambridge University Press, 1971).

61 Pidgin examples from Loreto Todd, *Modern Englishes: Pidgins and Creoles* (Oxford: Blackwell, 1984, pp. 65, 275).

62 A good discussion of *koinēs* is Jeff Siegel, 'Koinēs and Koineization' (*Language in Society*, 1985, 14, 357–78).

63 Arnold Toynbee, *A Study of History* (2-volume abridgement by D.C. Somervell, London: Oxford University Press, 1956, Vol. 1, p. 469).

64 Todd, 1974, p. 24. Joseph de Acosta's book was published in Seville; Edward Grimstone's (1604) English translation was the *Naturall and Morall Historie of the East and West Indies.*

65 Todd, 1974, p. 271.

66 On constructed languages in general: Andrew Large, *The Artificial Language Movement* (Oxford: Blackwell, 1985); J. Knowlson, *Universal Language Schemes in England and France 1600–1800* (Toronto: University of Toronto Press, 1975); L. Couturat and L. Leau, *Histoire de la Langue Universelle* (Paris: Hachette, 1903); John Edwards and Lynn MacPherson 'Views of constructed languages, with special reference to Esperanto' (*Language Problems and Language Planning*, 1987, 11, 283–304); Peter Forster, *The Esperanto Movement* (The Hague: Mouton, 1982).

67 E. Lieberman, 'Esperanto and trans-national identity: the case of Dr Zamenhof' (*International Journal of the Sociology of Language*, 1979, 20, 89–107).

68 Lieberman, 1979, p. 96. See also the biography of Zamenhof: Edmond Privat, *The Life of Zamenhof* (Bailieboro, Ontario: Esperanto Press, 1980).

69 Large, 1985.

70 K. Vossler, *The Spirit of Language in Civilization* (London: Routledge, 1932, p. 167).

71 Bertrand Russell on Esperanto: *The Autobiography of Bertrand Russell 1872–1914*

(New York: Bantam, 1968).

72   A. Tauber, *George Bernard Shaw on Language* (London: Peter Owen, 1965, p. 158).

73   H.L. Mencken, *The American Language* (New York: Knopf, 1977, p. 772).

74   George Steiner, *After Babel* (London: Oxford University Press, 1975, p. 202).

75   Steiner, 1975, p. 470.

76   Humphrey Carpenter, *The Letters of J.R.R. Tolkien* (Boston: Houghton Mifflin, 1981, p. 231).

77   Large, 1985, p. 200.

78   Dale Spender, *Man Made Language* (London: Routledge & Kegan Paul, 1985).

79   An interesting new book is Marina Yaguello, *Lunatic Lovers of Language: Imaginary Languages and their Inventors* (London: Athlone, 1992); she discusses not only 'serious' inventors but some of the others, too (e.g., De Vertus, who wrote on 'primitive language and its origin in lunar ideography').

80   Lieberman, 1979, p. 100.

81   See Lieberman, 1979, for notes and a critique of Flugel's study of Esperanto.

82   Forster, 1982; Edwards and MacPherson, 1987.

83   George Orwell observed that 'for sheer dirtiness of fighting, the feud between the inventors of various of the international languages would take a lot of beating' ('As I please', *Tribune*, 28 January 1944). Reprinted by Sonia Orwell and Ian Angus, *The Collected Essays, Journals and Letters of George Orwell*, Vol. 3 (Harmondsworth: Penguin, 1970, pp. 107–8). Interestingly, Orwell's aunt Nellie Limouzin lived in Paris with the noted Esperantist, Eugene Adam. In the early 1920s he founded the *Sennacieca Asocio Tutmonda*, a world society of non-nationalists which, by the end of the decade, claimed 6,000 members. Adam himself engaged in endless debate, which may have prompted Orwell's observation. See Michael Sheldon, *Orwell* (New York: HarperCollins, 1991).

84   Steiner, 1975, p. 233.

85   During the Second World War, the American forces used English–Navajo bilinguals as radio operators and, not content to use Navajo itself, the signalmen devised what was recently referred to as the 'world's most unbreakable code' (noted in the *New York Times*, 20 September 1992).

86   Steiner, 1975, p. 225.

87   Steiner, 1975, p. 46.

88   Ludwig Wittgenstein, *Tractatus Logico-Philosophicus* (London: Routledge & Kegan Paul, 1974).

89   Steiner, 1975, p. 224.

90   Steiner, 1975, p. 285.

91   'Logos' to the Greeks meant both 'word' and 'reason' and it was the Stoics who first identified human creativity and reason with the divine and all-pervasive Mind. Without having heard of Christianity, Philo Judaeus (fl. 20 BC–40 AD) actually called this 'logos' the 'only-begotten son' and, in Christ, Philo's 'logos' thus really became the 'word made flesh' (see Owen Barfield, *History of English Words*. London: Faber & Faber, 1953).

92   Steiner, 1975, p. 239.

93   Steiner, 1975, pp. 250–1.

94   In his foreword to Barfield's book (1953), W.H. Auden observed that 'understanding what another human being says to us is always a matter of translation' (p. 8).

95   Steiner, 1975; see also J. Large, *The Foreign Language Barrier* (Oxford: Blackwell, 1983) and L.G. Kelly, *The True Interpreter: A History of Translation Theory and Practice in the West* (Oxford: Blackwell, 1979).

96 Joachim du Bellay, *The Defence and Illustration of the French Language,* translated by Gladys Turquet (London: Dent, 1939, pp. 35–6). Originally published in 1549.

97 Steiner, 1975, p. 256.

98 Emile Zola, *L'Assommoir* (Harmondsworth: Penguin, 1970, p. 16). Originally published in 1876.

99 Zola, 1970, p. 18.

100 Zola, 1970, p. 18.

101 Emile Zola, *Germinal* (Harmondsworth: Penguin, 1954, p. 16). Originally published in 1885.

102 Josef Skvorecky, 'Literary murder at 5¢ a word' (*English Today,* 1985, 4, 39–42).

103 Sarah Hemming, 'Found in translation' (*Independent,* 25 October 1990). In French, Hamlet's soliloquy has a slightly different temper:

> Etre ou n'être pas, la question est là:
> Est-il plus noble de laisser son âme subir la volée,
> De pierres et de flèches d'un sort humiliant,
> Ou de prendre les armes contre un océan de tourments
> Et de périr en les affrontant.

104 There always exists the possibility of translation *errors,* of course. Crystal (1987) lists a few, some funny, others serious. When a UN delegate said 'L'Afrique n'érige plus des autels aux dieux', it was translated, on the basis of a mis-hearing, as '. . . des hôtels odieux'. In America, Khrushchev was told that he was 'barking up the wrong tree' but this was translated into Russian as 'baying like a hound'. Consider the verb *to table.* In America, it means to postpone consideration of a motion or a proposal, usually *sine die,* while in Britain it signifies the opposite – to present for discussion. In 1962, at the Geneva Disarmament Talks, the American and British contingents spent some time arguing before discovering that they both wanted to discuss a British motion. One of my favourite errors occurred in an American war film, subtitled in French. One of the soldiers peers into the distance, and another says, 'Tanks?' The subtitle reads 'Merci'. See D.J. Enright's review of Anthony Burgess, *A Mouthful of Air* (London: Hutchinson, 1992) in the *Times Literary Supplement* (13 November 1992).

105 Nonsense remains nonsense in translation, although it can certainly be cleverly done.

> 'Twas brillig and the slithy toves
> Did gyre and gimble in the wabe:
> All mimsy were the borogoves,
> And the mome raths outgrabe.
>
> Bewahre doch vor Jammeroch!
> Die Zähne knirschen, Krallen Kratzen!
> Bewahr' vor Jub jub-Vogel, vor
> Frumiösen Banderschnatzen!
>
> Son glaive vorpal en main il va-
> T-à la recherche du fauve manscant;
> Puis arrivé à l'arbre Té-Té,
> Il y reste, réfléchissant.

These verses from *Jabberwocky – Der Jammerwoch – Le Jaseroque* are by Lewis Carroll, Robert Scott and Frank Warrin. See Victor Proetz, *The Astonishment of Words* (Austin: University of Texas Press, 1971).

A further possibility is for translation to lead unintentionally to nonsense or undesirable phrasing. ' "Body by Fisher", describing a General Motors product, translated as "Corpse by Fisher", in Flemish, which did not help sales.... When General Motors put out its Chevrolet Nova, apparently no one thought of foreign sales. Nova, when spoken as two words in Spanish, means "It doesn't go".... Cue toothpaste, a Colgate–Palmolive product, was advertised in France without translation errors, but Cue happens to be the name of a widely circulated book on oral sex. A laundry soap ad in Quebec promised users "clean genitals". "Come alive with Pepsi" almost appeared in the Chinese version of *Reader's Digest* as "Pepsi Brings Your Ancestors Back from the Grave".' (Anonymous, 'Xenophobia', *Harper's*, May 1981, pp. 64–5).

106   Here are some other famous observations on translation through the ages. In his *Convivio* (*c.*1305), Dante expressed a still-common view that the higher flights of literature, those touched by the Muses, cannot be translated without loss:

> Nulla cosa per legame musaico
> armonizzata si può de la sua
> loquela in altra transmutare, senza
> rompere tutta sua dolcezza e armonia.
>
>   (Steiner, 1975, pp. 240–1).

Andrew Marvell (1621–1678) wrote a poem, *To his Worthy Friend Doctor Witty upon his Translation of the Popular Errors*, in which he observed:

> He is translation's thief that addeth more,
> As much as he that taketh from the store of the first author.

See H. Margoliouth, *The Poems and Letters of Andrew Marvell* (London: Oxford University Press, 1927). This sentiment was echoed a little later by Alexander Pope (1688–1744) in his preface to *The Iliad*:

> It is certain no literal Translation can be just to an excellent Original in a superior Language: but it is a great Mistake to imagine as many have done that a rash Paraphrase can make amends for this general Defect.

See *The Iliad of Homer*, edited by Maynard Mack (London: Methuen, 1967, p. 17). It was of course Pope's own translation of *The Iliad* that prompted Richard Bentley's (1662–1742) famous remark: 'It is a pretty poem, Mr. Pope, but you must not call it Homer' (see Samuel Johnson's *Life of Pope*). In more recent times we find George Borrow (1803–1881) observing bluntly (in *Lavengro*) that 'translation is at best an echo' (London: Oxford University Press, 1951, p. 175). Originally published in 1851. And Vladimir Nabokov, more poetic and more condemnatory, asks in *On Translating Eugene Onegin*:

> What is translation? On a platter
> A poet's pale and glaring head,
> A parrot's screech, a monkey's chatter,
> And profanation of the dead.

107   Ferdinand de Saussure (translator, Wade Baskin), *Course in General Linguistics*

(London: Peter Owen, 1960, p. 205). Of course, the idea of *un patriotism de clocher* predates Saussure's usage which is not, itself, a new coinage. *Clocher* alone signifies *la paroisse* or one's *pays natal*. A person *qui n'a vu que son clocher* is a bumpkin.

108 'Nous avons cru pouvoir conserver cette pittoresque expression de l'auteur [i.e., de Saussure], bien qu'elle soit empruntée à l'anglais (*intercourse*, prononcez *interkors* ...), et qu'elle se justifie moins dans l'exposé théorique que dans l'explication orale' (Ferdinand de Saussure, *Cours de Linguistique Générale*, Charles Bally and Albert Sechehaye (eds), Paris: Payot, 1980, p. 281).

109 de Saussure/Baskin, 1960, p. 206.

110 Benjamin Barber, 'Jihad vs McWorld' (*Atlantic Monthly*, March 1992, p. 53).

3 BILINGUALISM

1 There is a large and often quite technical literature on bilingualism. Some of the most useful recent works are Suzanne Romaine, *Bilingualism* (Blackwell, 1989); Hugo Baetens Beardsmore, *Bilingualism: Basic Principles* (Clevedon, Avon: Multilingual Matters 1986, 2nd edn); Kenji Hakuta, *Mirror of Language* (New York: Basic Books, 1986); Colin Baker, *Key Issues in Bilingualism and Bilingual Education* (Clevedon, Avon: Multilingual Matters, 1988); François Grosjean, *Life with Two Languages* (Cambridge, Massachusetts: Harvard University Press, 1982); Josiane Hamers and M. Blanc, *Bilingualité et Bilinguisme* (Brussels: Pierre Mardaga, 1983 – in English, Cambridge University Press, 1989). Each of these has an extensive bibliography. A good brief account is W. Mackey, 'Bilingualism and multilingualism' (in U. Ammon, N. Dittmar and K. Mattheier (eds), *Soziolinguistik*, Berlin: De Gruyter, 1987).

2 Leonard Bloomfield, *Language* (New York: Holt, 1933).

3 Uriel Weinreich, *Languages in Contact* (The Hague: Mouton, 1953).

4 Einar Haugen, *The Norwegian Language in America* (Philadelphia: University of Pennsylvania Press, 1953).

5 William Mackey, 'The description of bilingualism' (*Canadian Journal of Linguistics*, 1962, 7, 51–85).

6 Baker, 1988, p. 2.

7 Weinreich, 1953.

8 L.G. Kelly, *Description and Measurement of Bilingualism* (Toronto: University of Toronto Press, 1969) remains of some general value here. See also Romaine, 1989.

9 Baetens Beardsmore, 1986; Romaine, 1989.

10 Baetens Beardsmore, 1986, p. 7.

11 On p. 437 of Leonard Bloomfield, 'Literate and illiterate speech' (*American Speech*, 1927, 2, 432–9). This article is reprinted in Dell Hymes, *Language in Culture and Society* (New York: Harper & Row, 1964).

12 On p. 12 of Arthur Conan Doyle, 'A study in scarlet' (*The Complete Sherlock Holmes Long Stories*, London: John Murray, 1966).

13 Marilyn Martin-Jones and Suzanne Romaine, 'Semilingualism: a half-baked theory of communicative competence' (*Applied Linguistics*, 1985, 6, 105–17). A dubious concept from the first, semilingualism is now largely dismissed out of hand by modern linguists. Thus, Christina Bratt Paulston notes that 'semilingualism does not exist' and Tove Skutnabb-Kangas observes: 'In the

scientific debate the word has outlived its usefulness and should go ... [It is not] a linguistic or scientific concept at all ... it is a political concept.' Both writers are quoted by Baetens Beardsmore, 1986, p. 13.

14 See the 'fallacy of unobtainable perfection', in which lack of perfection is used as the basis for rejecting an argument or a position (Madsen Pirie, *The Book of the Fallacy*, London: Routledge & Kegan Paul, 1985).

15 John Milton, 'Of education' (*Prose Writings*, London: Dent, 1958, p. 323).

16 In 1886, Douglas Hyde defended Irish as the language best suited to the Gael's 'organs of speech' (p. 670 in 'A plea for the Irish language', *Dublin University Review*, 1886, 2, 666–76). A few years later, Máire Ní Mhurchadha agreed, seeing Irish as the natural clothing of the Irish mind ('The educational value of the Gaelic revival', *Irish Educational Review*, 1907, 1, 158–65). And R. Fullerton observed that the Irish brain was 'attuned' to thought in an Irish manner; in effect, the language was already inside Irish heads – teaching it, then, involved a drawing-out rather than a putting-in! ('The place of Irish in Ireland's education', *Irish Educational Review*, 1912, 5, 456–66).

17 Jules Ronjat, *Le Développement du langage observé chez un infant bilingue* (Paris: Champion, 1913); see also Baetens Beardsmore, 1986.

18 Werner Leopold's four volumes are collectively entitled *Speech Development of a Bilingual Child* (Evanston, Illinois: Northwestern University Press). Volume 1 (1939) deals with early vocabulary development, Volume 2 (1947) with the learning of sounds, Volume 3 (1949) with grammar and Volume 4 (also 1949) with a diary kept from the age of two.

19 George Saunders, *Bilingual Children: Guidance for the Family* (Clevedon, Avon: Multilingual Matters, 1982); E. Harding and P. Riley, *The Bilingual Family: A Handbook for Parents* (Cambridge: Cambridge University Press, 1986); E. de Jong, *The Bilingual Experience: A Book for Parents* (Cambridge: Cambridge University Press, 1986). The publishers of Saunders's book also issue a regular *Bilingual Family Newsletter.*

20 See David Singleton, *Language Acquisition: The Age Factor* (Clevedon, Avon: Multilingual Matters, 1989) and Birgit Harley, *Age in Second Language Acquisition* (Clevedon, Avon: Multilingual Matters, 1986).

21 George Orwell, 'England your England' (*Inside the Whale and Other Essays*, Harmondsworth: Penguin, 1964, p. 74). Originally published in *The Lion and the Unicorn* (London: Secker & Warburg, 1941).

22 Robert Gardner and W.E. Lambert, *Attitudes and Motivation in Second-Language Learning* (Rowley, Massachusetts: Newbury House, 1972); Ellen Ryan and Howard Giles, *Attitudes Towards Language Variation* (London: Edward Arnold, 1982); Howard Giles and Nikolas Coupland, *Language: Contexts and Consequences* (Milton Keynes: Open University Press, 1991); Howard Giles and Peter Robinson, *Handbook of Language and Social Psychology* (Chichester and New York: Wiley, 1990).

23 Bernard Spolsky, 'Bridging the gap: a general theory of second language learning' (TESOL Quarterly, 1988, 22, 377–96) and *Conditions for Second Language Learning* (Oxford: Oxford University Press, 1989).

24 John Firth, *The Tongues of Men and Speech* (London: Oxford University Press, 1970, p. 211).

25 Weinreich, 1953.

26 D. Spoerl, 'Bilinguality and emotional adjustment' (*Journal of Abnormal and Social Psychology*, 1946, 38, 37–57).

27 Baker, 1988, has a good discussion of bilingualism and intelligence.

28 Otto Jespersen, *Language* (London: Allen & Unwin, 1922, p. 148).

29 On p. 393 of F. Goodenough, 'Racial differences in the intelligence of school children' (*Journal of Experimental Psychology*, 1926, 9, 388–97).

30 See Benno Müller-Hill, *Murderous Science* (London: Oxford University Press, 1988) for an account of the 'scientific' selection of Jews and others in Germany, 1933–1945.

31 On problems with intelligence testing, see Andrew Colman, *Facts, Fallacies and Frauds in Psychology* (London: Hutchinson, 1987); R. Fancher, *The Intelligence Men* (New York: Norton, 1985); and Stephen Gould, *The Mismeasure of Man* (New York: Norton, 1981).

32 Elizabeth Peal and W.E. Lambert, 'The relation of bilingualism to intelligence' (*Psychological Monographs*, 1962, 76, 1–23). Reprinted in Gardner and Lambert, 1972.

33 Peal and Lambert (in Gardner and Lambert), 1972, p. 277.

34 Baker, 1988, p. 19.

35 Barry McLaughlin, *Second-Language Acquisition in Childhood* (Hillsdale, New Jersey: Erlbaum, 1978, p. 206).

36 George Steiner, *After Babel* (London: Oxford University Press, 1975); Weinreich, 1953.

37 Examples 1 and 2 are from Romaine, 1989; example 3 is from Beryl Benderly, 'The multilingual mind' (*Psychology Today*, March 1981, 9–12). Slightly different from these examples is 'foreign accent syndrome'. A recent case involved a 32-year-old American with no experience of foreign languages, who suffered a stroke, began speaking with a 'Scandinavian' accent, and appeared unfamiliar with English. At work here seems to be a brain malfunction which produces speech sounding like a foreign accent. Perhaps this is accounted for by listeners' perceptions, but other cases have involved apparent German, Spanish, Welsh, Scottish, Irish and Italian accents, and one wonders, then, about the circumstances which control the accent variety which emerges (reported in *English Today*, 1991, 27, 30).

38 Figure 3.1 is from Joan Rubin, *National Bilingualism in Paraguay* (The Hague: Mouton, 1968, p. 109).

39 Weinreich, 1953, p. 1.

40 Examples 1, 2, 4 and 5 are from Romaine, 1989; example 3 is from Baetens Beardsmore, 1986.

41 For some of the listed words, I found John Ayto, *Dictionary of Word Origins* (New York: Arcade, 1990) to be useful.

42 *Globe and Mail* (Toronto), 14 July 1992, commenting on the entry for Quebec English in Tom McArthur, *Oxford Companion to the English Language* (Oxford: Oxford University Press, 1992).

43 Joachim du Bellay, *The Defence and Illustration of the French Language* (London: Dent, 1939, pp. 81–82).

44 Examples from Robert McCrum, William Cran and Robert MacNeil, *The Story of English* (New York: Viking, 1986) and Mary Salter, 'A gorgeous "na" melody' (*Atlantic Monthly*, October 1981, 8–19).

45 Some of Orwell's ideas here were first aired in his regular 'As I please' column (*Tribune*, 21 April 1944). Reprinted in Sonia Orwell and Ian Angus (eds), *The Collected Essays, Journals and Letters of George Orwell* (Harmondsworth: Penguin, 1970); see Vol. 3, pp. 155–8. Later the views were more developed in 'Politics and the English language' (*Horizon*, April 1946). Reprinted in *Inside the Whale and Other Essays*, 1964, pp. 143–57; also in Vol. 4 of the *Collected Essays*. The quotations are from 'As I please', p. 157 and 'Politics and the English language', pp. 147–8.

46 Weinreich, 1953, p. 60.
47 If code-switching is often seen negatively, so too is bilingualism itself. During his tour of Britain (*The Kingdom by the Sea*, Harmondsworth: Penguin, 1984), Paul Theroux found himself wondering:

> whether the Welsh could be explained in terms of being bilingual, which is so often a form of schizophrenia, allowing a person to hold two contradictory opinions in his head at once, because his opinions remain untranslated. The Welsh had that mildly stunned and slap-happy personality that I associated with people for whom speaking two languages was a serious handicap. It made them profligate with language, it made them inexact, it had turned them into singers – well, that was no bad thing, they said. I did not think it was a question of good or bad, but only a kind of confusion.
>
> (pp. 163–4)

Well, Theroux shows himself to be no linguist (or psychologist) and, when he goes on to remark that bilingual signs in Wales are 'as unnecessary as the road signs in Canada, but like Canada's they [serve] a political purpose – a cheap sop tossed to the nationalists' (p. 154), he no doubt makes enemies on both sides of the Atlantic. Finally, Theroux reveals an ambivalent attitude (at best) towards Welsh itself: a 'whining, West Indian lilt ... with slushy throat-clearing ... full of interesting words ... some were grunts' (p. 164). I wonder if he's been back to St Dogmaels?

48 On the value and uses of code-switching, see Carol Scotton and William Ury, 'Bilingual strategies: the social functions of code-switching' (*International Journal of the Sociology of Language*, 1977, 13, 5–20) and Carol Scotton, 'The possibility of code-switching: motivations for maintaining multilingualism' (*Anthropological Linguistics*, 1982, 24, 432–44). A recent study suggests that code-switching, hitherto thought to occur only after the age of three or so, can be found among two-year-olds. The basic problem here was to demonstrate that this early mixing was not simple confusion but, rather, context-sensitive. See Elizabeth Lanza, 'Can bilingual two-year-olds code-switch?' (*Journal of Child Language*, 1992, 19, 633–58).

49 Robert Graves, *Goodbye to All That* (Harmondsworth: Penguin, 1960, p. 246). Originally published in 1929.

50 Bertrand Russell, *Unpopular Essays* (London: Allen & Unwin, 1950, p. 217). Gladstone it was, by the way, who reputedly gave us the word *antidisestablishmentarianism* – commonly held by schoolchildren to be the longest English word; no doubt it has long been replaced by some chemical monster.

51 Martin Joos, *The Five Clocks* (New York: Harcourt, Brace & World, 1967). Joos derives his title, incidentally, from an Irish joke:

> Ballyhough railway station has two clocks which disagree by some six minutes. When one helpful Englishman pointed the fact out to a porter, his reply was 'Faith, sir, if they was to tell the same time, why would we be having two of them?'

52 Joos, 1967, p. 19.
53 Joos, 1967, pp. 25–6.
54 Joos, 1967, pp. 36–7.
55 Joos, 1967, p. 19.
56 Reasons for language variation has been a neglected topic until fairly recently;

see Erving Goffman, 'The neglected situation' (*American Anthropologist*, 1964, 66, 133–6) and *Forms of Talk* (Oxford: Blackwell, 1981). See also Giles and Coupland, 1991.

57 Figure 3.2 is from p. 35 of Penelope Brown and Colin Fraser, 'Speech as a marker of situation' (in Klaus Scherer and Howard Giles (eds), *Social Markers in Speech*, Cambridge: Cambridge University Press, 1979). The whole Scherer and Giles book is valuable on this topic.

58 See E.G. Lewis, 'Bilingualism and bilingual education: the ancient world to the Renaissance' (in Joshua Fishman, *Bilingual Education*, Rowley, Massachusetts: Newbury House, 1976).

59. p 11 in William Mackey, 'La genèse d'une typologie de la diglossie' (*Revue Québécoise de linguistique théorique et appliquée*, 1989, 8, 11–28).

60 Charles Ferguson, 'Diglossia' (*Word*, 1959, 15, 325–40). Reprinted in Pier Paolo Giglioli, *Language and Social Context* (Harmondsworth: Penguin, 1972).

61 Ferguson, 1959 (in Giglioli), p. 236.

62 See Joshua Fishman, 'Bilingualism with and without diglossia: diglossia with and without bilingualism' (*Journal of Social Issues*, 1967, 23, 29–38). Reprinted, and slightly expanded, in *The Sociology of Language* (Rowley, Massachusetts: Newbury House, 1972). A good discussion of the 'original' diglossia, its 'extension', and complications arising is found in Ralph Fasold, *The Sociolinguistics of Society* (Oxford: Blackwell, 1984). In a brief article, Giuseppe Francescato also discusses some complications, particularly with Fishman's four-category scheme: 'Bilingualism and diglossia in their mutual relationship' (in J. Fishman, A. Tabouret-Keller, M. Clyne, B. Krishnamurti and M. Abdulaziz (eds), *The Fergusonian Impact*, Berlin: de Gruyter, 1986). See also André Martinet, 'The dynamics of plurilingual situations' in the same volume. A whole issue of the *Southwest Journal of Linguistics* (1991, 10) was devoted to studies of diglossia; this comprises Alan Hudson's discussion of the area as a whole, followed by ten case studies, and concludes with a piece by Ferguson in which he considers the strength and weaknesses of his original formulation.

63 See William Mackey, 'The polyglossic spectrum' and Asmah Haji Omar, 'Sociolinguistic varieties of Malay' (both in Fishman *et al.*, 1986); and A. Elgibali, 'The language situation in Arabic-speaking nations' (in Christina Bratt Paulston (ed.), *International Handbook of Bilingualism and Bilingual Education*, Westport, Connecticut: Greenwood, 1988).

64 See Ronald Wardhaugh, *An Introduction to Sociolinguistics* (Oxford: Blackwell, 1986). For a useful critique of bilingualism and diglossia which, among other things, notes that the association of diglossia with stability can be misleading, and which discusses the phantom of language 'choice' in models of social bilingualism in which languages and domains are rigorously categorized, see Marilyn Martin-Jones, 'Language, power and linguistic minorities: the need for an alternative approach to bilingualism, language maintenance and shift' (in Ralph Grillo (ed.), *Social Anthropology and the Politics of Language*, London: Routledge, 1989).

65 Some reckon Fishman's extension has trivialized Ferguson's original discussion of diglossia, especially for the Arabic case which was so central to it; some others, indeed, have even felt that diglossia should be reserved *only* for Arabic! Finally, Elgibali (1988) observes that the real nature of diglossia can be grasped 'only if one recalls the supreme authority of the Qur'an in all matters, especially language' (p. 58).

66 See Kenneth McRae, *Conflict and Compromise in Multilingual Societies*, Vols 1 and 2 (Waterloo, Ontario: Wilfrid Laurier University Press, 1983 and 1986);

Kenneth McRoberts, 'Federalism and political community' (a series of articles in the *Globe and Mail* (Toronto), 19 March to 2 April 1990); Colin Williams, 'Official language districts' (*Ethnic and Racial Studies*, 1981, 4, 334–47); and John Edwards, 'Ethnolinguistic pluralism and its discontents' (*International Journal of the Sociology of Language*, in press).

4 LANGUAGES IN CONFLICT

1 The attitude of Rivarol has led to the term 'un rivarolisme' (for which I am grateful to Professor William Mackey). Certainly, the idea that French is a uniquely limpid medium remains strong. Wolf Lepenies recently asked, 'Did you ever, in a discussion among French intellectuals, hear someone ask: "What did you mean by saying this?" "Could you please repeat what you just said?" I bet that you will never have heard words to that effect because this would be more than just impolite, it would be an unpardonable offence against the French language itself.' ('Speak in tongues to be a big cheese', *Times Higher Education Supplement*, 20 March 1992).

2 Eric Lenneberg, *Biological Foundations of Language* (New York: Wiley, 1967, p. 367).

3 Ernest Gellner, 'The new idealism: cause and meaning in the social sciences' (in I. Lakatos and A. Musgrave (eds), *Problems in the Philosophy of Science*, Amsterdam: North Holland, 1968, p. 388).

4 On the difficulties of 'getting inside' foreign cultures with accuracy, see Karl Heider, 'The Rashomon effect: when ethnographers disagree' (*American Anthropologist*, 1988, 90, 73–81).

5 See John Carroll, *Language, Thought and Reality: Selected Writings of Benjamin Lee Whorf* (Cambridge, Massachusetts: MIT Press, 1972).

6 Geoffrey Pullum, *The Great Eskimo Vocabulary Hoax and Other Irreverent Essays on the Study of Language* (Chicago: University of Chicago Press, 1991).

7 Joachim du Bellay, *The Defence and Illustration of the French Language* (London: Dent, 1939, pp. 46–7).

8 See John Honey, *The Language Trap* (Kenton, Middlesex: National Council for Educational Standards, 1983); and the rebuttal by John Edwards in a review article (*Journal of Language and Social Psychology*, 1983, 2, 67–76).

9 Even dictionary definitions of dialect and accent help to sustain the view that nonstandard language is less correct language. The *Oxford English Dictionary*, for example, notes that dialect may be considered as:

> one of the subordinate forms or varieties of language arising from local peculiarities of vocabulary, pronunciation, and idiom.

This definition is implicitly held by those for whom the term 'dialect' conjures up an image of some rustic, regional speech pattern. On 'accent' the *OED* is not much better; it is, we find, a mode of utterance which:

> consists mainly in a prevailing quality of tone, or in a peculiar alteration of pitch, but may include mispronunciation of vowels or consonants, misplacing of stress, and misinflection of a sentence.

Again, this does not correspond well with the value-free judgements of linguists.

10 Peter Trudgill, *Accent, Dialect and the School* (London: Edward Arnold, 1975, p. 26).

11 William Labov, *Language in the Inner City* (Philadelphia: University of Pennsylvania Press, 1976). Studies of 'Black English' should not lead us to think that it is some monolithic, unchanging variety. There are regional varieties within it. While the work of Labov and others has focused upon inner-city usage, other investigations demonstrate that not all of the features found there are characteristic of *all* Black speech. A study of rural speech in Nova Scotia has found, for example, recognizably 'black' language which does not include the grammatical variants associated with urban forms (see John Edwards, 'Reactions to three types of speech samples from rural black and white children in Nova Scotia', in L. Falk and M. Harry (eds), *The English Language in Nova Scotia*, in press). There is also current interest in the question of whether or not Black speech, generally, is diverging more from white (see William Labov, 'Are black and white vernaculars diverging?' *American Speech*, 1987, 62, 3–80; Geneva Smitherman, 'Black English, diverging or converging?' *Language and Education*, 1992, 6, 47–61). Finally, a recent study by Barbara Speicher and Seane McMahon has shown varying attitudes towards 'Black English' within the Black community itself ('Some African-American perspectives on Black English Vernacular', *Language in Society*, 1992, 21, 383–407).

12 R.W. Chapman, 'Oxford English' (*Society for Pure English*, 1932, 4) (no. 37).

13 Henry Wyld, 'The best English: a claim for the superiority of Received Standard English' (*Society for Pure English*, 1934, 4) (no. 39).

14 Much of interest concerning Chapman, Wyld and many others interested in maintaining 'standards' is found in Tony Crowley, *The Politics of Discourse* (London: Macmillan, 1989).

15 See H. Giles, R. Bourhis, P. Trudgill and A. Lewis, 'The imposed norm hypothesis: a validation' (*Quarterly Journal of Speech*, 1974, 60, 405–10); and H. Giles, R. Bourhis and A. Davies, 'Prestige speech styles: the imposed norm and inherent value hypotheses' (in W. McCormack and S. Wurm, (eds), *Language and Society: Anthropological Issues*, The Hague: Mouton, 1979).

16 See Trudgill, 1975.

17 See John Edwards, *Language and Disadvantage* (London: Cole & Whurr, 1989) and Peter Trudgill, *On Dialect* (Oxford: Blackwell, 1983).

18 R. LaPiere, 'Attitudes versus actions' (*Social Forces*, 1934, 13, 230–7).

19 W.E. Lambert, R. Hodgson, R. Gardner and S. Fillenbaum, 'Evaluational reactions to spoken languages' (*Journal of Abnormal and Social Psychology*, 1960, 60, 44–51). Reprinted in R. Gardner and W.E. Lambert, *Attitudes and Motivation in Second Language Learning* (Rowley, Massachusetts: Newbury House, 1972). See also Edwards, 1989, for fuller details.

20 M. Bragg and S. Ellis, *Word of Mouth* (London: BBC Television, 1976).

21 John Edwards and Maryanne Jacobsen, 'Standard and regional standard speech: distinctions and similarities' (*Language in Society*, 1987, 16, 369–80).

22 E. Ryan, H. Giles and R. Sebastian, 'An integrative perspective for the study of attitudes toward language variation' (in E. Ryan and H. Giles (eds), *Attitudes Towards Language Variation*, London: Edward Arnold, 1982).

23 See James Bradac, 'Language attitudes and impression formation' (in H. Giles and W.P. Robinson (eds), *Handbook of Language and Social Psychology*, Chichester and New York: Wiley, 1990); Christopher Zahn and Robert Hopper, 'Measuring language attitudes: the speech evaluation instrument' (*Journal of Language and Social Psychology*, 1985, 4, 113–23).

24 William Mackey, 'The importation of bilingual education models' (in J. Alatis (ed.), *Georgetown University Round Table on Languages and Linguistics*, Washington: Georgetown University Press, 1978, p. 7).

25 See the article on Gresham's Law by C. Harris (in J. Eatwell, M. Milgate and P. Newman (eds), *The New Palgrave: A Dictionary of Economics*, London: Macmillan, 1987).

26 T. O'Rahilly, *Irish Dialects Past and Present* (Dublin: Institute for Advanced Studies, 1932).

27 See D.A. Binchy, 'Review of *Gaelic and Scottish Education and Life: Past, Present and Future* (J.L. Campbell)' (*The Bell*, 1945, 10, 362–6).

28 Sydney Brooks, *The New Ireland* (Dublin: Maunsel, 1907, p. 22).

29 D. Gregor, *Celtic: A Comparative Study* (New York: Oleander, 1982).

30 Norman Denison, 'Language death or language suicide?' (*International Journal of the Sociology of Language*, 1977, 12, 13–22).

31 Jean Aitchison, *Language Change: Progress or Decay?* (London: Fontana, 1981).

32 Denison, 1977, p. 21.

33 See Ronald Wardhaugh, *Languages in Competition* (Oxford: Blackwell, 1987); Robert Cooper, *Language Spread* (Bloomington: Indiana University Press, 1982).

34 J. Platt, H. Weber and M. Ho, *The New Englishes* (London: Routledge & Kegan Paul, 1984); J. Pride, *New Englishes* (Rowley, Massachusetts: Newbury House, 1982); *World Englishes* and *English World-Wide* (journals published by Pergamon and John Benjamins, respectively).

35 The conflict between French and English is a particularly interesting one. The former is finding itself increasingly threatened globally, even in areas (the former French colonies in Africa, for example) in which its hegemony seemed, even quite recently, virtually unchallengeable. Closer to home, the power of English in the European Community is proving worrisome. Some 250 French intellectuals recently signed a statement of support, arguing in *Le Monde* that 'if [the EC] is to have only one language, we fail to see why it should be that of the United States': see Pauline Couture, 'Québécois voices' (*Globe and Mail* (Toronto), 14 July 1992). French scientists, too, are concerned: Claude Roux failed in a promotion attempt at the Centre National de la Recherche Scientifique and claimed (correctly, as it turned out) that his lack of publication in English was a central factor (David Bakewell, 'Publish in English, or perish', *Nature*, 23 April 1992). A recent book on the spread of English emphasizes the dangers to French (Claude Truchot, *L'Anglais dans le monde contemporaine*, Paris: Robert, 1990); see also Edwards, 1985; Wardhaugh, 1987.

36 John Edwards, *Language, Society and Identity* (Oxford: Blackwell, 1985).

37 John Edwards, 'Gaelic in Nova Scotia' (in C. Williams (ed.), *Linguistic Minorities, Society and Territory*, Clevedon, Avon: Multilingual Matters, 1991); John Edwards, Daniel MacInnes and Winston Jackson, 'Gaelic language attitudes in Nova Scotia: findings from a biased sample' (*International Journal of the Sociology of Language*, in press); Victor Durkacz, *The Decline of the Celtic Languages* (Edinburgh: John Donald, 1983).

38 Charles Dunn, *Highland Settler* (Toronto: University of Toronto Press, 1974, p. 134).

39 p. 70 in John Campbell, 'Scottish Gaelic in Canada' (*An Gaidheal*, 1948, 43, 69–71).

40 C. Ó Danachair, 'The Gaeltacht' (in B. Ó Cuív (ed.), *A View of the Irish Language*, Dublin: Government Stationery Office, 1969, p. 120).

41 Ernest Gellner, *Thought and Change* (London: Weidenfeld & Nicolson, 1964, p. 162).

42 It was Marcus Lee Hansen who observed that historical societies in America were often established by third-generation members; see 'The third generation

in America' (*Commentary*, 1952, 14, 492–500). In refuting 'Hansen's Law', John
Appel claimed, however, that such organizations were founded earlier, by
ethnic leaders, for specific ideological purposes (*Immigrant Historical Societies in
the Unites States, 1880–1950*, New York: Arno Press, 1980); see also Peter Kivisto
and Dag Blanck, *American Immigrants and their Generations: Studies and Commen-
taries on the Hansen Thesis after Fifty Years* (Urbana: University of Illinois Press,
1990).

43 Edwards, MacInnes and Jackson, in press.

44 D. Campbell and R. MacLean, *Beyond the Atlantic Roar: A Study of the Highland
Scots* (Toronto: McClelland & Stewart, 1974, p. 178).

45 R. Fullerton, *The Prudence of St Patrick's Irish Policy* (Dublin: O'Brien & Ards,
1916, p. 6).

46 D. O'Donoghue, 'Nationality and language' (in Columban League (ed.), *Irish
Man – Irish Nation*, Cork: Mercier, 1947, p. 24).

47 Daniel Dewar, *Observations on the Character, Customs and Superstitions of the Irish:
and on some of the Causes which have retarded the Moral and Political Improvement of
Ireland* (London: Gale & Curtis, 1812).

48 Christopher Anderson, *A Brief Sketch of Various Attempts which have been made to
diffuse a Knowledge of the Holy Scripture through the Medium of the Irish Language*
(Dublin: Graisberry & Campbell, 1818, p. 59).

49 Henry Mason, *History of the Origin and Progress of the Irish Society, established for
Promoting the Education of the Native Irish, through the Medium of their own Language*
(Dublin: Goodwin, Son & Nethercott, 1846, p. 9).

50 Nancy Dorian, 'Language loss and maintenance in language contact situations'
(in R. Lambert and B. Freed (eds), *The Loss of Language Skills*, Rowley,
Massachusetts: Newbury House, 1982, p. 47).

51 Glyn Williams, 'Language group allegiance and ethnic interaction' (in H. Giles
and B. Saint-Jacques (eds), *Language and Ethnic Relations*, New York: Pergamon,
1979, p. 58).

52 Ralph Linton, cited by Uriel Weinreich, *Languages in Contact* (The Hague:
Mouton, 1974, p. 101).

53 Max Weber, *Essays in Sociology* (London: Routledge & Kegan Paul, 1961,
p. 171).

54 See Antonio Gramsci, *Selections from Political Writings* and *Selections from Cultural
Writings* (London: Lawrence & Wishart, 1978 and 1985).

55 p. 11 in Hugh Trevor-Roper and George Urban, 'Aftermaths of empire'
(*Encounter*, 1989, 73, 3–16).

56 Gellner, 1964, p. 160.

57 Weinreich, 1974, p. 108.

58 Osborn Bergin, cited by Tomás Ó hAilín, 'Irish revival movements' (in B. Ó
Cuív (ed.), *A View of the Irish Language*, Dublin: Government Stationery Office,
1969, p. 91).

59 Glanville Price, *The Languages of Britain* (London: Edward Arnold, 1984, p. 143).

60 p. 5 in Michael Tierney, 'The revival of the Irish language' (*Studies*, 1927, 16,
1–10).

61 Moshe Nahir, 'The five aspects of language planning' (*Language Problems and
Language Planning*, 1977, 1, 107–23).

62 P.B. Ellis and S. mac a'Ghobhainn, *The Problem of Language Revival* (Inverness:
Club Leabhar, 1971).

63 Chaim Rabin, 'A tentative classification of language planning aims' (in Joan
Rubin and Björn Jernudd (eds), *Can Language be Planned?* Honolulu: University
Press of Hawaii, 1971).

64   p. 268 in D. P. Moran, 'The Gaelic revival' (*New Ireland Review*, 1900, 12, 257–72).

65   Desmond Fennell, 'Can a shrinking linguistic minority be saved?' (in E. Haugen, J. McClure and D. Thomson (eds), *Minority Languages Today*, Edinburgh: Edinburgh University Press, 1981, p. 30).

66   pp. 11, 31 and 32 in Joshua Fishman, 'What is reversing language shift (RLS) and how can it succeed?' (*Journal of Multilingual and Multicultural Development*, 1990, 11, 5–36); see also *Reversing Language Shift* (Clevedon, Avon: Multilingual Matters, 1991).

67   Alf Mac Lochlainn, 'Gael and peasant' (in D. Casey and R. Rhodes (eds), *Views of the Irish Peasantry*, Hamden, Connecticut: Archon, 1977, p. 34).

68   American work on dictionaries of the Assyrian, Sumerian, Demotic Egyptian, Hittite and other languages is clearly worthy and scholarly. Sometimes referred to as 'necrolexicography', it is nicely unencumbered by real speakers. If, as we saw in Chapter 1, it is not the best of times for many living varieties, 'there has never been a better time to be a dead language' – so observes Cullen Murphy on p. 20 of 'Huiswants es' (*Atlantic Monthly*, August 1992, 18–22). The title, incidentally, is a standard Hittite greeting – 'Be alive'.

69   See John Campbell, *Songs Remembered in Exile* (Aberdeen: Aberdeen University Press, 1990).

70   p. 301 in Moshe Nahir, 'Language planning goals' (*Language Problems and Language Planning*, 1984, 8, 294–327).

71   James Joyce, *Ulysses* (New York: Random House, 1961, p. 14).

72   Dermot Trench, *What is the Use of Reviving Irish?* (Dublin: Maunsel, 1907).

73   p. 65 in Nancy Dorian, 'The value of language-maintenance efforts which are unlikely to succeed' (*International Journal of the Sociology of Language*, 1987, 68, 57–67).

74   Ellis and mac a'Ghobhainn, 1971, p. 143.

5 LANGUAGES AND IDENTITIES

1   See W. Isajiw, 'Definitions of ethnicity' (in Rita Bienvenue and Jay Goldstein (eds), *Ethnicity and Ethnic Relations in Canada*, Toronto: Butterworths, 1985); see also John Edwards, *Language, Society and Identity* (Oxford: Blackwell, 1985).

2   Fredrick Barth, *Ethnic Groups and Boundaries* (Boston: Little, Brown, 1969).

3   T. Shibutani and K. Kwan, *Ethnic Stratification* (New York: Macmillan, 1965, pp. 40–1).

4   Max Weber, *Economy and Society* (New York: Bedminster, 1968, p. 389).

5   Isajiw, 1985, p. 14.

6   Herbert Gans, 'Symbolic ethnicity' (*Ethnic and Racial Studies*, 1979, 2, 1–20).

7   Gans, 1979, p. 1.

8   Gans, 1979, p. 10.

9   See Ma Shu Yun, 'Ethnonationalism, ethnic nationalism and mini-nationalism: a comparison of Connor, Smith and Snyder' (*Ethnic and Racial Studies*, 1990, 13, 527–41).

10   Elie Kedourie, *Nationalism* (London: Hutchinson, 1961, p. 9). It is a sad coincidence that, as I write this, I note in the *Times Literary Supplement* (10 July 1992) that Professor Kedourie died on 29 June. The last publication of this eminent scholar of nationalism was a review of two new books on Algeria; his death occurred on the same day as President Mohammed Boudiaf's assassination.

11 See Walker Connor, 'A nation is a nation, is a state, is an ethnic group, is a ...'
    (*Ethnic and Racial Studies*, 1978, 1, 377–400).

12 In his book *The Thirteenth Tribe* (London: Picador, 1980), Arthur Koestler saw
    the descendants of the biblical tribes as 'the classic example of linguistic
    adaptability', a strong demonstration of group identity outliving commu-
    nicative language shift:

> first they spoke Hebrew; in the Babylonian exile, Chaldean; at the time
> of Jesus, Aramaic; in Alexandria, Greek; in Spain, Arabic, but later
> Ladino – a Spanish–Hebrew mixture written in Hebrew characters, the
> Sephardi equivalent of Yiddish; and so it goes on. They preserved their
> religious identity, but changed languages at their convenience.
>
> (p. 157)

13 Wilhelm von Humboldt, 1797; cited by A. Grafton, 'Wilhelm von Humboldt'
    (*American Scholar*, 1981, 50, 371–81).

14 Again, Humboldt; cited by M. Cowan, *Humanist without Portfolio: An Anthology
    of the Writings of Wilhelm von Humboldt* (Detroit: Wayne State University Press,
    1963).

15 Johann Herder, 1772; cited by I. Berlin, *Vico and Herder* (London: Hogarth,
    1976).

16 Thomas Davis, 1843; see *Essays and Poems with a Centenary Memoir* (Dublin: Gill
    & Son, 1945).

17 The Azerbaijani literary historian, Kochärli, 1913; cited by Tadeusz Swie-
    tochowski, 'The politics of a literary language and the rise of national identity
    in Russian Azerbaijan before 1920' (*Ethnic and Racial Studies*, 1991, 14, 55–63).

18 The Scots Gaelic, Breton and Manx slogans are commonly encountered; there
    are such motto-like sentiments for all languages, certainly for all seen to be 'at
    risk'. See Douglas Gregor, *Celtic: A Comparative Study* (New York: Oleander,
    1980).

19 Friedrich von Schlegel, *Geschichte der Alten und Neuen Literatur* (1815).

20 This is from Alphonse Daudet's (1840–1897) famous little story, 'La dernière
    classe' (in his *Contes du Lundi*. Paris: Nelson, 1963). M. Hamel, the school-
    master, has his last day in class, for on the next the Germans take over in Alsace-
    Lorraine. It is necessary always, he tells his pupils, to guard and remember
    French – 'la plus belle langue du monde, la plus claire, la plus solide'.

21 Spoken by Eamon de Valera, a man who made little real effort to give Irish
    more than symbolic status, but who clearly and cannily assessed the benefits of
    linguistic lip-service (see T. R. Dwyer, *Eamon de Valera*, Dublin: Gill & Macmillan,
    1980).

22 See the discussion in Edwards, 1985.

23 Conor Cruise O'Brien, *Passion and Cunning* (London: Weidenfeld & Nicolson,
    1988).

24 David Mandelbaum, *Selected Writings of Edward Sapir* (Berkeley: University of
    California Press, 1963, p. 88).

25 Sapir (Mandelbaum), 1963, p. 118.

26 G.N. Clark, cited by John Spencer in 'Language and development in Africa' (in
    N. Wolfson and J. Manes (eds), *Language of Inequality*, The Hague: Mouton,
    1985, p. 389).

27 E.G. Lewis, 'Bilingualism and bilingual education: the ancient world to the
    Renaissance' (in Joshua Fishman, *Bilingual Education*, Rowley, Massachusetts:
    Newbury House, 1976, p. 172).

28 Lewis, 1976, p. 180.

29 Ernest Gellner, *Nations and Nationalism* (Oxford: Blackwell, 1983, p. 127).

30 Einar Haugen, 'The language of imperialism' (in Wolfson and Manes, 1985).

31 Johann Fichte, *Addresses to the German Nation* (New York: Harper & Row, 1968, pp. 58–9).

32 Anthony Smith, *Theories of Nationalism* (London: Duckworth, 1971, p. 182); see also Smith's new *National Identity* (Harmondsworth: Penguin, 1991).

33 See the recent treatment by Gordon Craig, 'Herder: the legacy' (in Kurt Mueller-Volmer (ed.), *Herder Today*, Berlin: de Gruyter, 1990); see also J. Penrose and J. May, 'Herder's concept of nation and its relevance to contemporary ethnic nationalism' (*Canadian Review of Studies in Nationalism*, 1991, 18, 165–78).

34 Kedourie, 1961, p. 68.

35 Many are extremely suspicious of nationalism, of course, and some concur with Kedourie; Noam Chomsky, for example, sees nationalism as 'a very horrifying thing' and George Steiner has described it as 'the venom of our age' (see John Edwards, 'Ethnolinguistic pluralism and its discontents', *International Journal of the Sociology of Language*, in press).

36 Smith, 1971, pp. 18–19.

37 H. Psichari, *Oeuvres complètes de Ernest Renan* (Paris: Calmann-Lévy, 1947, p. 899).

38 Renan (Psichari), 1947, p. 903.

39 Anthony Smith, 'The supersession of nationalism?' (*International Journal of Comparative Sociology*, 1990, 31, 1–31).

40 Joseph Magnet, 'Language rights as collective rights' (in Karen Adams and Daniel Brink (eds), *Perspectives on Official English*, Berlin: de Gruyter, 1990, pp. 295–6).

41 Magnet, 1990, p. 293.

42 Jeffrey Simpson, 'A collision of minorities' (*Globe and Mail* (Toronto), 23 December 1988).

43 William Tetley, 'Why not let the majority have its way on signs?' (*Globe and Mail* (Toronto), 17 January 1989).

44 Thomas Walkom, 'A fight about power, not rights' (*Globe and Mail* (Toronto), 28 December 1988).

45 Walkom, 1988.

46 Pierre de Bané, 'A shameful strategy' (*Globe and Mail* (Toronto), 27 June 1989).

47 See Edwards, 1985.

48 p. 230 in Charles Ferguson, 'Diglossia revisited' (*Southwest Journal of Linguistics*, 1991, 10, 214–34).

49 Einar Haugen, *The Ecology of Language* (Stanford: Stanford University Press, 1972, p. 325).

50 p. 203 in E. Allardt, 'What constitutes a language minority?' (*Journal of Multilingual and Multicultural Development*, 1984, 5, 195–205).

51 See Paul White, 'Geographical aspects of minority language situations in Italy' (in C. Williams (ed.), *Linguistic Minorities, Society and Territory*, Clevedon, Avon: Multilingual Matters, 1991).

52 The Volga-German example comes from Dirk Hoerder, 'Reflections on ethnic cultures under multiculturalism' (Conference on *The Future of Your Past*, Toronto, November 1991); the table itself is taken from John Edwards, 'Notes for a minority-language typology' (*Journal of Multilingual and Multicultural Development*, 1990, 11, 137–51).

53 Charles Ferguson, 'The language factor in national development' (in F. Rice (ed.), *Study of the Role of Second Languages in Asia, Africa and Latin America*, Washington: Center for Applied Linguistics, 1962); and 'National sociolinguistic profile formulas' (in William Bright (ed.), *Sociolinguistics*, The Hague: Mouton, 1966).

54 William Stewart, 'An outline of linguistic typology for describing multilingualism' (in Rice, 1962); and 'A sociolinguistic typology for describing national multilingualism' (in Joshua Fishman (ed.), *Readings in the Sociology of Language*, The Hague: Mouton, 1968).

55 See Haugen, 1972.

56 Harald Haarmann, *Language in Ethnicity* (Berlin: de Gruyter, 1986).

57 See Howard Giles and Nikolas Coupland, *Language: Contexts and Consequences* (Milton Keynes: Open University Press, 1991).

58 For detailed treatment of my typological work, see Edwards, 1990; also 'Socioeducational issues concerning indigenous minority languages' (in J. Sikma and D. Gorter (eds), *European Lesser-Used Languages in Primary Education*, Leeuwarden: Fryske Akademy/Mercator, 1991) and 'Sociopolitical aspects of language maintenance and loss' (in W. Fase, K. Jaspaert and S. Kroon (eds), *Maintenance and Loss of Minority Languages*, Amsterdam: John Benjamins, 1992).

6 THE PRESCRIPTIVE URGE

1 Quintilian, *De Institutione Oratoria* (translated by H.E. Butler, London: Heinemann, 1921). Cited by Tony Crowley, *Proper English* (London: Routledge, 1991, p. 129).

2 The citation is from an unnamed purist, in Robert Hall, *Linguistics and Your Language* (New York: Doubleday Anchor, 1960, p. 54). This book is the second, revised edition of the 1950 work called *Leave Your Language Alone* – a title which makes clear the non-interventionist stance of modern linguistics, as well as the belief that *all* varieties are equally 'correct'.

3 Samuel Johnson, *The Plan of a Dictionary of the English Language* (London: Knapton *et al.*, 1747, p. 32); see also following entry.

4 Samuel Johnson, *A Dictionary of the English Language* (London: Knapton, *et al.*, 1755). The quotation is from the *Preface* to the dictionary; both are unpaginated. A facsimile edition of Johnson's dictionary – which is accompanied by the *Plan* – was published in London in 1990, by Longmans (who had been part of the original Knapton *et al.* consortium which published the original).

5 Johnson, 1755.

6 Johnson, 1755.

7 Cited by G.M. Trevelyan, *Illustrated English Social History* (Vol. 3) (London: Longmans, 1951, p. 110).

8 Cited by James Boswell, *The Life of Samuel Johnson* (London: Collins, n.d., pp. 104–5).

9 Cited by Robert Burchfield, *Unlocking the English Language* (New York: Hill & Wang, 1991, p. 121). Some of the information about Cobbett was gleaned from two treatments by Robertson Cochrane in his 'Word play' column (*Globe and Mail* (Toronto), 20 and 27 June 1992).

10 George Orwell, 'Politics and the English language' (in *Inside the Whale and Other Essays*, Harmondsworth: Penguin, 1964, p. 143).

11 Orwell, 1964, p. 156.

12 Whitney Bolton, 'William Caxton' (in Tom McArthur (ed.), *Oxford Companion to the English Language,* Oxford: Oxford University Press, 1992, p. 200).

13 Cited by G.N. Trevelyan, *Illustrated English Social History* (Vol. 1) (London: Longmans, 1949, pp. 78–9).

14 John Ayto, 'English: failures of language reforms' (in I. Fodor and C. Hagège (eds), *Language Reform: History and Future* (Vol. 1), Hamburg: Helmut Buske, 1983, p. 88).

15 Cited by John Joseph, *Eloquence and Power* (London: Pinter, 1987, p. 108).

16 Robert Hall, *External History of the Romance Languages* (New York: Elsevier, 1974, p. 174); Hall is useful throughout this section.

17 Hall, 1974, p. 174.

18 Hall, 1974, p. 176.

19 Ronald Wardhaugh, *Languages in Competition* (Oxford: Blackwell, 1987, p. 100).

20 See R. Wardhaugh, 1987 and Ralph Grillo, *Dominant Languages* (Cambridge: Cambridge University Press, 1989). See also Renée Balibar, *L'Institution du Français* (Paris: Presses Universitaires de France, 1985).

21 The biography of *Bertrand Barère: A Reluctant Terrorist* is by Leo Gershoy (Princeton: Princeton University Press, 1962).

22 Wardhaugh, 1987, p. 102.

23 Wardhaugh, 1987, p. 103.

24 For the Ordonnance de Villers-Cotterêts see Joseph, 1987 and Wardhaugh, 1987.

25 See Hall, 1974; Johannes Kramer, 'Language planning in Italy' (in Fodor and Hagège, 1983, Vol. 2); Jonathan Steinberg, 'The historian and the *questione della lingua*' (in P. Burke and R. Porter (eds), *The Social History of Language,* Cambridge: Cambridge University Press, 1987).

26 With increasing pressure for regional autonomy among northern Italians, who see their fortunes stifled by ineffectual southerners, we may see this old slogan replaced by '... in bocca milanese'. The Lombard League received 8 per cent of the overall Italian vote, and 20 per cent in the north, in the April 1992 election. In December 1992, these figures rose to 14 per cent and 40 per cent, respectively. The League is now the major political force in the north, in control of several important cities; country-wide, it is the second political party.

27 Again, Hall, 1974 is useful, especially on the Italian academies. The date (1572) of the founding of the Accademia della Crusca is open to question, since informal meetings of what was to become the Accademia began in the mid-sixteenth century; official recognition came, as noted, with the sponsorship of Duke Còsimo. On the occasion of its fourth centenary, the Accademia published *The Fairest Flower: The Emergence of Linguistic National Consciousness in Renaissance Europe* (Firenze, 1985); it contains some excellent studies.

28 Hall, 1974, p. 180.

29 Joshua Fishman, 'The impact of nationalism on language planning' (in Joan Rubin and Björn Jernudd (eds), *Can Language be Planned?* Honolulu: University Press of Hawaii, 1971, p. 10).

30 See G. Guitarte and R. Torres-Quintero, 'Linguistic correctness and the role of academies in Latin America' (in Joshua Fishman (ed.), *Advances in Language Planning,* The Hague: Mouton, 1974).

31 Randolph Quirk, *Style and Communication in the English Language* (London: Edward Arnold, 1982, pp. 67–8).

32 Robert McCrum, William Cran and Robert MacNeil, *The Story of English* (New York: Viking, 1986, p. 129).

33 Cited by Ayto, 1983, p. 92. The quotation is from Dryden's dedication to his play, *The Rival Ladies.*

34 Cited by McCrum *et al.*, 1986, p. 129.

35 See Ayto, 1983.

36 Cited by Tom McArthur, 'Academy' (in McArthur, 1992, p. 8).

37 Cited by Crowley, 1991, p. 31.

38 Crowley, 1991, p. 37.

39 A recent call for an English academy was made in 1984 by Professor Braj Kachru, a well-known writer on English and Englishes. Believing that English lags behind Spanish and French here, Kachru stressed that an 'academy of correction' was not envisaged; rather, he hoped for some sort of international clearing-house or think-tank (*Times Higher Education Supplement*, 28 September 1984).

40 Cited by Crowley, 1991, p. 19; the relevant sections of Locke's *Essay* are reproduced in Crowley's book.

41 Crowley, 1991, p. 68.

42 Modern lexicographers are less Quintilian-like and, even in 1877, Alexander Ellis (a co-worker with James Murray, the editor of the *Oxford English Dictionary*) was able to observe that 'hearing from a peasant's mouth is always safer than from a gentleman's and far better than from a lady's' (K. Murray, *Caught in the Web of Words*, New Haven: Yale University Press, 1977, p. 75).

43 See J.R. Hulbert, *Dictionaries: British and American* (London: André Deutsch, 1955).

44 Crowley, 1991, p. 128.

45 See David Crystal, *Cambridge Encyclopedia of Language* (Cambridge: Cambridge University Press, 1987).

46 See Shirley Heath, 'A national language academy? Debate in the new nation' (*International Journal of the Sociology of Language*, 1977, 11, 9–43); see also Glendon Drake, *The Role of Prescriptivism in American Linguistics, 1820–1970* (Amsterdam: John Benjamins, 1977).

47 Heath, 1977, p. 30.

48 Noah Webster, *Grammatical Institutes* (Hartford: Hudson & Goodwin, 1783, p. 7).

49 Tony Crowley, *The Politics of Discourse* (London: Macmillan, 1989).

50 Crowley, 1989, p. 165.

51 Crowley, 1989, p. 180.

52 Crowley, 1989, p. 183.

53 Examples are from William Lutz, 'The world of doublespeak' (in Christopher Ricks and Leonard Michaels (eds), *The State of the Language*, London: Faber & Faber, 1990).

54 Philip Howard, *The State of the Language* (New York: Oxford University Press, 1985, p. 63).

55 Howard, 1985, pp. 58–9.

56 Stanislav Andreski, *Social Sciences as Sorcery* (London: André Deutsch, 1972); see also John Harley, 'The smell of the lamp: bad writing in the behavioural sciences' (*Canadian Journal of Education*, 1983, 8, 245–62).

57 Dwight Bolinger, *Language: The Loaded Weapon* (London: Longmans, 1990).

58 See Drake, 1977 on the violent popular reaction to Webster's *Third New International Dictionary* (1961), which was produced on descriptivist principles: language constantly changes, change is normal, spoken language *is* the language, 'correctness' rests upon usage and all usage is relative.

59 In June 1989, the Prince of Wales was highly critical of a recent report on

English in the national curriculum; he talked of academic 'nonsense' and the need for a 'basic framework' and formal drills. He even complained that he had to correct all the letters sent from his own office. This occasioned, of course, a good deal of response, both from academics and others – but W.F. Deedes, writing in the *Daily Telegraph* (30 June) observed – no doubt correctly – that Prince Charles had said what the man on the Clapham omnibus was thinking. In December 1989, the heir to the throne made some further observations: modern usage was seen as appalling, and the common argument was made for some golden age – 'if English is spoken in Heaven ... God undoubtedly employs Cranmer as his speechwriter'. Prince Charles went on:

> Looking at the way English is used in our popular newspapers, our radio and television programmes, even in our schools and theatres, they [a great many people] wonder what it is about our country and our society that our language has become so impoverished, so sloppy and so limited – that we have arrived at such a dismal wasteland of banality, cliché and casual obscenity.
>
> (cited by Crowley, 1991, p. 9).

60 W. Haas, 'On the normative character of language' (in *Standard Language: Spoken and Written*, Manchester: Manchester University Press, 1982, p. 3).

61 George Thomas, *Linguistic Purism* (London: Longman, 1991, p. 13).

62 Hall, 1974.

63 Goethe, cited by Thomas, 1991, p. 101. Goethe also wrote a poem called *Die Sprachreiniger*, in which he lamented the drawing of a 'Pestkordon' around Germany to keep out 'Kopf, Körper und Schwanz von fremden Wort'.

64 On linguistic purism see also Björn Jernudd and Michael Shapiro, *Politics of Language Purism* (Berlin: de Gruyter, 1989); and Joseph, 1987.

65 See Karen Adams and Daniel Brink, *Perspectives on Official English* (Berlin: de Gruyter, 1990); James Crawford, *Bilingual Education* (Trenton, New Jersey: Crane, 1989) and *Language Loyalties* (Chicago: University of Chicago Press, 1992); *International Journal of the Sociology of Language*, 1986, 60; Dennis Baron, *The English-Only Question* (New Haven: Yale University Press, 1990); John Edwards, 'Social purposes of bilingual education' (in G. Imhoff (ed.), *Learning in Two Languages*, New Brunswick, New Jersey: Transaction, 1990).

66 Edwards, 1990, p. 50.

67 Edwards, 1990, p. 63.

68 According to the last census, Germans are the largest American ethnic group.

69 I am indebted to those who presented papers at a recent conference, 'Canons in the Classroom', held in my university (October 1992). I have drawn particularly from the papers of Elizabeth McKim ('The *Norton* by any other name: anthology selection and the inevitable canon'), Bob Moore ('Reading between the canon and the curriculum') and A.C. Hamilton ('Northrop Frye and the literary canon'). After choosing the title for this section, I discovered a book with the same title – *Loose Canons: Notes on the Culture Wars*, by Henry Gates (Oxford: Oxford University Press, 1992). Gates's agenda is one of canon expansion; he wishes to see room made for those who have been hitherto 'voiceless'. See also what was Sidney Hook's final article, 'Is teaching "Western Culture" racist or sexist?' (*Encounter*, 1989, 73(3), 14–19), in which he essentially supports the idea that the canon represents the best thought available.

70 On language planning, see Carol Eastman, *Language Planning* (San Francisco:

Chandler & Sharp, 1983); Juan Cobarrubias and Joshua Fishman, *Progress in Language Planning* (Berlin: Mouton, 1983); Chris Kennedy, *Language Planning and Language Education* (London: Allen & Unwin, 1984).

71 John Edwards, *Language, Society and Identity* (Oxford: Blackwell, 1985). Critical observations on language planning may be found in James Tollefson, *Planning Language, Planning Inequality* (London: Longman, 1991) and in Glynn Williams, *Sociolinguistics* (London: Routledge, 1992).

72 Einar Haugen, 'Dialect, language, nation' (*American Anthropologist*, 1966, 68, 922–35); see also Moshe Nahir, 'The five aspects of language planning' (*Language Problems and Language Planning*, 1977, 1, 107–23).

7 LANGUAGES, CULTURES AND EDUCATION

1 John Edwards, *Language, Society and Identity* (Oxford: Blackwell, 1985).

2 See Edwards, 1985; John Higham, *Send These to Me* (New York: Atheneum, 1975); John Edwards, *Linguistic Minorities, Policies and Pluralism* (London: Academic Press, 1984); and Philip Gleason, 'Pluralism and assimilation: a conceptual history' (in Edwards, 1984).

3 See Horace Kallen, 'Democracy versus the melting pot' (*The Nation*, 18 and 25 February 1915); and *Culture and Democracy in the United States* (New York: Boni & Liveright, 1924).

4 Barbara Lal, *The Romance of Culture in an Urban Civilization* (London: Routledge, 1990).

5 Gunnar Myrdal, *An American Dilemma: The Negro Problem and Modern Democracy* (New York: Harper & Row, 1944).

6 See Edwards, 1985.

7 Andrew Greeley, cited by Arthur Mann, *The One and the Many* (Chicago: University of Chicago Press, 1979, pp. 17–18).

8 p. 53 in Benjamin Barber, 'Jihad vs McWorld' (*Atlantic*, March 1992, 53–63).

9 Barber, 1992, p. 53.

10 Michael Novak, cited by Philip Gleason on p. 17, 'Confusion compounded: the melting pot in the 1960s and 1970s' (*Ethnicity*, 1979, 6, 10–20); Novak's own *The Rise of the Unmeltable Ethnics* (New York: Macmillan, 1971) is a typical paean to multiculturalism of the period.

11 Nathan Glazer and Daniel Moynihan, *Beyond the Melting Pot* (Cambridge, Massachusetts: MIT Press, 1963).

12 Herbert Gans, 'Symbolic ethnicity: the future of ethnic groups and cultures in America' (*Ethnic and Racial Studies*, 1979, 2, 1–20) and 'Second-generation decline: scenarios for the economic and ethnic futures of the post-1965 American immigrants' (*Ethnic and Racial Studies*, 1992, 15, 173–92).

13 Gans, 1992, p. 175.

14 p. 233 in Thomas Sowell, 'Ethnicity in a changing America' (*Daedalus*, 1978, 107, 213–237).

15 Gans, 1992, p. 175.

16 Jean Burnet, 'The policy of multiculturalism within a bilingual framework' (in A. Wolfgang (ed.), *Education of Immigrant Students*, Toronto: Ontario Institute for Studies in Education, 1975, p. 211).

17 See John Porter, *The Vertical Mosaic* (Toronto: University of Toronto Press, 1965); also his 'Dilemmas and contradictions of a multi-ethnic society' (*Transactions of the Royal Society of Canada*, 1972, 10, 193–205) and *The Measure*

of Canadian Society (Toronto: Gage, 1979).

18 p. 100 in Manoly Lupul, 'The political implementation of multiculturalism' (*Journal of Canadian Studies*, 1982, 17, 93–102).

19 See Guy Rocher, *Le Québec en mutation* (Montreal: Editions Hurtubise, 1973).

20 Raymond Breton, 'Multiculturalism and Canadian nation-building' (in A. Cairns & C. Williams (eds), *The Politics of Gender, Ethnicity and Language in Canada*. Toronto: University of Toronto Press, 1986, p. 53).

21 James Fleming, 'Multiculturalism' (*Canadian Ethnic Studies Association Bulletin*, 1982, 9, 9).

22 Michael Tenszen, 'Most oppose melting pot, Murta says' (*Globe and Mail* (Toronto), 14 May 1985).

23 'Mr. Murta's mosaic' (*Globe and Mail* (Toronto), 15 May 1985).

24 *Globe and Mail*, 15 May 1985.

25 A. Walmsley, 'Uneasy over newcomers' (*Maclean's*, 1989, 102, 28–9). Very recent polls have found Canadians to be 'in their most hostile mood in some time toward immigrants'. Have we seen an end, some asked, of the general public tolerance which, even though largely passive, has been prized in Canada? Interestingly, this survey found *Québécois* among the *most* tolerant (*Globe and Mail* (Toronto), 14 September 1992).

26 K. O'Bryan, J. Reitz and O. Kuplowska, *Non-Official Languages: A Study in Canadian Multiculturalism* (Ottawa: Supply & Services Canada, 1976); see also J. Berry, R. Kalin and D. Taylor, *Multiculturalism and Ethnic Attitudes in Canada* (Ottawa: Supply & Services Canada, 1977).

27 R. Breton, J. Reitz and V. Valentine, *Cultural Boundaries and the Cohesion of Canada* (Montreal: Institute for Research on Public Policy, 1980, p. 384).

28 John Edwards and Joan Chisholm, 'Language, multiculturalism and identity: a Canadian study' (*Journal of Multilingual and Multicultural Development*, 1987, 8, 391–408); see also John Edwards and Lori Doucette, 'Ethnic salience, identity and symbolic ethnicity' (*Canadian Ethnic Studies*, 1987, 19, 52–62), in which a relationship was found between claiming ethnic-group membership and supporting *active* government policies on multiculturalism.

29 Breton, 1986, pp. 47–8.

30 See John Edwards, 'Ethnolinguistic pluralism and its discontents' (*International Journal of the Sociology of Language*, in press) and 'The power of nationalism: the Canadian referendum of 1992' (*Proceedings of the International Conference on Maintenance and Loss of Minority Languages*, in press).

31 John Stuart Mill, *Considerations on Representative Government* (London: Dent, 1964, p. 362). Originally published in 1861.

32 Mill, 1861/1964, p. 366.

33 B. Connors, 'A multicultural curriculum as action for social justice' (in S. Shapson and V. D'Oyley (eds), *Bilingual and Multicultural Education: Canadian Perspectives*, Clevedon, Avon: Multilingual Matters, 1984, p. 106).

34 Connors, 1984, p. 110.

35 See Jim Cummins, 'Empowering minority students' (*Harvard Educational Review*, 1986, 56, 18–36); D. Spener, 'Transitional bilingual education and the socialization of immigrants' (*Harvard Educational Review*, 1988, 58, 133–53).

36 Edwards, 1985, p. 131.

37 Maureen Stone, *The Education of the Black Child in Britain: The Myth of Multiracial Education* (London: Fontana, 1981).

38 S. Tomlinson, 'Home, school and community' (in M. Craft (ed.), *Education and Cultural Pluralism*, London: Falmer, 1984, p. 149).

39 H.L. Mencken, cited in Martin Joos, *The Five Clocks* (New York: Harcourt, Brace

& World, 1967, p. xiv). Perhaps, in these politically-correct times, I should admit that not all narrow schoolteachers are female.

40 See John Edwards, *Language and Disadvantage* (2nd revised edn) (London: Cole & Whurr, 1989).

41 In Britain, the recent report of the Committee of Inquiry into the Teaching of the English Language (the Kingman Report, published in 1988), with its recommendation for more formal grammar instruction, and the new British national curriculum, have occasioned much debate. See, for example, the papers in *Language and Education*, 1988, 2(3); also Michael Stubbs, 'The state of English in the English state' and Chris Winch 'Standard English, normativity and the Cox Committee report,' both in *Language and Education*, 1989, 3(4), pp. 235–50 and 275–93, respectively. Harold Rosen, 'The nationalisation of English' (*International Journal of Applied Linguistics*, 1991, 1, 104–17), provides a critical assessment of the Cox Report (1989) and the compulsory teaching of standard English.

42 John Edwards and Margaret McKinnon, 'The continuing appeal of disadvantage as deficit' (*Canadian Journal of Education*, 1987, 12, 330–49); see also John Edwards, 'Language and educational disadvantage' (in Kevin Durkin (ed.), *Language Development in the School Years*, London: Croom Helm, 1986).

43 This is, again, a topic I've treated in detail elsewhere; see Edwards, 1985. Most of the book-length treatments of bilingualism cited in chapter 3 can also be consulted here.

44 See E.G. Lewis, 'Bilingualism and bilingual education: the ancient world to the Renaissance' (in Joshua Fishman, *Bilingual Education*, Rowley, Massachusetts: Newbury House, 1977).

45 T. Haaroff, *The Schools of Gaul* (Oxford: Clarendon, 1920, p. 226).

46 Fishman, 1977.

47 Ronald Reagan, cited by John Edwards, 'Social purposes of bilingual education' (in G. Imhoff (ed.), *Learning in Two Languages*, New Brunswick, New Jersey: Transaction, 1990, p. 50).

48 See Edwards, 1990.

49 Elie Kedourie, *Nationalism* (London: Hutchinson, 1961, pp. 83–4).

50 Useful treatments of immersion education include: W. Lambert and G. Tucker, *Bilingual Education of Children* (Rowley, Massachusetts: Newbury House, 1972); Merrill Swain and Sharon Lapkin, *Evaluating Bilingual Education* and Stan Shapson and Vincent D'Oyley, *Bilingual and Multicultural Education* (both Clevedon, Avon: Multilingual Matters, 1982 and 1984); Fred Genesee, 'The Canadian second language immersion program' (in Christina Paulston (ed.), *International Handbook of Bilingualism and Bilingual Education*, New York: Greenwood, 1988); *Canadian Modern Language Review*, 1989, 45(3) – apart from this whole issue on immersion, this journal frequently publishes articles on the subject.

51 p. 182 in Merrill Swain, 'English-speaking child + early French immersion = bilingual child?' (*Canadian Modern Language Review*, 1976, 33, 180–7); see also S. Lapkin, M. Swain and V. Argue, *French Immersion: The Trial Balloon that Flew* (Toronto: Ontario Institute for Studies in Education, 1983).

52 William Mackey, 'Safeguarding language in schools' (*Language and Society*, 1981, 4, 10–14).

53 Hector Hammerly, 'The immersion approach' (*Modern Language Journal*, 1987, 71, 395–401). See also *French Immersion: Myths and Reality* (Calgary: Detselig, 1989).

54 R. Lister, 'Speaking immersion' (*Canadian Modern Language Review*, 1987, 43,

701–17).

55 See the works just cited, and the interchange between Hammerly and Swain/ Lapkin in the *Modern Language Journal* (1990, 74, 66–71). See also Carl Dodson's interesting doubts about immersion – on the grounds that a method based upon imitation of first-language learning cannot ignore the fact that a first language already exists – in his 'A reappraisal of bilingual development and education' (in H. Baetens Beardsmore (ed.), *Elements of Bilingual Theory*, Brussels: Vrije Universiteit, 1981).

56 Mackey, 1981, p. 13.

57 Fred Genesee, 'Bilingualism and biliteracy: a study of cross-cultural contact in a bilingual community' (in John Edwards (ed.), *The Social Psychology of Reading*, Silver Spring, Maryland: Institute of Modern Languages, 1981); see also Calvin Veltman, 'Comment' (*International Journal of the Sociology of Language*, 1986, 60, 177–81).

58 Peter Trudgill, *Sociolinguistics* (Harmondsworth: Penguin, 1974, p. 86); see also Philip Smith, *Language, the Sexes and Society* (Oxford: Blackwell, 1985).

59 Trudgill, 1974, p. 85.

60 Janet Holmes, *An Introduction to Sociolinguistics* (London: Longman, 1992).

61 Holmes, 1992.

62 Mary Haas, 'Men's and women's speech in Koasati' (*Language*, 1944, 20, 142–9); see also Ralph Fasold, *Sociolinguistics of Language* (Oxford: Blackwell, 1990) and Trudgill, 1974.

63 Japanese examples are from Holmes, 1992.

64 Chiquito examples are from Trudgill, 1974.

65 Kūrux examples are from Francis Ekka, 'Men's and women's speech in Kūrux' (*Linguistics*, 1972, 81, 21–31); see also Fasold, 1990.

66 See Trudgill, 1974.

67 See Holmes, 1992; the term was coined by A. Bodine, 'Sex differences in language' (in B. Thorne and N. Henley (eds), *Language and Sex: Difference and Dominance*, Rowley, Massachusetts: Newbury House, 1975).

68 John Fischer, 'Social influences on the choice of a linguistic variant' (*Word*, 1958, 14, 47–56).

69 Trudgill, 1974.

70 Holmes, 1992.

71 Peter Trudgill, *On Dialect* (Oxford: Blackwell, 1983); on 'covert prestige', see also John Edwards, 'Social class differences and the identification of sex in children's speech' (*Journal of Child Language*, 1979, 6, 121–7).

72 There is information, from a variety of contexts, that where a large prestigious language threatens a smaller one, and where language shift is occurring, women are likely to be early 'shifters': see Holmes, 1992, Edwards, 1985, and Philip Smith, 'Sex markers in speech' (in Klaus Scherer and Howard Giles (eds), *Social Markers in Speech*, Cambridge: Cambridge University Press, 1979).

73 See Robin Lakoff's 'Language and women's place' (*Language in Society*, 1973, 2, 45–79) and her book of the same title (New York: Harper & Row, 1975); see also the discussion in Holmes, 1992.

74 See Holmes, 1992.

75 H. Leet-Pellegrini, 'Conversational dominance as a function of gender and expertise' (in H. Giles, W.P. Robinson and P. Smith (eds), *Language: Social Psychological Perspectives*, Oxford: Pergamon, 1980, p. 103).

76 See the recent collection of papers in *International Journal of the Sociology of Language*, 1992, 94.

77 Francine Frank and Frank Anshen, *Language and the Sexes* (Albany: State

University of New York Press, 1983, p. 46).
78 Otto Jespersen, *Language* (London: Allen & Unwin, 1922).

8 CONCLUSIONS

1 Christopher Ricks and Leonard Michaels, *The State of the Language* (London: Faber & Faber, 1990, p. xvii).
2 Perhaps the reference to Priscian is unfair; after all, he is hardly unique in the annals of prescriptivism. Still, his sixth-century *Partitiones* and *Institutiones Grammaticae* were very influential, and his name has become synonymous with grammatical narrowness. Thus, *diminuere Priscianis caput* is to violate the rules of grammar. The earlier Samuel Butler, whom I cited in Chapter 1, observed in *Hudibras*:

> And hold no sin so deeply red
> As that of breaking Priscian's head.

In his *Satyr upon the Imperfection and Abuse of Human Learning*, Butler reiterated the idea:

> And counted breaking Priscian's head a thing
> More capital than to behead a king.

Later, Alexander Pope said, in *The Dunciad*:

> Some free from rhyme or reason, rule or check,
> Break Priscian's head, and Pegasus's neck.

Finally here, Shakespeare has the schoolmaster Holofernes refer to Nathaniel the curate's rather hackneyed Latin by saying, 'Priscian a little scratched; 'twill serve'. It is in this same scene from *Love's Labour's Lost* (V:i) that Moth, the page to the ridiculous Don Adriano, says to Costard the clown that these pedants 'have been at a great feast of languages, and stolen the scraps'.
3 Judith Brett, 'The bureaucratization of writing' (*Meanjin*, 1991, 50, 513–22).
4 See chapter 6.
5 Peter Ladefoged, 'Discussion note: another view of endangered languages' (*Language*, 1992, 68, 809–11).

INDEX OF NAMES

INDEX OF SUBJECTS

INDEX OF LANGUAGES AND
LANGUAGE FAMILIES

(see also Tables 2.3, 2.4 and 5.1; Map 2.1)